Beyond the Balfour Declaration

The 100-Year Quest For Israeli–Palestinian Peace

Beyond the Balfour Declaration

LESLIE TURNBERG

First published in Great Britain in 2017 by
Biteback Publishing Ltd
Westminster Tower
3 Albert Embankment
London SE1 7SP

ISBN 978-1-78590-136-2

10 9 8 7 6 5 4 3 2 1

A CIP catalogue record for this book is available from the British Library.

Set in Baskerville

Printed and bound in Great Britain by
CPI Group (UK) Ltd, Croydon CR0 4YY

Contents

Acknowledgements	vii
Preface	ix
Introduction	xi
Maps	xxii
PART I	1
Chapter 1: 1898–1923: Twenty-Five Years of Turmoil	3
Chapter 2: The Balfour Declaration	25
Chapter 3: Many Resolutions but No Resolution	41
Chapter 4: War, Armistice but Few Intimations of Peace	57
Chapter 5: At the United Nations	65
Chapter 6: More Wars and Abortive Peace Proposals	69
Chapter 7: The 1967 War	77
Chapter 8: The Palestinians	91
Chapter 9: Anwar Sadat Takes Over in Egypt, 1971	99
Chapter 10: Rabin, Begin and Sadat	105
Chapter 11: President Carter and Camp David	111
Chapter 12: The PLO and War in Lebanon	123
Chapter 13: More Lost Opportunities	131
PART II	139
Introduction: Inching towards Peace	141
Chapter 14: Tentative Steps towards Oslo	147

Chapter 15: How Extremists Began to Win the Future 159
Chapter 16: Peace with Jordan but Not with Syria 169
Chapter 17: More Faltering Steps towards Peace 173
Chapter 18: The Road to Camp David II 181
Chapter 19: Ariel Sharon Elected, 2001 193
Chapter 20: The Road Map and Unilateral Withdrawal 199
Chapter 21: Olmert Takes Over, 2006 203
Chapter 22: The Syrian Track 211
Chapter 23: Abbas, Netanyahu, Obama and a Roller-Coaster Ride 221
Chapter 24: In the Eye of the Storm 231
Chapter 25: Public Pressures and Government Constraints 237
Chapter 26: External Affairs 247
Chapter 27: Options for Peace 257
Chapter 28: What Would a Final Status Agreement Look Like? 265

Notes 273
Bibliography 279
Index 287

Acknowledgements

THERE WAS MUCH SCEPTICISM amongst friends about the wisdom of writing a book on the Israeli–Palestinian conflict when so much had already been written. I justified entering a field rich in literature, at least to myself, on the grounds that I too needed to better understand the background. And if I was uncertain, maybe others were too.

My sense was that the centenary year of the Balfour Declaration would bring out strong views about the validity of that Declaration, and hence about the legitimacy of Israel itself. Some would feel that Balfour's Declaration was the biggest error of judgement that a government could make while others would believe that it was the remarkable culmination of a desire to correct hundreds of years of injustice to a persecuted race. This is a field in which beliefs, not always based on facts, are strongly held. If I have managed to fill at least some of the gap between opinion and evidence, I will feel justified in having put pen to paper.

Needless to say I have relied heavily on many people to help me avoid too many errors of fact or judgement. It is impossible to name them all here but some stand out and I cannot fail to mention the enormous debt I owe to them.

For the fruitful conversations I have had with Jonathan Parris, Ron Prosor, Dan Schueftan, Tom Segev, and Yossi Beilin, I am truly grateful. I have had much encouragement from many individuals including

Natan Sachs, Lord Roddy Balfour, Rabbi Lord Jonathan Sacks and many others.

Special thanks are due to some who have had the patience to go through my manuscripts with an eagle eye. Sir David Manning made hugely important suggestions for improvements. Shmuel Barr cast a very perceptive and critical eye on my writings, while Mustafe Abbasi helped me understand Palestinian history rather better. I thank Anton Alexander for drawing my attention to the importance of the threat of malaria in early twentieth-century Palestine. It was Gilad Eisen, however, who made line-by-line suggestions for improvement. It was he who made sure to point out my errors and without his input I feel sure that the book would have been the poorer.

Needless to say, any remaining errors and misapprehensions are entirely my own.

I am deeply grateful to all these individuals.

I am grateful to Stand with Us for allowing me to reproduce the maps on pp. xxii and xxiii.

I was delighted that the current Earl, Lord Roddy Balfour, agreed to write the Preface. It has been a privilege and a pleasure to have his support.

At Biteback, my editors, Jonathan Wadman and Olivia Beattie, have been enormously supportive in shepherding me through the editing process. My gratitude to them is unbounded.

Writing has been a pleasure but it would not have been possible if I had not hidden myself away from social contact at times, not least from my wife Edna. It is to her patience, support and encouragement that I dedicate this book.

February 2017

Preface

I WAS VERY HONOURED when Leslie Turnberg asked me to compose a preface to this book, written to coincide with the 100th anniversary of the Balfour Declaration, signed by my forebear, Arthur, and Foreign Secretary at the time, in a letter to Lord Rothschild. In it, he expressed His Majesty's Government's support for making the old Biblical lands of Palestine once more a home for Jewish people, a large number of whom had been evicted from Russia and elsewhere in the pogroms of the previous decades. It was this humanitarian aspect of the Declaration of which our family are most proud.

Notwithstanding this humanitarian imperative, many post-1948 commentators, after the formal creation and UN recognition of the state of Israel, have sought to blame the Declaration as the fountain of all conflict in the cauldron of the Middle East since then. Of course I have followed events in the region keenly and if ever the aphorism 'my enemy's enemy is my friend' was true then it has been there. At many times, and this probably applies to the very present, the regional conflicts have been power-mongering between the many countries and an ever-escalating struggle for supremacy between Shia and Sunni Muslims.

The Declaration never anticipated the Holocaust thirty years later or the pressures a burgeoning Palestinian population would bring to a very small area over which all the Abrahamic faiths claim viscerally felt rights. The wish expressed in the Declaration that creating a Jewish homeland should not interfere with the current inhabitants at the time has clearly been overtaken by these events and factors. Nonetheless, it is our family's sincere hope that some resolution can be found for the problem, which will probably require much shuttle diplomacy, some giving of ground by Israel and some arm-twisting of the Palestinian militants (most of whom are sworn to destroy Israel) by neighbouring Arab states.

Of course this has all been tried before, and written about, but for myself, finding a book which deals with the whole of the past 100 years and which is concise and readable has too often found me putting down a tome which isolated a period of time and was likely to be verbose as a result.

Thus it was that when I was introduced to Leslie he told me he was writing this book and offered it to me to read in its raw draft form. I was immediately drawn to his style and his pinpointing of key moments and the circumstances building up to them or their after-effects. He maintains a wonderful pace to keep the reader from getting bogged down and it is his enormous research and ability to winnow out the unimportant which make the book so readable to somebody like myself, an average reader and student of current affairs and history. I commend it to anybody who feels that getting a good understanding of the machinations surrounding Palestine in the last 100 years is just too big a task to undertake. Leslie Turnberg has done all the heavy-lifting for that reader.

The 5th Earl of Balfour
February 2017

Introduction

SATURDAY EVENING, 4 NOVEMBER 1995, and Yitzhak Rabin, Prime Minister of Israel, is being given an enthusiastic reception by 100,000 Israelis. They are gathered in Tel Aviv at the rally in support of his peace initiatives. He is elated and hugely encouraged. He steps down from the platform with Shimon Peres a few steps behind him and heads for the bulky armoured Cadillac waiting to take him away. The security guards have been casually watching the crowds, missing a young Jewish student, Yigal Amir, standing patiently nearby and are slow to react when he walks behind Rabin, pulls out his gun and shoots him three times in the back. It is a miracle that Rabin's wife, Leah, at the last moment persuaded him to wear the bullet-proof vest he had resisted for so long. He falls to the ground, shaken and bruised, but is otherwise unhurt. He is quickly helped into his car and driven away.

It is then that he realises how fragile the peace process is and how quickly it could be destroyed by an act of terror.

Rabin strengthens his determination to move rapidly to full statehood for the Palestinians from the limited autonomy accepted after the Oslo agreements of 1993. The architect of Oslo, Yossi Beilin, is by now able to present him with a worked-up plan that has been agreed in further secret meetings with Mahmood Abbas of the PLO: Palestinian statehood on the West Bank and Gaza, withdrawal from all Israeli settlements apart from those immediately adjacent to the border with an equal area of Israeli land given over in compensation, acceptable security arrangements for Israel, part of East Jerusalem to be ceded to the new state and a limited return of refugees with compensation for others.

Within two years all this will be achieved despite efforts to derail the process with repeated Hamas terrorist attacks and acts of violence against Israelis and, in retaliation, against Arabs by Jewish extremists. The Palestinian economy grows as improved relations with Israel evolve. Peace with Jordan was already made in 1994 and now the scene is set for a peace treaty with Syria and Lebanon.

Of course, this is not what happened. Rabin persistently refused to wear body armour and Amir's shots were fatal. Although there is every possibility that this rosy outcome would not have been achieved, never before had the two-state peace solution seemed nearer.

The history of the Middle East is littered with acts of violence by determined opponents who have confounded the possibility of a peace. Of course many other factors have played a part in the failure but that is the sad story of the 100 years since the Balfour Declaration.

The seemingly high-minded purpose of that Declaration, to provide a homeland in Palestine for a persecuted people while at the same time protecting the rights of the indigenous Palestinian Arab population, has proved to be hopelessly optimistic. Those who drafted it could hardly have imagined that the conflict between Jews and Arabs, Zionists and Palestinians, would remain unresolved for so long. And now, in its centenary year, doubts about the validity of the Declaration are again being raised. Some regard the Declaration as a terrible mistake leading to disastrous consequences while others see it as a remarkable and rare act of magnanimity by an imperial nation.

It was the recent fashionable questioning of the basis of Balfour, and even the legitimacy of Israel's right to exist, that tempted me into writing this book.[1] I have been encouraged too because it is hard not to be aware of how large the gaps are between perception and reality. It is difficult to disagree with Richard Crossman when he wrote about 'the violent partisanship of a public opinion which is formed on second-hand judgements' and 'the irresponsibility of those who find it easy to make up their minds far away from the scene of the action'.[2]

Facts are hard to come by in arguments about who or what is to blame for the continuing stand-off. So my aim has been to provide a succinct history since 1917 of efforts to reach a resolution that has been so elusive and to focus on why, despite numerous valiant efforts, agreements that have seemed so tantalisingly close have always failed. I want, too, to tackle head on the question of the validity of the Balfour Declaration. The growth of anti-Semitism on the back of a wave of extremism, and reaction to it, has added a further impulse to my efforts to write about events in one part of the Middle East. It will not go unnoticed that I am not a historian and that I live many miles away from the Holy Land but I take comfort from the fact that this has allowed me to write for a general public from what I hope is a balanced perspective.

I was aware that I was entering a field that is rich in literature. Despite Israel's relative youth a huge number of excellent books have been written about efforts to make peace between it and its neighbours. I have pitched my own views between those who feel that Israel can do little wrong on the one hand[3] and those of the many revisionist historians on the other.[4] Both seem to me to be selective in their use of facts although neither is guilty of purveying the gross distortion of the evidence to which some writers stoop.[5] Somewhere between Israeli hubris and revisionist cynicism is where I have tried to set my thoughts.

I am far from alone in this space. Israel's vibrant democracy throws up a full range of opinions and its media possess enough critics of government policy to satisfy any sceptic.

Several themes emerge from the morass of information and misinformation about Israel and the Middle East. The Balfour Declaration was no more than an indication of British government thinking in 1917 and took the shape of a letter to Lord Rothschild. It was never a legally binding document although its impact was far reaching. It was, however, more than simply an expression of favourable views in that it bore the stamp of official approval. But the legal basis for Israel's future existence lies in the international recognition given by the League of Nations in 1922 and by the United Nations in 1947.

Of course there was much painful negotiation between 1917 and 1947 but the Balfour Declaration could so easily have been lost on many occasions. If, for example, British Prime Minister David Lloyd George's secret negotiation with the Turks for a separate World War I peace in 1916 and 1917 had been successful, the Ottomans might have been able to retain their Middle East empire and the Zionist dream would have been abandoned or at least postponed.[6]

While antipathy to Jewish immigration within Palestine was manifest in violent local opposition during the first half of the twentieth century, antagonism was not obvious in the rest of the Muslim world. The Grand Sharif Hussein in Mecca and his son Faisal were supportive of Chaim Weizmann and his plan for a Jewish influx into what they considered a remote backwater. The Arabs felt much more betrayed by the Anglo-French Sykes–Picot Agreement of May 1916. This, and later post-World War I agreements, divided up the rest of the Middle East by straight lines in the sand regardless of tribal and religious divisions. Today's militant Muslim factions are now busily revising these imposed borders in a devastating and destructive way.

It is difficult for me to accept the view that the creation of Israel is somehow responsible for the mayhem now raging elsewhere in the Middle East. The idea that if Israel did not exist we would not have seen the Arab Spring and the Winter that followed, the rise of IS and Al Qaeda, or the splintering of Syria and Iraq, to say nothing of the fundamentalist turmoil in north Africa, is stretching the evidence more than a little. In his book on the causes of the rise of Islamic Jihad and the turmoil in the Middle East, Patrick Cockburn does not mention Israel or Palestine.[7]

In Israel–Palestine there are Palestinians, especially in Hamas, who constantly preach that all the land between the river Jordan and the

Mediterranean Sea should be theirs while there are right-wing Israelis who believe fundamentally that Judea and Samaria, that is the whole of the West Bank, should be part of a greater Israel. But these are the views of a minority; the majority of public opinion on both sides favours a peaceful two-state solution, although even that is now threatened. It is depressing to hear from Khalil Shikaki, director of the Palestinian Centre for Policy and Survey Research in Ramallah, that his public opinion polls are showing the highest-ever number of Palestinians who believe a two-state solution is no longer possible.[8] This is also true of Israeli public opinion, but here the reason is even more disturbing. On both sides there is a strong belief that it is the other side that does not want peace even though they themselves may desire it – a complete misunderstanding of the opposition's views. When I told my Israeli granddaughter that I was writing a book on the 'peace process' she said, 'What peace process?' She simply confirmed what I already knew, that cynicism in Israel about the prospects for peace is almost universal.

Israeli taxi drivers are neither short of views nor shy of expressing them. My recent driver spoke for the prevalent Israeli view that the Palestinians 'would like to drive us into the sea'. Palestinians on the other side see the expansion of Israeli settlements as erasing a future Palestine on the West Bank from the map. Negotiations have repeatedly stalled as serious disagreements on such hard cases as Jerusalem, refugees and borders have remained intractable. While all governments make mistakes, few have such potentially devastating consequences as those made in Israeli–Palestinian affairs. It is painful now to note the misunderstandings, misconceptions and missed opportunities that abound.

Abba Eban famously said that 'the Palestinians never miss an opportunity to miss an opportunity'. He also said that 'nations often behave wisely once they have exhausted all the other alternatives'.[9] It is not clear that Israel or the Palestinians have exhausted all the alternatives yet. History has shown how, far too often, both leaderships have been driven by reaction to extremist actions, and the extremists are well aware of it.

It is not difficult to be despondent. The possibility of progress, even in simply re-opening discussions, seems to grow increasingly remote and the price of failure makes it less worthwhile to take risks. The many pessimists point to the innumerable failed attempts to bridge the gaps. They say that success is always foiled by 'events' – one or other party is accused of reneging on a promise, an act of terror, an assassination, a devastating suicide attack or even a walk on the Temple Mount – that blow any progress out of the water. The history of repeated failures has left many turning back to the status quo as a preferable alternative.

Not everything has stood still, however. The three 'Noes' of the Arab League in 1967, in which they concluded that there could be no negotiation, no recognition and no peace with Israel after the 1967 war, were followed many years later by the Arab Peace Initiative, in which the possibility of three 'Yeses' was raised. Peace agreements with Egypt in 1979 and with Jordan in 1994 have stood the test of time, demonstrating what might be possible given enough commonality of interests. Even the thirty or more years of Yasser Arafat's reluctance to recognise Israel's right to exist changed to an uneasy acceptance by the Palestinians of its presence, if not its Jewishness, in the Middle East.

So is there any room for optimism?

Clearly 'optimism' is hardly the word and one has to take a very long-term view if one is not to be consumed by pessimism. The potential dividends are far too large and continuing failure is damaging to both sides. It is clear that at the end of the day only direct negotiation between Israel and the Palestinians can yield lasting results. Whatever encouragement or pressure the Americans, the Europeans or other Arab states may offer, and these can undoubtedly be valuable, it is the parties themselves that have to agree solutions they can find acceptable.

All negotiations involve discussions, not only across the table with the opposition but also along the table with colleagues on the same side, while at the same time there is another negotiation behind the table with your population. Negotiators closeted away in a room may be able to reach agreement but getting the public to sign up to those agreements is quite another matter. Daniel Taub, Israel's ambassador to the UK until 2015 and an ex-member of the team negotiating with the Palestinians, said that there is yet another dimension: time. Here one is negotiating for one's parents and grandparents in the past and, simultaneously, for the future of one's children and grandchildren. Too often he felt that negotiations focused on the history of grandparents instead of on the future for grandchildren.[10] Despite that profound thought it has proved impossible for negotiators to jettison history entirely.

The difficulties lie not so much in being able to provide an outline of what a reasonable and acceptable final position might look like. That has been on the table in various guises for some time: two autonomous states with secure borders, withdrawal from outlying settlements and land swaps for others, a resolution of the position of refugees with a limited return of some and acceptable compensation for others and, most difficult of all, agreement on an arrangement for Jerusalem. Security and a morale-boosting sense of justice for both Palestinians and Israelis are basic requirements. This is easy to state from a safe distance but the fact that the end game has been so elusive demonstrates that no one, so far, has been able to overcome the innate fears, prejudices and mistrust of two sides that start from quite different and conflicting positions both historically and psychologically.

The Palestinians are constantly reminded that what they thought of as their land was taken over by an influx of Jews to solve a European catastrophe not of their making. There is an Arab view too that land that had once been Muslim is for ever theirs and anyone other than a true believer is regarded as a usurper. The Palestinians' sense of resentment has not been reduced as they and their Arab allies have been repeatedly beaten in a series of wars starting in 1947. Defeat is painful and feeds a lingering bitterness and desire for revenge.[11] The Palestinian media never let the people forget their sense of subjugation and victimhood. Nor was this humiliation softened when they were expelled or fled in 1948 to a Jordan that then included the West Bank, where they were treated as second-class citizens, and to Syria and Lebanon, where they have suffered the indignity of being kept in refugee camps, without rights, ever since. This Palestinian narrative, feeding a burning frustration, has to be faced if a resolution of the conflict is to be reached.[12] Many Israelis believe that it is now doubtful whether the Palestinians can ever bring themselves to accept a Jewish state in the Middle East.

The Israeli narrative is based upon a quite different take on events. They remember that the Jews have lived in Palestine since biblical times and for centuries before Islam emerged as a religion. Every year their festival of Passover reminds them of their exodus from Egypt in the thirteenth century BCE. They see the archaeological evidence of their presence wherever the surface is scraped: at Megiddo and Tel Shearim, in the City of David and the walls of Herod's Temple, at Masada and in the Dead Sea Scrolls of Qumran. They point to the tombs of their patriarchs at Hebron, Nablus and Bethlehem, and their daily prayers are full of yearning for a return. They have had a continuous presence in the Holy Land despite efforts to expel them and they made up the majority of the Jerusalem population for well over 100 years before 1917. Recent efforts by UN committees to wipe away the Jewish connection to the land fly in the face of all the evidence on and in the ground. Zionists point out that Israel is the only Jewish country in the world amongst a large number of Muslim countries. Their population of six million Jews is minute in comparison with the 300 million Arabs in surrounding countries. Its land mass, at 8,000 square miles no bigger than Wales, is hardly visible on maps of the Middle East.

Centuries of persecution and pogroms across Russia and Europe made their yearnings more poignant. Little wonder then that they believe that they have a legitimate right to the land and that history, both ancient and recent, is on their side. The Balfour Declaration of 1917 simply gave that yearning some legitimacy. And they have recognition by the United Nations as a nation state in international law.

Rightly or wrongly, these are the basic positions from which the two sides face each other.

International opinion of Israel and Israelis has fluctuated widely. By the 1930s their transformation was complete, from 'Fiddler on the Roof' peasants bent short-sightedly over religious tomes to bronzed muscular farmers making the deserts bloom and living the seemingly perfect socialist experiment in the kibbutzim. The remarkable and stirring rescue of hostages at Entebbe by Israeli forces in 1976 completed the switch from victims to heroes and suddenly Jews in the diaspora were able to hold their heads up and wear their skull caps in public without danger of persecution. World opinion soon changed as the Palestinian Arabs took the place of the Jews as the new victims and the Jews began to be portrayed as the oppressors. From victims to perpetrators of victimhood in one generation. It is the unfortunate case that 'world opinion', in so far as it is represented by the United Nations General Assembly, now the epicentre of much criticism, is strongly influenced by a large number of countries that themselves have rather unsavoury reputations. Almost every resolution against Israel is easily carried by the large number of Arab countries and their allies, many of whom lack any semblance of democracy and barely represent the opinions of their own people, let alone 'world opinion'. Israel is now both intimidated and intimidating. Ambivalence and controversy characterise not only its international reputation but also its multifarious internal political and societal divisions.

In this book I have tried to examine the ways in which efforts have been made to resolve the major sources of dispute and why they have failed; where progress has been made and where the situation has been made worse by interventions; what should be avoided and what encouraged; in other words, what might be done to avoid the errors of the past. I have tried to gain an understanding of where both sides have come from, their differing histories and psychological backgrounds.

But I take the possibility that I will be able to come up with any solutions with a large measure of humility. I can hardly be unaware of how impossible it has been to predict the tumultuous events in the Middle East of the last few years. I know too that peace is never the end point. It is merely the exchange of a dangerous unstable state of belligerency for one that is less dangerous: the absence of war. Friendship and good relationships have not automatically followed peace treaties in Northern Ireland, in Kosovo or between Egypt and Israel. But these treaties are vastly better than no peace treaty.

Much of history is a series of missed opportunities, sometimes followed by regret. Israel and the Palestinians have had their fair share. Of course everything is clear in retrospect and life seems full of lost opportunities. Wisdom after the event is universal. So I am aware of the need to avoid laying too much blame for errors of judgement and the results of missed opportunities from many years ago. In writing about historic events it is impossible to know all that was in the minds of those having to take difficult decisions and what influences were being brought to bear on them. It is difficult, however, to avoid some speculation about what might have happened given different decisions, if only to try to avoid making similar mistakes. I do so here but have tried to avoid accusations of guilt.

From time to time the idea of a one-state solution is raised. Although I have little sympathy for this proposal and believe it may be unworkable it is supported by significant and respected figures.[13] But there are increasing numbers of thinkers on both sides who feel that the two-state solution is also increasingly unworkable and are looking for alternative types of arrangement. These too will form part of my examination of future prospects for a resolution acceptable to both parties.

I have strived to ensure the accuracy of what I write by consulting as many of the original sources as possible and by assessing the views of multiple witnesses of the same historic events. I have interviewed many individuals who have been directly involved in key negotiations and have tried to give a reasoned view of how the parties have reached their current position. The first half of the book focuses on the history while in the second part I enlarge on more recent events and provide an analysis of current prospects for a resolution to this long-running unhappy saga.

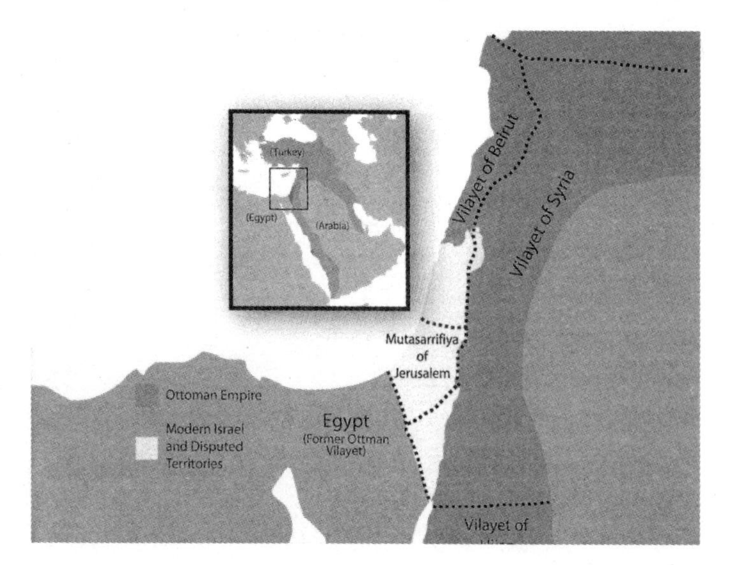

1914. The Ottoman Empire. Palestine is a series of vilayets and sanjaks (regions and districts).

1917. Palestine as envisaged by Balfour as a home for the Jews.

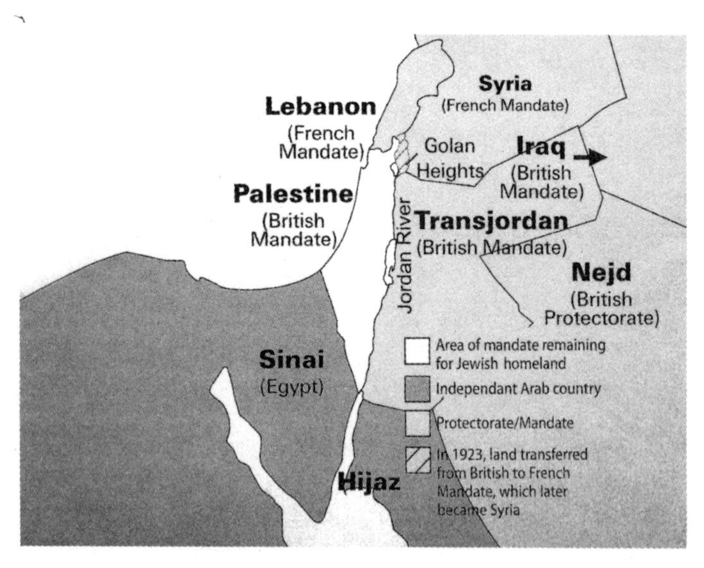

1922. Creation of Transjordan and reduction of Palestine by 70 per cent. Accepted by Weizmann.

1937. Peel Commission Plan for Partition. Reluctant acceptance of markedly reduced Jewish area by Ben Gurion but rejected
by Palestinian Arabs.

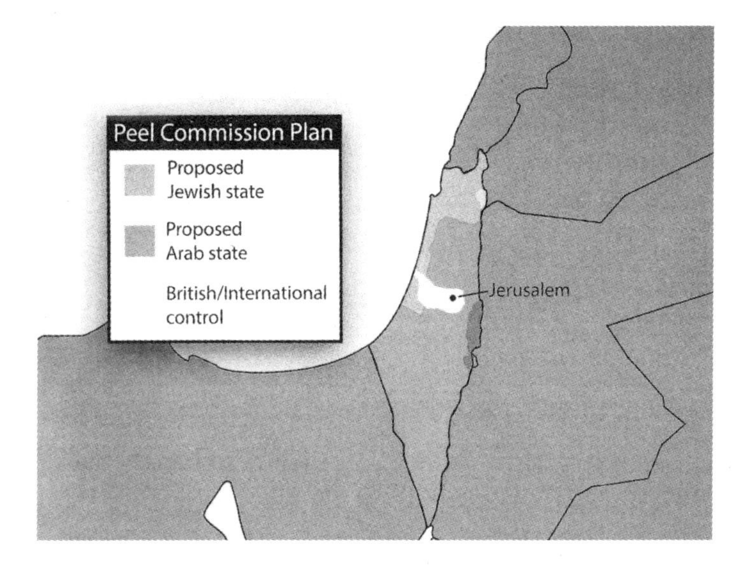

1947. UN Partition Plan. Borders difficult to sustain.

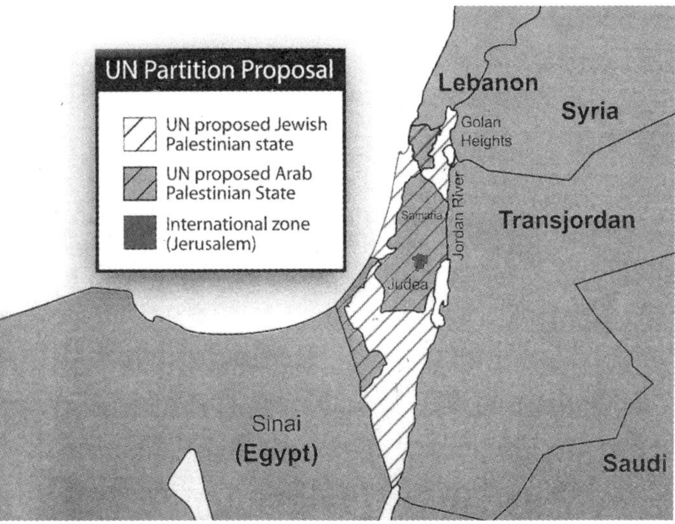

BELOW LEFT
1949. Armistice lines after War of Independence. Jordan takes over West Bank until 1967.

BELOW RIGHT
1979. Current borders between Israel and Palestinian Territories.

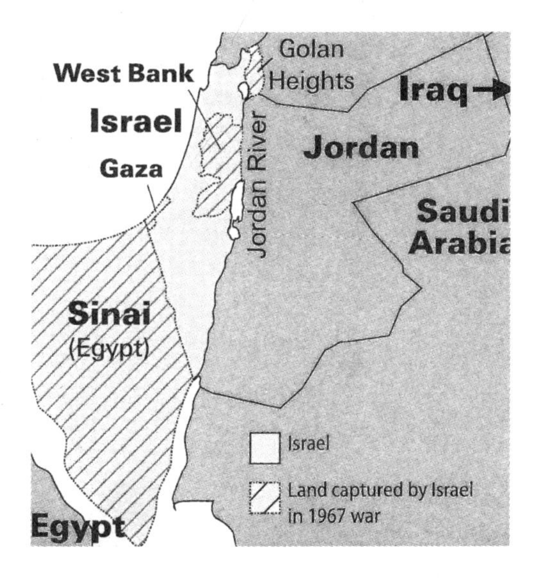

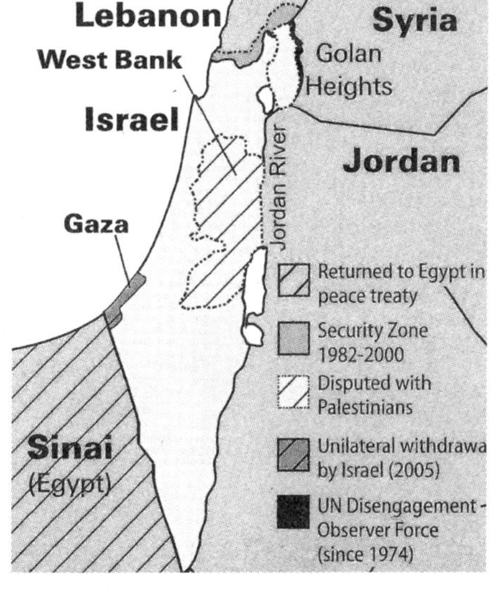

PART I

CHAPTER 1

1898–1923: Twenty-Five Years of Turmoil

THERE IS A TENDENCY to lay many of the troubles in the Middle East at the feet of Balfour but it is clear that first oppression by the Ottomans and then duplicity on the part of the British and French caused much resentment and ill-feeling amongst the Arabs. We must go back before the Balfour Declaration of 1917 and in any case well before 1948 to understand the strikingly different positions of today's Israelis and Palestinians.

The early twentieth century had already been a period of disillusion and betrayal in Arab eyes. They looked back to what they had lost since the golden age of Islam that had lasted for more than 700 years. It had spread its religion, language and culture around the Mediterranean as far as Spain but by 1453 had become splintered by internal tribal and religious disputes. Then, expelled by the Christian incursion into the Iberian Peninsula their position was weakened further as they became unable to resist the Turkish tribes sweeping through the Middle East. The Ottoman Empire, wrested from the Byzantines, stretched from Morocco in the west to Mesopotamia in the east, incorporating much of south-eastern Europe and the Middle East.

Although the Ottomans were Muslim and the Sultan took on the role of Caliph, the Arabs were kept on a tight rein from Constantinople. The Turks knew how to divide and rule, while the Middle East was split largely along tribal and ethnic lines.

Palestine had been part of Syria in this vast Ottoman Empire for almost 400 years when in 1900 its borders merged with Mesopotamia in the east and the desert in the south. Apart from Jerusalem, its separate distinctive nature did not figure highly in the Arab consciousness. At the beginning of the twentieth century, 'there is no real sense of Palestinian self-determination and there is no Palestinian national movement to speak of. Arab nationalism is awakening at a distance: in Damascus, in Beirut, in the Arabian Peninsula. But in Palestine there is no cogent national identity.'[1]

Even Syria was described as 'merely a geographical term corresponding to no National sentiment in the breasts of the inhabitants'.[2] However, this was not quite the whole picture.

Although most of Palestine was arid and inhospitable, this was not the case around Nablus or the seaports of Acre and Jaffa. Nablus was a thriving agricultural and commercial centre for much of the nineteenth and early twentieth century, exporting cotton and linen during the early years and then the highly regarded Nablus soap, made from olive oil, in later years.[3] By the time the British Army entered Palestine in the Great War, the Palestinian population, recognisable mainly by dress, customs and dialect, was being pressed by leading families to become part of the wider Arab world of Syria.[4] A small number of 'notable' families controlled commercial activities in this part of Palestine. It was they who exerted the most influence but relationships with the Ottomans were often strained and a battle for control was always in the offing. Elsewhere in Palestine most of the land was barely cultivated or cultivatable, malaria infested and poor *fellahin* did their best to farm the land around their villages while the Bedouin, with whom they were often in conflict, wandered the edges of the settled areas.

The Palestinians were mainly Sunni Muslims but small numbers of Jews and a larger number of Christians lived mostly peacefully in the community. Not all Palestinians were indigenous and in the 1920s and 1930s a number migrated from other Arab countries, attracted by the increasing job opportunities following the influx of Jews.[5] The British authorities, at this time, were rather more assiduous in clamping down on illegal Jewish immigration than on illegal Arab immigration.

Dissolution of the Ottoman Empire[6]

By 1900 the Ottoman Empire was weakening. It was being nibbled away in the north by Austro-Hungary and Russia while, in the Middle East, Arab nationalism was rearing its head. Increasingly restive under the yoke of the Ottomans, the Arabs were beginning to struggle for freedom. Self-rule and a re-institution of Arabic as their language were strong motivators and a number of Arabic secret societies based in Damascus and Beirut were plotting against the weakening Turks. The onset of World War I seemed to offer an opportunity when hopes were raised by a series of tempting and competing offers from the British and French on the one hand and the Germans on the other. Both sides of the European conflict were keen to woo the Arabs in the not unreasonable belief that an ally in the Middle East would be valuable in their war effort. Protection of their oil interests, which were beginning to be recognised as invaluable, and of their route to India through the Suez Canal weighed heavily on Britain. The Germans worked with the Arabs on a plan for a pan-Islamic jihad against the British and the French.* But by 1915 negotiations with the British certainly raised Arabic hopes, only for their sense of betrayal to become so much worse when the promises they thought had been agreed were not fulfilled.

The key players in the intrigue that followed included: the Grand Sharif Hussein of Mecca; two of his sons, Faisal and Abdullah; T. E.

* Much later, during World War II, the Germans again worked on an alliance with the Arabs and used the new common enemies, Russia, communism and the Jews, as a lure. They were successful in raising a number of divisions of Muslim soldiers to the Wehrmacht and the SS in that conflict. The (failed) Iraqi uprising against the British came as a result of Nazi support. The Allies too were not far behind in their efforts to bring the Arabs on board but they were more successful in raising Jewish forces in Palestine.

Lawrence (Lawrence of Arabia); Sir Henry McMahon; and Gertrude Bell, a remarkable Englishwoman and close friend of many Arab tribal leaders. We will hear more of them and also of Sir Mark Sykes and François Georges-Picot shortly.

The British, in a Machiavellian series of manoeuvres, tried to woo both the Arabs and Turks to their side.[7] They had opened discussions with the Turks to try to wean them off their allegiance to the Germans, with promises about a continuing future for their empire in the Middle East, at the same time urging the Arabs to revolt against the Turkish regime.[8] They were also wooing the American Jewish community with promises of a homeland for Jews in Palestine, in the (mistaken) belief that they were powerful enough to persuade the American leadership to enter the war. Within the Foreign Service there were two significant misapprehensions. First, that the Grand Sharif Hussein spoke for all the Arab tribes and had a huge army he could call upon and second, that the Jews had a powerful network of operatives who could influence opinion world wide. Neither of these bore much resemblance to their true position.

There were many balls being juggled in the air in 1916 but the major driver of British ambitions was to ensure that the battle in Flanders was won and Britain was making all sorts of promises to the Arabs, the Turks and the Jews as well as the French, whom they were desperate to keep on side. In the event the Turks did not bite but the Arabs did, agreeing at first to what was also being offered to the Jews.

The British were not the only ones capable of double-dealing. Grand Sharif Hussein in Mecca was in conversations with the Turks at the same time as he was speaking to the British. The Turks were demanding that he take up arms in a jihad against the British in Egypt with its strategically important Suez Canal.[9] He and his sons, Faisal and Abdulla, were, however, more interested in examining what was on offer from what they thought was a more trustworthy Britain. They certainly trusted the British more than the French, whom they knew to have strong ambitions of their own for the Middle East.

The fact that Hussein, a Muslim of strong faith, was siding with the uncircumcised Western 'infidel' of Britain against the Caliph was remarkable in itself but he clearly had his eye set on an Arabic hegemony with himself as its head. His sons were indeed eventually installed as Hashemite rulers in Iraq and Jordan but only after many tears and much bloodshed.

After some soul-searching and with the support of most other Arab leaders in the secret societies of Damascus, Sharif Hussein decided to throw his lot in with the UK. But of course he demanded a price. This took the form of the 'Damascus Protocol', in which the cost of entering the war against Turkey was independence and self-rule for the Arab nations.[10] Hussein's 'protocol' envisaged a vast area covering the whole of Arabia, from the borders of Turkey in the north to Egypt in the south and from the Mediterranean in the west to Persia in the east, all to be placed under his leadership. Not everyone in the British-Middle East administration was happy with the idea of Hussein as ruler over so many disparate Arab tribal regions and Ibn Saud, Hussein's rival for leadership, was less than enamoured with Hussein's self-proclaimed style as King. But it was the Damascus Protocol that formed the basis of the unhappy correspondence between Hussein and Sir Henry McMahon, the British high commissioner in Cairo, who made what were taken to be clear British promises. Although Palestine was not specifically mentioned, an area including the 'districts of Damascus, Homs, Hama and Aleppo' was to be excluded from the purported new Arabic Kingdom.

The room for misunderstanding was considerable. It was not helped by the circumlocution of Hussein's language, which was lavishly embellished and circuitous, or by the fact that McMahon knew little or no Arabic. The problem was compounded when the translation into Arabic of McMahon's letter lost the subtlety (and deviousness) of the original English version. The omission of an apparently crucial comma caused problems when it was later recognised that the English version left open the prospect of a French takeover of Syria while the

Arabic version seemed to promise it to Hussein.[11] The subsequent offer of the thrones of Trans-Jordan and Iraq to Hussein's sons might have been an attempt by the British to placate the Hashemites.

It was then that, in Arab eyes, a series of disastrous developments occurred. Hussein thought he was clear in what he had been offered. The British, however, obfuscated over the details and argued about where exactly the boundaries of the proposed Arabia were to be, especially around the western parts of Syria including Palestine. The British sought to leave final 'details' over differences of interpretation until after the war and Hussein went along with that since time was running out and by then he needed the British as much as they needed him. The Young Turks were busily weeding out Arab plotters in Damascus and Hussein feared for his own life and that of his son Faisal. The British offer of arms and £125,000 per month in gold sovereigns may have oiled the wheels. In any event it was not until 1917 that a particular fondness for Palestine was planted in the Arab soul and, as events unfolded, Hussein did not feel so strongly then about that part of what he thought of as his kingdom. He was more concerned about French aspirations in the region. But it was the difference between the meaning of such words as 'independence', which is what the Arabs thought they had negotiated, and 'spheres of influence' and 'oversight', which the British and French fondly assumed they had agreed, that was later to cause so much of the trouble.

Sykes–Picot Proposals, 1916

Much has been written about the Sykes–Picot proposals and about the way in which they were the cause of much of the subsequent mistrust of Britain across the Middle East. It is, therefore, worth spending a moment outlining the genesis of this Anglo-French agreement and its impact even though in the end it was not implemented exactly as originally envisaged.[12]

At about the same time as McMahon was entering an encouraging correspondence with Hussein the UK government was under pressure to ensure that the Middle East did not fall into the hands of the Central Powers. It could not rely on the Arab chieftains, many of whom favoured the Germans. Nor did it have much faith that left to themselves the Arabs could keep a peaceful and secure control over such a huge stretch of land as the post-conflict Arabia envisaged in Hussein's Damascus Protocol. An alternative scenario was sought and Sir Mark Sykes, a considerable authority on the Middle East, was asked to come up with options for the governance of Arabia. He and François Georges-Picot, from the French Foreign Office and at the embassy in London at the time, produced their plan.

Sir Tatton Benvenuto Mark Sykes, a fascinating man, had used his considerable intelligence and charm in the service of Britain to good effect.[13] He held strong opinions but altered them rapidly when circumstances changed. A graduate of St John's College, Cambridge, he had written four books by the age of twenty-five. He was able to bring to his books knowledge of the Middle East gleaned during many trips to the region with his father and later as an attaché at the British embassy in Constantinople. He was a valuable bridge between the War Office, the War Cabinet and the Foreign Office in discussions on the Middle East. A classicist, he was responsible for renewing Greek and Roman names for Palestine, Iraq and Syria and it was he who chose the colours for the flags later used for the new countries of Jordan, Iraq and Kuwait.

Initially, his attitude to the Jews did not differ much from the commonly accepted negative views of the time but while he reflected opinion of them as 'despised and weak' in a letter to Faisal, he grew to admire Chaim Weizmann and worked on Faisal to reach an accommodation with him. By 1916 he was able to tell a Jewish audience that 'it might be the destiny of the Jewish race to be the bridge between Asia and Europe, to bring the spirituality of Asia to Europe and the vitality of Europe to Asia'.

While working at the Peace Conference in Paris in 1919, he died suddenly at the Hotel Lotti of Spanish flu at the age of thirty-nine. There was a strange resurgence of interest in him in 2007 when his lead-lined coffin was dug up to try to isolate the Spanish flu virus from his body in an effort to develop a vaccine. It was thought that his body, and the virus, might be well preserved. Unfortunately the coffin had split and the body badly decomposed. The scientists had to make do with poor specimens.

François Georges-Picot had a lower profile but knew Syria and Lebanon well, having been France's consul general in Beirut before the war, and was an advocate of a greater Syria incorporating Lebanon and much of Mesopotamia. He went on to become ambassador to Argentina and died aged eighty-one in 1951. He managed to achieve much for his country by his strong advocacy for the French case for oversight of Syria and Lebanon in his sometimes heated discussions with the British Cabinet. His role in the Sykes–Picot Agreement is his greatest claim to fame, or infamy, depending on your point of view. That, and perhaps the fact that he was the grand-uncle of Valéry Giscard d'Estaing, later President of France. His body has not turned out to be of interest.

The Sykes–Picot plan divided the land into British and French spheres of influence with one area, encompassing Syria and Lebanon, to be placed under French control while most of Mesopotamia was to be given over to the British. Palestine was to be overseen by an undefined international body since both countries had designs on it. Russia was to be given much of Turkey and in particular a port on the Black Sea. Limited autonomy was to be allowed for the Arabs themselves as Britain and France oversaw their emergence as sovereign powers.

Sykes had given assurances to Hussein about the scope of the agreement. He pointed out that Article 1 stated that 'France and Great Britain are prepared to recognise and protect an independent Arab State or Confederation of Arab States'. But he may not have been clear that it went on to state that 'in Area (a), France, and in Area (b) Great

Britain, shall have priority of right and enterprise and local loans … and shall alone supply advisors etc'.[14]

The proposal was certainly welcomed by the French, who had long-standing economic and cultural interests in Syria and Lebanon. And while there were dissenting voices in the UK, it gave the British a buffer in the north, provided by the French, between themselves and what was to have become Russian Turkey while keeping France at a safe distance from Egypt and the Suez Canal. Further justification for this division of the spoils was found when the Secretary of State for India, Austen Chamberlain, recognised that Baghdad was largely Shia and would offer resistance to rule from the Sunni Mecca of Hussein.

What both the British and French completely ignored were the sectarian divisions that were unleashed. The arrogant assumption that these divisions could be overridden by Western-style nationalism was a huge error whose repercussions are now being played out in the disintegration of national borders imposed then. The British oversight of the Middle East may have been seen as a way of influencing the whole region to join its side but the idea that the 'Arab World' could be treated as a single entity was soon shown to be far too naïve. The French were more concerned with securing the Christian Maronites of the Levant as a bulwark against the Arab nationalism that was threatening their interests in north Africa.

Half the population of the Iraq that later emerged were Shiites and a quarter were Kurds, neither of whom were too wedded to the aims of pan-Arabism, yet it was the Sunni faction, despite their numerically smaller presence, that took the reins of office. In Syria on the other hand, the Alawite section of the Shia took over despite the overwhelming numbers of its Sunni population. A complete mix-up! It is surprising that these regimes remained stable for so long. Only extremely tight and sometimes vicious dictatorial control was able to maintain that posture. It was this fundamentally unsustainable position that is now being overwhelmed, first in the Arab Spring and popular uprisings and then by Islamic fundamentalist factions. It is clear that imposing

Western-style structures on sectarian divisions across the Middle East was resented at the time and led to today's instability. Jordan is the exception and that regime has managed to survive because it has a predominantly Sunni population ruled by an enlightened and moderate monarch strongly supported by Britain and the USA.

At the time the Sykes-Picot Agreement helped Britain keep their French allies on board. The French were reluctant to accept the British need to send troops from the European lines to the Middle East and they were already unhappy that the McMahon negotiation was giving too much away to the Arabs. Sykes–Picot offered a way out.

Once formulated, the plan was shared in secret with the Russians, who accepted what was offered with alacrity. The plan had been kept secret for obvious reasons but after the Russian Revolution in 1917 brought the Bolsheviks to power they, wanting to disassociate themselves from imperial colonisation, withdrew their agreement to annex Turkey. They also immediately publicised details of the plan, much to the embarrassment of the British and the dismay of the Arabs.[15]

The Sykes–Picot Agreement clashed with the Hussein–McMahon understanding and with reassurances given to Hussein by T. E. Lawrence. However, as we will see, it was overtaken by agreements reached between David Lloyd George and Georges Clemenceau in 1919 that were even more constraining on the prospects for Arab self-determination.

Although the Arabs felt that they were being double-crossed, the British, in a typical bout of justification, believed that they could reconcile the Arab desire for self-determination with what they felt would simply be their oversight, support and sphere of influence. Lord Curzon, in the UK government, recognised that Sykes–Picot was a 'facade' but went along with it on the characteristic British grounds that they could govern better than anyone else. Others had purer intentions and believed that it was in the Arabs' best interests to have a benign supporter of their own ambitions. Whatever the intentions, many Arabs did not see it that way and the realisation that they had been merely pawns in the game being played out in Europe left them frustrated but powerless.

The Arab uprising against the Turks, encouraged by the McMahon–Hussein correspondence in 1916–17, was of only modest value in the war effort but the Sykes–Picot plan caused enormous ill-feeling. By the end of the war the situation had changed in many ways and the plan as originally conceived seemed no longer appropriate. Britain no longer needed a French buffer between itself and what now remained as non-Russian Turkey. And it no longer needed Hussein or his sons.

And, of course, the Balfour Declaration had been announced.

It was in this complex situation that Europe and the Middle East were about to be carved up in Paris. For the Arabs, Balfour was simply a further demonstration of Western perfidy.

The Birth of Zionism

The towering figures of early Zionism are undoubtedly Theodor Herzl and Chaim Weizmann and without them it is unlikely that we would have seen the birth of a Jewish state. Herzl was not the first to suggest it and many others contributed, as we will see, but it is to them that Israel owes its existence.

The realisation that there was no future for the Jews in Europe followed centuries of persecution and pogroms. Then the assassination of Tsar Alexander II of Russia in 1881 by a group of eight young revolutionaries unleashed a further wave of pogroms against the Jews of the Pale of Settlement even though only one of the eight, a young woman, Gesya Gelfman, was Jewish.[16] These officially instigated pogroms, numbering in their hundreds, were supplemented by drunken mobs who rampaged through the villages as the police stood by. Alexander III, successor to the throne, ably assisted by Konstantin Pobedonostsev, decreed that a third of the Jews should be converted, another third expelled and the final third starved to death. The notorious Kishinev pogrom of 1903 saw over a million Jews flee Russia and the one in Odessa in 1905, in which 2,500 Jews were murdered, added a further incentive.

Most of the émigrés went to the USA but about 35,000 socialist idealists went to Palestine with that gleam of utopia in their eyes. This *aliyah* (organised immigration into Palestine) accelerated the rise of Zionism and despite Arab fear and hostility Palestine was rather more bearable for Jews than the oppression they had left behind. But the increasing purchase of land was a cause of considerable conflict. Absentee Arab land owners in Beirut and Damascus, receiving a meagre income from poor farmers, were happy to sell their land at exorbitant prices to the Jews but local Muslim leaders saw that the loss in this narrow strip of territory between the sea and the river Jordan would threaten their livelihood and confiscate what they believed was theirs. Others saw it as a threat to the trade route between Syria and Egypt and to their guardianship of the Haram al-Sharif (Temple Mount) and the Al-Aqsa mosque in Jerusalem. It is not much wonder that there was increasing strife in the first decades of the twentieth century.

The philosopher Moses Hess had advocated emigration to a Jewish state in Palestine in his 1862 book, *Rome and Jerusalem*, and the idea of a home for the Jews in Palestine was far from new in Britain. The seeds had already been sown in Acre by the unlikely person of Napoleon in 1799 when he promised to restore Palestine to the Jews. He soon revoked that idea but in Britain during much of the nineteenth century evangelical Christian movements espoused the conversion of the Jews and their restoration to Palestine. Prominent Christian figures learnt Hebrew and many, both in Britain and in America, supported their return to their homeland. Sir Moses Montefiore had already visited Palestine early in the century and started investing in agricultural settlements in Safed and in vineyards elsewhere in the north while novels by George Eliot and Benjamin Disraeli (*Daniel Deronda* and *Tancred* respectively) later in the century extolled the case for a Palestinian home for the Jews. In 1840 *The Times* published a tract advocating such a course,[17] and although much of this enthusiasm was driven by a desire to convert the Jews to Christianity there was certainly much sympathy for their sorry plight. Lord Shaftesbury, a strong advocate for Jewish conversion, lobbied his Prime Minister, Lord Palmerston, to have them returned to Palestine.[18] Palmerston himself, even better disposed towards the Jews, had tried to persuade the Turkish Sultan of the advantages of allowing them to emigrate into Palestine,[19] and, in 1839, told the British vice-consul in Jerusalem that it was his duty 'to afford Protection to the Jews generally'. Shaftesbury wrote about 'a country without a Nation', referring to an underpopulated Syria, including Palestine, and 'a Nation without a country'.[20] Although he was not the first to use this phrase,[21] and while the country was by no means entirely an empty plot, it was to become a slogan for the Zionists. In America, leading Zionist Henrietta Szold was speaking of a return to a homeland for the Jews in Palestine immediately before Herzl published his fateful book (see below). By the time the Balfour Declaration was published the idea of a Jewish Palestine was well understood.

Meanwhile in western Europe anti-Semitism seemed at first to be falling during the Enlightenment as the poor downtrodden peasant Jews of Russia and Poland moved to Berlin and Vienna. Their assimilation and, in many instances, conversion to Christianity offered the prospect of normality. It led many Jews to a complacent and deluded sense of safety. According to Weizmann, his colleagues in German felt that once the Germans had had their eyes opened to the excelle qualities of the Jews, all would be well. 'A little enlightenment, j ciously applied, and anti-Semitism would simply vanish.'[22] And while it did. But soon anti-Semitism was converted to racism a Jew was made to recognise that he could never get rid of h identity no matter how assimilated he was.

Theodor Herzl

In the final decade of the nineteenth century this situation absolutely clear to the writer Theodor Herzl, prompting him to begin his life's work and to set down his ideas in *The Jewish State* (1896). It was he who made a nascent Zionism a political reality. Although Zionism was discussed by leading Jewish figures for most of the late nineteenth century, it was very much an internal set of discussions amongst like-minded Jews and lacked any focus. It was Herzl who recognised the need to engage politically with an international non-Jewish audience if there was to be any solid future for Zionism and the Jews.

Born in 1860 in Budapest, Herzl's assimilated family moved to Vienna when he was eighteen years old. There he qualified as a lawyer but soon became better known for writing plays and books before he moved on to journalism. Jews had prospered in many fields in his Vienna. More than half the lawyers and doctors were Jewish, the liberal press was largely in Jewish hands and cultural life, music and the arts were dominated by Jewish patrons.[23] The city of Mahler and Freud, Wittgenstein and Zweig and Schönberg, it was cultured and civilised but despite all this remarkable assimilation into Viennese life anti-Semitism grew.

Herzl came to Zionism late but he was made to realise that as a Jew he was prevented from entering the civil service and kept out of the inner circles of aristocratic society. The election of a virulently anti-Semitic mayor, Karl Lueger, in 1895 was a clear indication of the future direction for Jews and it was this very public ostracism, despite assimilation, that fired Herzl's Zionism. He was probably ignorant of the work of Hess or of Leo Pinsker, a Jewish physician in Odessa, who had already in 1882 pointed out that anti-Semitism was an incurable disease that could only be overcome by self-liberation. The reception given to Jews in the streets of Paris, where Herzl had been sent to report on the Dreyfus affair for the *Neue Freie Presse*, gave him no comfort and the many grossly anti-Semitic papers and books being published at that time struck him 'between the eyes'. Eugen Dühring's disturbed and disturbing essay of 1891, 'The Jewish Problem as a Problem of Race, Morals and Culture', was pivotal to his conversion.

It was this type of racial anti-Semitism that gave rise to his purely secular Zionism with its strongly political rather than religious bias. He

was never an observant Jew. He did not have his sons circumcised and they converted to Christianity in later life. But he realised that the only salvation for the Jews would be a state of their own and, by 1895, he had devoted himself to developing practical schemes for such a state.

He set about three tasks: gaining support internationally from without the Jewish community, creating a focused organisation for the Jews and pursuing a wide publicity campaign. He understood that it was essential to gain the attention and support of heads of state and travelled widely to try to enlist them. The Ottomans then ruled the Middle East and support from the Sultan of Turkey would clearly be important if land in Palestine was to be found. The Sultan was under pressure and short of money. Perhaps a deal could be struck. Kaiser Wilhelm of Germany was a key figure too but while Herzl briefly gained his attention, with neither him nor the Sultan did he gain anything more. He was more successful in London where he met Joseph Chamberlain, Britain's Colonial Secretary, who, after some thought, suggested the possibility that the Jews might be able to develop their homeland in east Africa. This came to nought, as we will see, but at least Herzl had aroused some sympathy for the notion of a Jewish state at a senior level in the UK government.

But the publication of *Der Judenstaat* ('The Jewish State') came as a bombshell to the Jews. Herzl made it clear that he was writing about a practical and practicable possibility and not just 'imponderables floating high in the air'. It was not simply the word 'state' in the title, although that alone was startling enough; it was the detailed description of what a Jewish state would look like and the steps needed to bring it to fruition that created such an impact. It would need financial backing, not just from philanthropy but from the issue of stock and the sale of property and possessions of those who left for the new land. He described in some detail the steps needed, including the formation of a Jewish company, a bank and a society of Jews to organise the gradual emigration to the new land.[24] The purchase of land, the setting up of the legal and constitutional organisations, trade, commerce and working practices, even a seven-hour working day, were all described. He was a democrat but his idea of democracy was somewhat to the right of centre. 'I think a democratic monarchy and an aristocratic republic are the finest form of Government' and 'A democracy without a sovereign's useful counterpoise ... tends to idle discussion in Parliaments, and produces that objectionable class of men – professional politicians'.[25] Ah! Yes. He initiated a series of International Zionist Congresses, the first in 1897, to take forward his ideas.

Devastated by what he had heard of the plight of Russian Jewry, Herzl was tempted to accept Chamberlain's suggestion of a Jewish homeland in east Africa (in what became Kenya but was known as the 'Uganda' scheme), as an immediate solution. It was soon dropped, however, as it became clear at the Zionist Congress of 1904 that the Russian members themselves were vehemently opposed to the idea.

He never ceased trying to convince world leaders and governments of the justice and value of the cause and he managed to sow the concept internationally of a Jewish homeland in Palestine. It was an uphill struggle for much of the time, to persuade not only others but also the Jews themselves with their often conflicting ideas. In his short Zionist life – he died aged forty-three – Theodor Herzl endured constant struggle and pain, sacrificing health and family life to his cause. But his seminal work was crucial for Israel's future existence.[26]

Chaim Weizmann

In the UK it was Chaim Weizmann who played the most significant role in persuading the government of the importance of a Jewish homeland. It came as a surprise to me to know that he is little recognised by the current generation of young Israelis but paradoxically, it was his strongly pro-British stance, absolutely pivotal in 1917 but anathema in the 1930s and 1940s, that led to his fall from favour.

He had a number of advantages. Born in a *shtetl* in the Russian Pale in

1874, he experienced first-hand the plight of Russia's Jews. He graduated in biochemistry in Berlin before spending time working on his research in Geneva and eventually making his way to Manchester. Here he found a supportive academic environment that suited him and his new wife. He became a British citizen and, working in the university as a reader in chemistry, he became a key national figure in industrial fermentation and went on to develop a process for the rapid production of acetone.

This was useful in the manufacture of cordite and had assumed some importance to a government anxious for a ready supply of explosives as the First World War began. Weizmann was asked to direct the British Admiralty Laboratories in London to further this work and it was there that he was able to take advantage of his privileged position. The First Lord of the Admiralty was then the young and frisky Winston Churchill, who exhorted him rapidly to produce large quantities of acetone. Weizmann was a very persuasive Zionist and had gathered a valuable group of colleagues – Simon Marks, Israel Sieff and Harry Sachar – in Manchester. In bringing C. P. Scott, editor of the *Manchester Guardian*, on board he achieved an important and powerful ally who, in 1906, introduced him first to Herbert Samuel, later president of the Local Government Board, and then to David Lloyd George. (While at the British Admiralty Laboratories he may have made further contact with Lloyd George, who in 1916 was Secretary of State for War.) His entry to the circles of the Foreign Office and the Prime Minister gave him the opportunity to expand on the Zionist cause. Extremely persuasive, he convinced Sir Arthur Balfour of the case for Palestine as the place for a Jewish homeland.

The Balfour–Weizmann Connection

They made an unusual pair, Balfour an English aristocrat and Weizmann a neatly bearded middle European Jew. Arthur Balfour had not been regarded seriously in Parliament at first. He gave the appearance of a detached, aloof man, aristocratically imperturbable and seemingly indolent but this was a superficial impression and a much more sympathetic picture is given of him by his niece and biographer, Blanche Dugdale.[27] He was certainly appreciated by a large circle of friends and was recognised as being extremely intelligent and amusing. Though logical and persuasive as a parliamentarian, he was not a politician in the modern sense and he did not obviously strive to climb any greasy poles. Stabbing opponents in the back was beyond him. But he was absolutely committed to his ideals with a strong British nationalistic, conservative backbone. Although he never married and had difficulty expressing emotion in his correspondence, he had no problem in enchanting, and being enchanted by, members of the opposite sex and probably had one prolonged liaison with a married woman.[28] He was a philosopher with his own set of ideas and had written several books including one titled *A Defence of Philosophic Doubt* in which he expressed his scepticism of both religious belief and blind acceptance of Darwin's scientific explanations of human evolution. There was rather more to him than is expressed in his much-quoted remark that 'nothing matters very much and few things matter at all'.

Winston Churchill described him as having the 'uplifted mental and moral vision' of 'a great Pope', adding, 'he was the best mannered man … considerate in every society and with great and small alike … All his life he dwelt in circles of admiring friends.'[29] His tendency to lean against any convenient wall and his reclining posture on the parliamentary benches seemed to mirror his laid-back approach to life so it was a surprise to some when in 1887 he was appointed Chief Secretary for Ireland by Lord Salisbury, the Prime Minister. But then it was realised that Salisbury (Robert Cecil) was his uncle, and when 'Bob's your uncle' anything's possible. He turned out to be a very effective minister despite his reputation as an aristocratic amateur and he went on to become Prime Minister. Although this was not a happy experience for him he later became Foreign Secretary in the government of Lloyd George and it was in that position he took up Weizmann's cause.

Much has been made of the reasons behind Balfour's support for Zionism. Some say that he knew little of the Middle East and did not fully understand what the Declaration might mean for the Arabs. Others supposed that he felt guilt for his support, when Prime Minister, for the Aliens Act of 1905, which had been introduced to limit immigration from Eastern Europe, largely of Jews. A desire to woo powerful American Jews to the cause in the – mistaken – belief that they could influence their President to enter the war on the Allies' side may have played a part, while yet others believed that he was keen to place a people who were supportive of the West in a strategically important part of the world. And the fear that the Jews might heed the blandishments of the Germans or, later still, to ally themselves with the Bolsheviks were believed by some to be important reasons to keep the Jews on board. But these are not the main reasons. Strategic influences played only a modest part and although he may have been optimistic about Jew and Arab living together, he was far from ignorant of the Middle East. He was quite clear in his recognition of the 700,000 Arabs that 'now inhabit that ancient land'.[30] There seems little doubt that the main driver was his innate sense of justice for the Jewish cause. His interest in the Jews and their history was life long, originating in his Old Testament training. He told his niece that 'Christian religion and civilisation owes to Judaism an immeasurable debt, should be fully repaid'. His moral sense of indignation at talk of anti-Semitism pre-dated his hearing about Zionism. He had met Weizmann many years before when he was canvassing for his seat in Manchester and it was there that he first gained an interest in Zionism, and he said as much in his many speeches.[31] In his maiden speech to the House of Lords on 21 June 1922 he said, 'I have never pretended that it was purely from … materialistic principles that the Declaration of November 1917 originally sprung.' He went on to say that there was no parallel in world history to the position of the Jews:

> Here you have a small race, originally inhabiting a small country, I think about the size of Wales or Belgium … at no time in its history wielding

> anything that can be described as material power, crushed between great Oriental monarchies, its inhabitants deported, then scattered, then driven out of the country to every part of the world and yet maintaining continuity of religion and racial tradition of which we have no parallel elsewhere ... We cannot forget, how they have been treated during long centuries ... our whole religious organisation of Europe has ... proved itself guilty of great crimes against this race.

There can be little doubt that it was these high-minded motives that drove him to support the Zionist cause or that they belie accusations of hypocrisy sometimes ascribed to him. On his death bed in 1930 he told his niece that he felt that what he had been able to do for the Jews had been the thing he looked back on as 'most worth his doing'.[32]

Lloyd George's Support and Jewish Opposition

David Lloyd George, of strong Welsh Methodist background, well versed in the Bible and with a working knowledge of Hebrew, was also well disposed to the Jews. He had met Weizmann while he was working for the government at the Admiralty and his law firm, Lloyd George, Roberts and Co., had been engaged in the 'Uganda' scheme back in 1904. By the time he was Chancellor of the Exchequer he well understood the Zionist's case. He was, however, much more pragmatic than Balfour and played on the advantage of having a favourably disposed Jewish people on the Allies' side in the Middle East. Weizmann lost no time in keeping him up to date.

Weizmann also worked his charm on Sir Mark Sykes, of Sykes–Picot fame, who was converted from an initially anti-Semitic stance to one of support for the Zionists. The Zionists and Weizmann did not have it all their own way, however, and much of the resistance to the idea of a Jewish homeland came, not from anti-Semitic voices, but from fellow Jews. Indeed most of the significant members of the government were soon convinced of the idea. But a strong case against the Zionist cause was being mounted by prominent Jews, including Lucien Wolf and, later, Edwin Montagu, a member of the government, using arguments that are once again becoming familiar today.[33] Why should an assimilated Jew, well integrated into British society, want to be involved in a Jewish homeland elsewhere? If I am an Englishman who happens to be a Jew why do I need it? Furthermore, if such a homeland existed would it not cause more anti-Semitism than already exists and wouldn't there be pressure for every Jew to have to leave England? Would it not be preferable to encourage assimilation and better treatment of Jews in countries where they are less privileged than in England? And isn't this whole idea not only a ridiculous pipe-dream with no chance of success but, in simply trying to achieve it, likely to cause more difficulties for Arabs as well as the Jews around the world? These arguments were strongly made by Montagu in Cabinet meetings and in memos during 1917. Montagu, who was then Chancellor of the Duchy of Lancaster in Asquith's Government, had inherited enormous wealth from his banker father, Samuel Montagu, the 1st Lord Swaythling. He wrote from his position in the comfortable establishment, not dissimilar from that of Viennese and Berlin Jewry at the turn of the century.[34] He seemed rather more sympathetic to Indian nationalism later as Viceroy than to Jewish Zionist aspirations. While Montagu thought of himself first as an Englishman and then as a Jew, that opinion was not necessarily shared by others. Herbert Asquith, the Prime Minister and a friend of Montagu, was mildly anti-Semitic in the fashion of the day and it was clear to him that Montagu, whom he referred to as 'the Assyrian', was a Jew. The fact that Montagu later married Venetia Stanley, who had converted to Judaism to do so, and had been Asquith's long-time muse, did not improve his opinion.

Asquith was not alone in his anti-Semitism. Richard Crossman later wrote of the 'bacilli of anti-Semitism' lying deep in the unconscious of most non-Jews, underlining Weizmann's argument that the Jew would always need a country of his own if he was to be able to hold his head up. Weizmann had never suggested that all Jews should go there or that Jews could not prosper in any other country, but that without a country of his own, a Jew would always be at the mercy of the whim of others. And if there were Christian and Muslim countries, why not a Jewish one?

He did win the day in the end after a fraught time in which he sought the support of America, France and Russia. He contacted Supreme Court Justice Louis D. Brandeis, the most senior Jewish Zionist in the USA, and he in turn persuaded President Woodrow Wilson to give modest but vital support for the Zionist cause. Later Weizmann easily diverted an initially sceptical Henry Morgenthau, a senior Jewish member of an American mission sent to try to negotiate a separate peace with the Turks. Morgenthau had been the US ambassador to Turkey but soon became an important supporter of the Zionist cause inside the US establishment. The French too came on board after Nahum Sokolow, whom Weizmann had sent to Paris, convinced Jules Cambon, of the Foreign Ministry, to write a letter of support, albeit in rather reluctant terms but enough for the British Cabinet to go ahead. Russian Jewry was, of course, strongly supportive but the outcome was always hanging in the air until the last moment.

The fortunate coincidence of Montagu being sent out as Viceroy of India during the crucial discussions in the Cabinet when they finally produced the Declaration allowed Weizmann to heave a sigh of relief. The Americans suggested minor changes to the evolving Declaration that were all included in the final draft. However, the Zionists were not out of the woods even then because, as we saw earlier, Lloyd George was still, in 1917, pursuing secret negotiations with the Turks that would have allowed them to retain their Arabian dominion in exchange for a peace deal behind the Germans' back. If these negotiations had been successful there is little doubt that he would have reneged on any agreement with the Jews (and the Arabs), in exchange for an early peace.

CHAPTER 2

The Balfour Declaration

THE JEWISH HOMELAND QUESTION had been actively discussed in the British Cabinet for years before the Balfour Declaration saw the light of day. In 1915 Herbert Samuel presented a memorandum to his colleagues entitled 'The Future of Palestine' and the Foreign Secretary, Sir Edward Grey, spoke in support. The stage was set but much agonising went into the drafting of the Declaration and the form of words finally adopted left a great deal open to interpretation. It was sent in the form of a letter, signed by Balfour and dated 2 November 1917, to Lord Rothschild, leader of the Jewish community; the original is now in the British Library.

The critical sentence reads:

> His Majesty's Government view with favour the establishment in Palestine of a national home for the Jewish people, and will use their best endeavours to facilitate the achievement of this object, it being clearly understood that nothing shall be done which may prejudice the civil and religious rights of existing non-Jewish communities in Palestine, or the rights and political status enjoyed by Jews in any other country.

A continuing source of discontent arose when neither this nor any previous draft of the letter spoke of the 'rights and political status' of the non-Jewish residents, only their 'civil and religious rights'. It also spoke of *a national home*, not *the national home.*

It was almost certainly intended that the imprecise wording would tread as careful a line as possible between the competing demands of Jews and Arabs. There was a utopian dream of a Palestine with Jew and Arab living peacefully together that generated much optimism, at least amongst the Jews. It is difficult to imagine that the drafters fully understood how many problems were to arise as a result. A rather complacent view was held that Palestine, a collection of sanjaks or districts ruled from Beirut and Constantinople and sparsely populated, could readily accommodate an influx of Jews. Balfour fondly believed that the Arabs should be grateful for freeing them from the yoke of the Ottomans and would not begrudge 'that small notch' of land for the Jews.[1]

One month after the Balfour Declaration appeared, General Allenby entered Jerusalem and Ottoman rule in the Middle East was almost at its end.

The Declaration has been regarded by some as a rare act of magnanimity by an imperial nation and by others as the most regrettable of the disasters inflicted on the Middle East by the British. Now there is a fanciful view too that Britain would have had wonderful relations with the Arab world if it had only not issued the Balfour Declaration, forgetting perhaps that Sykes–Picot and later interventions had a rather more detrimental influence on relationships.

The announcement of the Declaration was greeted with great excitement by the Jews but took some time to be recognised as a highly significant milestone. Perhaps the reticence of the media on Balfour had something to do with the fact that it coincided with the first reports of the Russian Revolution. In a strange coincidence, while Weizmann was enthralling Jewish students with his exposition of the Zionist cause in a café in Geneva, another Jew, Leon Trotsky, was across the street in another café extolling the virtues of communism. Remarkably, both achieved their main purpose in 1917.

Reactions by Palestinian Arabs to the continuing stream of Jews entering Palestine before 1917 were exacerbated by Balfour but their strong antipathy was fired less by anti-Semitism then than by their being deprived of land. The fact that the British were offering something that was not theirs to give did not find much favour with the Palestinians. As recently as 2016, Riyad al-Maliki, the Foreign Minister of the Palestinian Authority, was seeking support from Arab leaders to bring a law-suit against Britain for the Balfour Declaration.[2]

However, Palestinian antagonism in 1917 to the Jewish influx was not mirrored as strongly elsewhere in the Arab world. Grand Sharif Hussein in Mecca, self-proclaimed spokesman for many Arab leaders, and his son Faisal, seemed less concerned with Palestine than with what might happen in the wider Middle East. This was certainly their view in discussions they had had with Sir Henry McMahon in 1916, and Faisal even signed an agreement to cooperate with Weizmann in January 1919 after a couple of amicable meetings. There is a photograph of the two of them dressed in full Arabic regalia, both looking serious and Weizmann looking faintly ridiculous. Faisal and Hussein were both favourably disposed to Jewish immigration into Palestine and *The Times* reported their strong support and friendship towards the Jews at the time. Hussein, undisturbed by the Declaration, or by the Jewish influx into Palestine, had his eye much more firmly set on the rest of Arabia for his kingdom. The daily Mecca newspaper, *Al-Qibla*, in March 1918 wrote about the Jews as the original sons of the sacred homeland, namely Palestine, and welcomed them as brethren.[3] Faisal talked of the two main branches of the Semitic family, Arab and Jew, who understood each other. 'The Arabs, especially the educated amongst us, look with the deepest sympathy on the Zionist movement,' he wrote to the Austrian-American jurist Felix Frankfurter.[4]

The Faisal–Weizmann Agreement, signed in Paris on 3 January 1919, laid out in full the acceptance of immigration of the Jews into Palestine, their setting up of a Jewish homeland and the definition of boundaries between the Arab state and Palestine. Unfortunately that was not to be the end. Faisal appended a significant postscript in English, in which he stated that the agreement was entirely dependent on the Arabs gaining their full independence. He was vehemently opposed to French aspirations in Syria and Lebanon and made this a condition of his agreement with Weizmann, who he felt could be a valuable ally with Britain against the French. It was the absence of the independence he sought that scuppered this agreement rather than a dispute between Arab and Jew.

It was inevitable that there would be a clash of interests. The Jewish influx encouraged by Balfour's Declaration and the mandate that followed were almost the last spasms of declining British imperialism, coming at just the moment when Arab nationalism was emerging. A recipe for bloodshed. Before World War I, few challenged European nations as they colonised foreign countries to 'civilise' the aboriginals. Only later did the doctrine of Woodrow Wilson arise with its antipathy to the idea of 'Empire' and colonisation came to be seen as immoral. It is not too surprising then that the arrival of the Jews in Palestine was regarded as yet another example of Western colonialism rather than the return of an ancient people to their original home.

But Weizmann was certainly a smooth operator. He even gained the support of T. E. Lawrence when he entertained him to tea at his house in London. He managed to head off an American Commission report that recommended a combined Syrian–Palestinian mandate and worked his magic at the 1919 Peace Conference in Paris as he spoke to everyone he could meet. An idea of his erudition and powers of persuasion can be gleaned from his many speeches given during these years.[5]

While the French remained sceptical, the British and Americans were largely supportive and when Britain was given the mandate for Palestine, Weizmann believed that the Jewish homeland was safe. His battles had only just begun.

Jerusalem

Nowhere in the Middle East evokes such strong emotions and sense of attachment. Simon Sebag Montefiore, in his book *Jerusalem: The Biography* (2011), chronicles the long, and too often violent and bloody, history of this city in all its gory details. For more than a thousand years before the birth of Christ it was the centre of Jewish life. With its Temple and Holy of Holies it was the seat of Jewish religious activity and has continued to be yearned for in the daily prayers of the diaspora ever since. It was the focus of Christianity for over 400 years. Jesus was resurrected here and the Church of the Holy Sepulchre gathers thousands of pilgrims every year. And since Mohammed ascended to heaven from the Dome of the Rock it has been a centre for Muslims. The Al-Aqsa Mosque, originally built in 691 CE, remains the third most important shrine for millions of Muslims. The fact that the Jewish Temple and the Dome of the Rock were built on the same piece of land compounds the problem of who should hold precedence over whom.

During the Spanish Inquisition Jews fled to the Middle East, many to Jerusalem, and by 1880 they formed the majority of its residents. By 1900 there were about 28,000, mainly Sephardic Jews, out of a total of 45,000 Jerusalemites and by 1914 they were being joined by increasing numbers of Russian émigrés. During much of the nineteenth century the Jewish, Muslim and Christian population lived in close proximity to each other, mostly enjoying friendly relationships. Arab and Jew have lived in peace for long periods of history but, as we have seen, that harmony can easily vanish when rivalries and jealousy are allowed to dominate and extreme polar opinions take over.

Jerusalem remains at the heart of the conflict, and resolving who should have ultimate responsibility for the city and how it is governed is an enormous challenge. Not that there has been any shortage of solutions proposed for Jerusalem by well-meaning people: no fewer than sixty-five different arrangements have been proposed, but none have proved acceptable to all so far. I expand later on some of the ideas for a future Jerusalem. Currently East Jerusalem is largely Palestinian while Jews predominate in the West and the whole is within Israeli jurisdiction. The Temple Mount is under Israeli sovereignty but religious administrative responsibility is in Jordanian hands.

The 1919 Paris Peace Conference

American antipathy to imperial aggrandisement, endorsed by Bolshevik Russia, forced the UK and France to re-think their ambitions for the Middle East. But if the Arabs felt that here was an opportunity to regain something of what they had lost with Sykes–Picot they were soon to be disappointed.

Although Woodrow Wilson, the American President, was pressing for self-determination for the Arabs, he was an innocent in the hands of the wily Europeans who manipulated the wording of agreements to suit their own ends while seeming to comply.[6] Clemenceau, with his walrus moustache and grey suede gloves that never seemed to leave his hands, was almost as smooth an operator as Lloyd George and after much debate it was finally agreed that the French should have a mandate for Syria and Lebanon and the British for Mesopotamia, on the grounds that mandates were much to be preferred to colonisation.[7] Mandates were to be time limited even though the limit and the time were not defined.

Palestine, which according to Sykes–Picot was to have been supervised by some international body of undetermined type, was now to be placed under a British mandate. The fact that the British Army was in evidence all over the Middle East and that General Allenby had been the first to enter the captured Jerusalem placed them in a powerful negotiating position. The French, although resistant to British claims, were keen to gain support for their division of the spoils of war in Europe and reluctantly agreed. Relations between the French and British were strained but the British accepted that Syria and Lebanon should be handed over to the French mandate while increasing their own hold over Mesopotamia and Palestine. This was the basis of an agreement reached, informally at first, in 1919 by Clemenceau and Lloyd George.[8] 'British conviction of superiority clearly meant that they could take charge of less fortunate souls.'[9] It was clearly recognised that the Arabs were ill-prepared to take on self-government in 1919.

While Britain and France might have imagined a relatively quiescent and grateful Arab acceptance of the munificent offer of support they were making, Prince Faisal and his compatriots, who were under pressure from the Arab nationalists in Damascus, felt differently. Faisal had appeared uninvited with T. E. Lawrence at the Peace Conference, an imposing and impressive figure who was nevertheless largely ignored. The Zionists had also appeared before the Peace Conference with a proposal for a Jewish state encompassing both sides of the river Jordan and they too were side-lined. Faisal left for Syria almost empty-handed but not before signing a document said to exclude Lebanon and Palestine from the land to be handed over to the Arabs at some future unspecified date. He had also signed the agreement with Weizmann referred to earlier and reached some sort of accord with Clemenceau in which he believed he had gained self-rule for the Arabs. This was a short-lived idea.

Not everyone in the UK government was easy with the decisions being made that side-stepped previous agreements reached with the Arabs. The mandates were put into practice before they had been formally agreed by the newly formed League of Nations. The League was, in any case, very much the instrument of the great powers in its early years and only later did it gain its relative independence.[10] George Curzon, later Lord Curzon and then a minister in the Foreign Office, William Ormsby-Gore and members of the government pointed out that the French 'takeover' of Syria and Lebanon not only contradicted the Hussein–McMahon agreement, but was illegal under fifty-year-old international laws that covered non-intervention in the affairs of Maronite Christian, Druze and Muslim communities. The French, on the other hand, responded that they could not be expected to abide by an agreement (Hussein–McMahon) which they were neither consulted on nor a party to. This little spat between the allies was soon overtaken by the British calculation that giving way to the French had advantages to them in allowing a re-negotiation of territorial allocations under the newly designated mandates.

The following year, 1920, was to be one of considerable intrigue.

Despite the Faisal–Clemenceau accord, the Greater Syrian Parliament in Damascus had already, by July 1919, rejected French designs. Arabic nationalism continued to gain strength and in January 1920 the Syrians declared independence. Faisal was crowned King in Damascus and his desire to frustrate the French strengthened his liaison with the British despite their support for the Zionists. But getting into bed with the British raised Arab antipathy. Many still looked back with regret at the demise of Ottoman rule. He nevertheless filled the gap in Syrian leadership until he was summarily dethroned, as we will see.

The San Remo Conference, 1920

It was against the background of the Syrian bid for independence that the British and French rapidly called the San Remo Conference in April 1920. That conference, incorporating both countries and chaired by an Italian with Japanese and American observers, lasted only seven days but its recommendations were momentous and its conclusions have reverberated down the years. Attended by Lloyd George and his Foreign Secretary, Lord Curzon, the conference saw the French represented by their Prime Minister, M. Millerand, and M. Berthelot of the Foreign Office. The conference confirmed the mandates, for France in Syria and Lebanon, and Britain in Mesopotamia and Palestine, but more importantly for the Jews it enlarged on the Balfour Declaration. The French characteristically tried to renege on their support for Balfour's Declaration but Curzon, a somewhat ambivalent supporter of Zionism, reminded them of the earlier written agreements of their own Foreign Office in the person of Jules Cambon. Berthelot bad-temperedly accepted and suggested that they move on to more important decisions than 'minor points such as Zionism'.

The Conference went on to stress the term 'national' home for the Jews, promoting the idea of the Jews as a nation, Curzon even used the term *the National Home*, and while Balfour spoke of the British exerting 'their best endeavours to facilitate' a home for the Jews, San Remo made it obligatory for the mandate to put it into effect. The recommendations from San Remo were approved at the Supreme Council of Allied Powers and re-affirmed in statute two years later, in 1922, by the League of Nations.

Meanwhile the French, in a demonstration of perfidy that outdid even the British, quashed Arab aspirations in Damascus with a display of military might in the battle of Maysalun. They then drove Faisal out of the city, whereupon he fled to the south, where he was later offered the throne of the newly formed Iraq by the British. Thereafter the French remained in control of Syria and Lebanon until 1946 when both countries gained full independence.

The British were struggling too in trying to placate the Arabs while holding on to Balfour's Declaration. This was not easy, and there was even a vote in the House of Lords, in 1922, to rescind the Declaration (but not in the lower House). But Palestine was not the only problem for the British and may not have been the most pressing at the time. In Ireland the 'Irish Free State' was struggling to emerge; in India troubles were stirring with the slaughter of unarmed Indians at Amritsar and Gandhi's nascent mission for independence; in Iraq a revolt against the newly mandated British masters saw more than 8,000 Arabs killed; and in Egypt a rebellion against the British proved difficult to contain. Little wonder that Colonial Secretary Churchill was distracted.

Before 1920 the boundaries of Palestine were fluid to say the least; Palestinians until then were said to think of themselves as Syrians in the Palestinian, southern part of Syria. It was Hadrian (he of the wall separating England from Scotland) who first named the area Syria-Palestina. However, by 1918 a distinct Palestinian nationalism was beginning to stir. Amongst prominent 'ruling' or 'notable' Palestinian families, opinion was beginning to be divided between those who were wedded to a Syrian-led pan-Arab nationalism and others who favoured a circumscribed Palestinian Arab nationalism.[11] When it became clear that the French were about to take over the mandate for Syria the Palestinian nationalists gained the upper hand and in any event Faisal's flirtation with the British and their Zionistic tendencies was already tipping the balance against the pan-Arabists. It is worth noting, however, that the birth of Palestinian nationalism was more than simply the result of anti-Zionism and the machinations of the French in Syria were probably more significant.

As we have seen, Palestine was by then rather more than just a 'desolate and unlovely' land, as Mark Twain described it, and it would be a mistake not to note the ongoing commercial activity around Nablus and the export of cotton, soap and citrus fruits from Jaffa that spoke of a more nuanced picture. But Twain's comment was true of large parts of the rest of Palestine where cultivation of a rocky or marshy land by the influx of Jews was an uphill struggle. Malaria was rife and had already had an impact on Allenby's troops as they marched in from the south in 1917. The disease was so endemic that Allenby's army was to collapse from malaria the following year, fortunately after having finally defeated the Turks. One of the first acts of the Jews entering Palestine, in the years after Balfour, was the destruction of the breeding grounds of the mosquitoes, to keep them free of this disease vector.

When Britain took on the trusteeship of the mandate it included not only the land between the river and the sea but also that east of the Jordan, shortly to become Trans-Jordan. The Jewish leadership had been led to believe that the Palestine they desired would include the whole area east and west of the Jordan but it was soon to learn otherwise. It is little wonder that Israel's present-day borders are subject to so much debate.

Cairo Conference, 1921

The British, in an effort to placate the Arabs, made a series of recommendations at a conference they convened in Cairo in 1921. It made rapid progress under the chairmanship of Winston Churchill. A line was drawn along the river Jordan to define the eastern border of

Palestine for the first time (albeit reducing its area by about 70 per cent), with the new country of Trans-Jordan lying east of the river. Although both were ostensibly part of the same Palestinian mandate they were in practice two distinct mandates. This was underlined when Faisal's brother Abdullah was named Emir of Trans-Jordan and became King Abdullah I of Jordan while Faisal himself had become Faisal I of Iraq.

Although here we are focusing on the division of Palestine along the Jordan, it was the lines drawn in the sand beyond that are the source of so much current unrest in the Middle East.[12] The Ottoman administrative system, in operation for more than 500 years, was ignored under the pressure to share out spheres of interest. The land had previously been divided into vilayets (provinces) overseen by a military governor and sub-divided, sometimes according to religious and ethnic divisions, into sanjaks (districts). The area of Syria and Palestine with its series of such divisions was ruled from Beirut and Damascus while Jerusalem had its own specific oversight by the Turks. They were able to exert control and maintain a peace of sorts in this way. Not so after Cairo when, in creating Iraq, a single artificial monarchy combined Sunni and Shiite Muslims and Sunni Kurds, who have rarely had harmonious relations. Ancient animosities emerged and caused chaos although it is remarkable that these states survived as long as they did. It was clearly a wholesale division of the Middle East, in which tribal boundaries were completely ignored. Today, almost a hundred years later, there is a resurgence of pan-Arab nationalism in which the straight national borders defined by the Allies in the twentieth century for Iraq, Jordan and Syria as well as Palestine are no longer acceptable to IS (the Islamic State of Iraq and the Levant). A caliphate over the whole of Arabia and beyond is the 21st-century aim of this group, along with a repair of the damaging divisions of Arabia, which they see as being caused by the infidel West. The disastrous legacy of that rapid decision in Cairo has been played out in much continuing bloodshed.

A similar set of problems arose in the already unstable Balkans, where a counterpoise that had been maintained for years under the

Ottomans was disrupted. But for the Jews it is worth noting that while they were unhappy that Palestine was now to be reduced by over 70 per cent and restricted to west of the river it was tacitly agreed at Cairo that all of the smaller Palestine, including the West Bank, was to be part of the Jewish homeland. The Arabs rejected this part outright while Weizmann complained but accepted the proposal despite the objections of the newly formed, and armed, Israeli force, Irgun. Further erosion of the Jewish homeland was to follow later, as we will see, and this gradual nibbling away has coloured the positions sometimes adopted by Israeli leaders in the peace negotiations of recent years.

It is of interest that Abdullah I of Jordan had early entered into a non-belligerency agreement with the Jewish leaders, although without any publicity. This agreement was unhappily set aside in 1948, but more of that later.

None of these manoeuvrings endeared the Western powers to the Arabs and it was not until many years later that complete independence was gained for all, except for the Palestinians. Jordan gained full independence from Britain in 1946 but was not recognised by the United Nations until 1955. Iraq was accepted as a sovereign state by the League of Nations in 1932 but the French clung on to Lebanon long after Syria gained independence.

This story of double dealing, broken promises and subterfuge between 1914 and 1922 created much of the disenchantment of Arabs for the Europeans. The Balfour Declaration of 1917 simply threw further fuel on the developing inflammatory situation. However, Balfour was clearly only one source of resentment and at the time was not thought of as threatening, at least by Hussein and Faisal.

League of Nations Recognition, 1922

Oversight of the mandates was handed to the newly formed League of Nations. Its early days were not promising and its independence from the great powers was limited. The countries covered by mandates did not gain much comfort from Appendix C of Article 22 of the Covenant of the League of Nations, which stated that advanced nations should administer 'peoples not yet able to stand by themselves under the strenuous conditions of the modern world'.[13]

Despite its rocky administrative beginnings, in 1922 the League laid the foundations for the inexorable trajectory to Jewish statehood. The agreements reached in 1920 in San Remo were accepted unanimously and in full by the fifty nations of the League and laid in statute. In view of doubts that have sometimes been expressed in recent years about the legitimacy of Israel's existence, it is worth examining the wording of the international agreement reached in 1922.

The relevant League of Nations document is very clear on the rights of Jewish self-determination as a nation. It states in the preamble:

'Whereas recognition has thereby been given to the historic connection of the Jewish people with Palestine and to the grounds for reconstituting their national home in that country.'

Article 2 states:

> The Mandatory shall be responsible for placing the country under such political, administrative and economic conditions as will secure the establishment of the Jewish national home, as laid down in the preamble…

Article 4:

> An appropriate Jewish agency shall be recognized as a public body for the purpose of advising and cooperating with the Administration of Palestine…

Article 6:

> The Administration … shall facilitate Jewish immigration under suitable conditions … [with certain protections for other sections of society]'

Article 7:

> Provisions [shall be] framed so as to facilitate the acquisition of Palestinian citizenship by Jews who take up their permanent residence in Palestine.

And Article 22:

> 'English, Arabic and Hebrew shall be the official languages of Palestine…'

It is hard to read this document, signed on 24 July 1922, as anything but an agreement that the Jews were being given nationhood in Palestine by the League of Nations and that it would lead inevitably to a Jewish state.

The 1922 mandate was put into effect on 23 September 1923. It was fully accepted by the United Nations when it succeeded the League in 1946.

During the whole period between 1919 and 1922 Weizmann had been doubling his efforts to persuade the great powers of the value of a Western-orientated and friendly Jewish homeland in Palestine and had been recruiting as many allies as he could find. The emerging and vibrant American Zionist movement, under the guidance of such powerful figures as Louis D. Brandeis, Felix Frankfurter, Rabbi Stephen Wise and Jacob de Haas, was deeply committed but soon a rift with Weizmann opened up. The Americans were more concerned with more practical matters on the ground, especially malaria eradication and the economic development of the Jews in Palestine while Weizmann remained focused on the need to continue gaining political support. It is unfortunate that their differences became more personal with the passage of time.

Looking at the years 1917–25, it is possible to discern the origins of future discontent. At the time much of the Arab leadership was unhappy to be saddled with mandatory rule. The lack of the freedom to govern themselves played heavily on them. They saw it as a manifestation of British imperial colonisation masquerading as a mandate, lending a further spur to their antipathy to Israel's presence in the Middle East. Concern about Jewish immigration was at first localised to Palestinian Arabs and only later did the rest of the Arab world take on their cause. And for the Jews, the nibbling away of the Palestine they thought they had been offered by Balfour, first on the east of the river Jordan and later in various partition plans, has rankled ever since. It is this that has added fuel to the drive of current right-wing Israelis for a greater Israel incorporating the West Bank; that, and the idea of a biblical Israel, an *Eretz Yisroel*, based on ancient history.

CHAPTER 3

Many Resolutions but No Resolution

DESPITE THE FACT THAT Israel is a full member state of the UN its legitimacy is sometimes questioned, especially, but not only, in the Middle East. Opponents of Israel point to the ambiguous wording of the many UN resolutions and government statements and declarations to lay doubt on its foundation. It is worthwhile therefore to go back to the original texts to tease out the basis of these criticisms and to try to clear up some of the misconceptions.

Firstly, the Balfour Declaration. It is clear that the British government was persuaded of the case for a Jewish homeland in Palestine and Cabinet discussions recorded at the time leading up to the Declaration were strongly in favour of it. Even though there was no mention of a Jewish state, merely a home, it is hard to imagine that no one recognised the possibility that statehood would follow at some time. Balfour was reported to have said as much in private conversations. It is not difficult to understand why there was such Arab objection as a consequence.

Much has been made of the phrase 'it being clearly understood that nothing shall be done which may prejudice the civil and religious rights of existing non-Jewish communities in Palestine'. This form of words was reiterated in the League of Nations mandate and the Treaty of Lausanne (see later). Here was the belief that Arab and Jew would live in peace and harmony. There were Muslims who spoke in those sorts of terms in London, notably Sheikh Ismail Abdul al-Akki and Wadia Kesrawani, and Sharif Hussein and his son King Faisal were also supportive. However, this was not the case on the ground in Palestine. No account was taken of the state of local belligerency, exacerbated by the Declaration, that already existed there between Arabs and Jews. The inconsistency between the two aims – a 'Jewish home' and 'protection of rights' – became obvious as the two parties fought each other. Little thought had been given to how one party should protect the rights of another party that was intent on killing them. The distinction between self-defence and acts of aggression was not always clear cut.

Efforts to try to row back from this unhappy position were made in the next few years. Once again, Weizmann's constant lobbying in London, and Geneva at the League of Nations, was critical and he headed off repeated Arab efforts to stop Jewish immigration.[1] Partition between Arab and Jewish Palestine, recommended in the Peel Report of 1937 and ten years later at the UN, cemented the antagonistic forces across the new borders.

There has also been much discussion in recent years about the Jewishness of the state of Israel. Mahmoud Abbas, President of the Palestinian Authority, has been reluctant to recognise that Israel is a Jewish state. He shuns the idea of a 'state for the Jewish people' and even a 'national home for the Jews', seemingly to protect the rights of the Arab minority in Israel or more likely because he wants to demonstrate an Arab hope of taking over the state by demographic means.

Some might say that this does not seem to be such a vital condition during any negotiations. After all, Israel and Israelis know that it is a Jewish state and although the Jewishness of the state was always tacitly understood this issue was never overt before the last ten years. However, a glance at the history of how important it was to the Jews in the formative years of the 1920s may provide some justification now for Prime Minister Netanyahu's belief that it is fundamental. Achieving recognition for self-determination as a Jewish nation was no simple task and the continuing need for the Jews to have a safe haven – a homeland they can always find when required – has never gone away. It is true too that as well as giving credence to Jewish nationhood, the League of Nations pronouncement also gave a much greater sense of identity to the Arab Palestinians.

More Trouble in the 1920s and 1930s

It is hardly surprising that outbreaks of violence occurred throughout this period. With each Arab atrocity came an equally vicious response. The mandate became a poisoned chalice to the British as they tried to keep order between the Jews and Arabs. While Winston Churchill and Balfour continued to espouse the Zionist cause, the military establishment in Palestine were reluctant supporters of the Jews for much of this time.

The situation was not made easier when Haj Amin al-Husseini was appointed Grand Mufti of Jerusalem in the belief that he would be able to bring order to the chaos in Palestine. A flamboyant charismatic man, whose family had appropriated the Husseini name, he had added the appendage *Haj* (pilgrimage) having been on a pilgrimage to Mecca and falsely proclaimed he was descended from the Prophet. He had grand aspirations to make his mark on political Islam. He used Jerusalem as a tool, claiming that Al-Aqsa was in danger of a takeover by the Jews. Despite his obvious and intense hatred of the Jews he was appointed Grand Mufti in 1921 by Lord Samuel, the Jewish high commissioner to Palestine, in a spectacularly misplaced effort to be seen to be entirely neutral in Arab–Jewish affairs. This is the Mufti who was responsible for inciting most of the violence against the Jews over the next fifteen years and blame for the vicious attacks, in which several hundred Jews and Arabs were killed, can be laid directly at his door. He later turned his ire on the British and in 1937 escaped to Lebanon and later to Damascus as he became too much of a handful for the mandate. He continued to sponsor violence until he re-appeared in Germany in 1941, where he became an ally of Hitler.[2]

Jewish enthusiasm for Palestine continued to grow as threats to the Jews' existence in Europe increased. By 1945 there were about 500,000 Jews in Palestine compared with 1.2 million Arabs but despite the discrepancy in numbers they had established not only a strong agricultural base but also an increasingly firm cultural foundation with hospitals, theatres and a university. Although the Palestinians had been successful around Nablus and Yaffo in growing cotton, olives and citrus fruits during the nineteenth century, the Jews were able to change what had largely been inhospitable land beyond these centres into blossoming orchards and vegetable gardens. And the Arabs watched with growing resentment, feeling that they were being dispossessed even though much of the land that had been sold was marshland or desert and sparsely populated. They felt left behind as they saw the Jews prospering.

The kibbutz movement bred strong independent young men and women who became increasingly self-reliant. They were the backbone of Jewish resistance to the efforts of the Arabs to eliminate them and stop their 'invasion' from Europe. They were not averse either to offensive actions of their own where they felt they were warranted in pursuit of the goal of a Jewish state.

Riots and outbreaks of violence continued throughout the 1920s and 1930s with particularly damaging assaults on kibbutzim between 1936 and 1939. This was the time when Orde Wingate, a British major, began to lead the Jewish opposition, the Haganah, against Arab gangs. Despite this picture of mutual antagonism there were many exceptions where Arab and Jew lived in reasonable harmony during this period. Mustafa Abbasi, Professor of Middle Eastern History at Tel-Hai College, told me that he remembers as a child his parents and grandparents speaking of their good relations with the Jews in Safed, the Chief Rabbi being a frequent visitor to their home during this period.

The Peel Commission and Partition

When an Arab general strike, lasting more than six months in 1936, caused more chaos, the British set up a commission under Lord Peel, grandson of Prime Minister Robert Peel. He was asked to come up with solutions that might placate both the Arabs and Jews, a fruitless task but one that reflected British thinking very clearly.

Peel rapidly realised after arriving in Palestine that there was no common ground between two people fighting for the same piece of land. The only hope lay in a surgical operation. His report in 1937, covering no less than 423 pages, represented a first stab at a plan envisaging a division of Palestine into a Jewish and an Arab state.[3] The latter was to be annexed to King Abdullah's Trans-Jordan while a thin sliver of land along the coast was to be the province of the Jews. Weizmann, although reluctant to see his idea of a homeland reduced to a fraction of the Palestine that Balfour had seemed to promise, urged acceptance, realising that here, for the first time, was a clear recognition of a Jewish sovereign 'state' as against a 'homeland'; and, again, Jewish immigration was encouraged. David Ben Gurion, by then the acknowledged leader of the Jews of Palestine, even more reluctant, eventually agreed. Within Israel, Ben Gurion is its most highly regarded founder and, along with Herzl and Weizmann, is one of the three most significant figures in its history. Born in Plonsk in Russian-dominated Poland in 1886, by his late teens he had rapidly established himself as a charismatic leader of men. His early socialism led to his arrest by the Russians and later to his leadership of left wing groups and the trade union movement in Palestine. He had emigrated in 1906 and soon joined an agricultural commune, a forerunner of the kibbutz movement, helped set up a Jewish self-defence group (Hashomer), and was deported by the Ottomans before returning to join the British Army's Jewish Legion. He remained a passionate socialist throughout his life, informal and decisive but privately reserved and intellectual. While Weizmann was busily engaged in quiet diplomacy with heads of state internationally during the 1930s, Ben Gurion was actively creating facts on the ground in Palestine. It is not difficult to understand why these two men did not see eye to eye as they differed on what was needed to create a Jewish state. The fact is, both approaches were vital but neither man could easily accept the other's approach. Leading the struggle on the ground, Ben Gurion was later able, through his dominant and dominating personality, to weld the disparate armed groups into the Israel Defense Forces (IDF) and it was natural that he should become Israel's first Prime Minister in 1948.

There has been some dispute about a letter Ben Gurion wrote to his son, Amos, from London in 1937 about the Peel proposals. He accepted them but wrote, in Hebrew, that the proposed Jewish state 'in only part of the land' was not the end but the beginning. The particularly contentious part of the letter, currently in the Israel Defense Forces archives, talks of expelling the Arabs but there are words crossed out before that which allow a different interpretation and on which critics of Israel and revisionist historians have focused. Ben Gurion recognised that 'we will get more than we already have' and 'I am confident that we would not fail in settling in the remaining parts of the country, through agreement and understanding with our Arab neighbours, or some other means … There is no Arab immigration problem. Arabs are not persecuted. They have a homeland and it is vast … The Jews could be equal allies, real friends, not occupiers or tyrants over them.' Edward Said paints a somewhat different picture. He suggests that the land was far from lacking people, that they were not all as impoverished as is sometimes made out, that later, in 1948, they did not simply flee but were forced out and that the Zionists were much more savage than the Palestinians.[4] Clearly the picture takes on a different appearance depending on where you sit, and while there may be a kernel of truth in Said's suggestion it is far from the whole truth.

The Arabs, however, vehemently rejected Peel, not least because the recommendations included the loss of orange groves and, more significantly, the transfer of large numbers of the population from the nascent Jewish 'state' in a third of the land west of the river Jordan. Only Abdullah amongst Arab leaders was in favour. Soon the plan was recognised as unworkable. The Woodhead Committee, which later examined the practicalities of introducing the Peel recommendations, realised that the political, administrative and financial difficulties were just too great and the proposals were quietly dropped.[5]

Meanwhile the position of the Jews in Germany was becoming increasingly fraught as Hitler came to power. Until then many Jews there had been in positions of influence and were seemingly well integrated. All that was to change in the 1930s although it is of interest that Hitler, who had already revealed his fearful anti-Semitism in *Mein Kampf*, did not object to getting rid of the Jews by letting them go to a state of their own, well away from Germany. He soon put a stop to that idea when ex-Grand Mufti Husseini intervened.

The White Paper, 1939

The Jews felt that the British civil and military authorities in Palestine were largely anti-Semitic. In a desire to lean towards the Arabs, regarded by them as the weaker party, they pressed the Jews harder. The Palestinian Arabs, however, saw things differently. They felt that the British with their innate sense of fairness leant too closely to the Jews and many Arabs lost their lives or were imprisoned by the British. For the British, in the middle, these were uncomfortable times.

By 1939, with a European war in the offing, the British were even more anxious to keep the Arabs on board. The result was the MacDonald White Paper putting the idea of a Jewish state off the agenda and placing a strict limit on Jewish immigration.[6] Churchill spoke out in the House of Commons against the restrictions,[7] but to no avail and it remained the British position until well after the end of the World War. It is difficult to overestimate the revulsion in which the British were held by the Jews in Palestine as they saw them condemning so many of their brothers and sisters to certain death in the camps of Europe. It was the attitude displayed by Lord Halifax when he was reported as saying 'There are times when considerations of abstract justice must give way to those of administrative expediency' that so incensed the likes of Menachem Begin, then the leader of Irgun, and determined his opposition to the British ever after.

Even before the war Ben Gurion had said, 'We will fight with the British as if there is no White Paper; we will fight the White Paper as if there were no war.' And they did.

An intriguing episode in 1942 saw the British in a schizophrenic stance in which one part was training and arming Palmach, the striking platoon of Haganah, to help protect Palestine should the Germans invade from north Africa, at the same time as the British military police was disarming Palmach and arresting its members. Only when Rommel was defeated at El Alamein and the German threat retreated did the arming and training of Jewish forces cease. The British clearly knew that the Jews would fight with them against the Germans come what may and decided to make more effort with the Arabs. They were fearful that the latter were being wooed by the Germans again and knew that the ex-Grand Mufti was well disposed in that direction.

The three years between 1945 and 1948 were unhappy ones for all in Palestine: the British, the Arabs and the Jews. Coming on the back of the horrors of the Holocaust the stresses and strains in Palestine became increasingly difficult to contain. Jewish immigration into Palestine had almost ceased by 1945 but the full realisation of the enormity of the Holocaust and the devastation of European Jewry soon became starkly obvious to the world. Six million had been slaughtered and now one million displaced and enfeebled survivors remained in limbo. What to do with them as evacuation of the concentration camps began? Palestine was seen as somewhere they might find refuge from a Europe that was trying to recover from its turmoil. But the British, responsible for the mandate, remained wedded to the 1939 'White Paper' and closed the doors. Their fears were that a large influx of Jews would create even more unrest amongst the Palestinians and with the increasing power of oil pressing the British to keep the Arabs elsewhere on board, they kept tight control over the number of Jews allowed into Palestine. Noam Chomsky wonders why the survivors could not have been given the choice of where to go.[8] Some were indeed allowed to go to the USA, South Africa and Canada so why Palestine? But he forgets that no other country was rushing to take them and the only hope for most was the Palestine that the Jews had long desired. The Americans had already, by 1924, adopted their Immigration Bill that placed strict limits on the number of eastern European immigrants.

The injustice of their position brought international opprobrium on the British, while Jewish resistance became much more active and violent. The 100,000 Jews who had fought alongside the British during the war were dismayed by the continuing impact of the 'White Paper'. The British became increasingly reviled as they continued to operate the strict limits on immigration and acts of violence were doubled against them. It was the splinter group Irgun (in full Irgun Tzvei Leumi, also known by the acronym Etzel), which had become disenchanted with the Jewish leadership's policy of restraint, that was causing most of the problems for the British.

Formed initially to defend the Jews against attacks by the Arabs during the 1930s, Irgun became increasingly aggressive, often to the dismay of the Jewish Agency. It joined the British in fighting the Germans but after the war things changed dramatically. The assassination of Lord Moyne, the British Minister of State in Cairo in 1944, by an even more extreme group, Lehi (Lohamei Herut Israel – Fighters for Freedom of Israel), created great animosity in Britain while the Jewish Agency was appalled and declared Lehi a terrorist organisation.

Moyne had been demonised because of his action in 1942 in sending back a ship, SS *Struma*, with its cargo of hundreds of Romanian Jews who were all killed when the *Struma* was later torpedoed in the Black Sea. His failure to agree to a deal with Adolf Eichmann, who had offered a million Jews for arms in 1944, did little to improve his reputation. But his assassination was a particularly damaging act for the Jews since Moyne had been converted by then to the idea of partition and Jewish statehood. It was greeted with outrage in Britain and put back the case for further migration and a Jewish state. Britain's security forces watched with apprehension the activities of Irgun operatives in London,[9] while the British Labour Party, which had been very supportive of the Zionist cause at the Labour Party meeting, soon changed tack when they came into office in 1945.

Irgun began raiding British troop quarters and post offices as well as responding to Arab attacks. When its operatives were arrested and executed by hanging its response was sickeningly rapid. Two British soldiers were hanged in retaliation, to be followed by a further series of raids on British instalments culminating in 1946 with the dynamiting of the King David Hotel in Jerusalem, where the British mandate offices were sited. Ninety-one people were killed including thirteen British soldiers.

Menachem Begin was the last leader of Irgun and his character must have been strongly influenced by this critical period in Israel's history. His sense that the Arabs were hell bent on the destruction of the homeland he had spent his life working towards and that they would never come to accept a Jewish state strengthened his resolve. He came to regard the British as almost as wicked as Hitler's Germany in their aggressive prevention of Jewish immigration from Europe, and their turning back of boat-loads of Holocaust survivors left a deep mark. Begin was a disciple of Ze'ev Jabotinsky, a clever and charismatic man with a very clear approach to the Arabs. Although he spoke of coexistence and of compassion and dignity he believed that only aggressive action would bring the Arabs to an acceptance of Jews and Israel. To Begin, violent action was needed to remove the British yoke entirely and this put him on a collision course with Ben Gurion. One does not have to look too far into Begin's history to understand his resolute brand of Zionism. He seemed never to recover from his sense of guilt at having fled Warsaw in 1939, leaving behind 90,000 members of his Zionist Behar organisation who were doomed to a certain death. The later news of the death of his father, brother and nephew, shot by the Germans and their bodies thrown into a river, left him devastated. Imagine then his feelings when, in 1943, he arrived in Palestine after a period in a Russian jail. His deeply buried fury must be responsible for his unbending belief in the right of the Jews to a state he had fought so hard to achieve. It surely determined his negotiating stance later when, as Prime Minister, he faced Anwar Sadat at Camp David.

At the other extreme stood Chaim Weizmann, who had spent his life negotiating with heads of state, and in particular with the British. He found violence abhorrent, believing in the value of patient persuasion, at which he had excelled. Between the two stood Ben Gurion, ever the pragmatist, who believed that aggression must be tempered by negotiation. He took a leaf out of Machiavelli's book, who advised that both attributes were necessary if a new state was to be formed.[10]

The League of Nations had already, before World War II, drawn attention to the fact that the 'White Paper' recommendations were in conflict with the conditions of the mandate. President Truman was now, after that war, pressing the British to allow 100,000 Holocaust survivors to immigrate to Palestine and was appalled when the British mandate dragged its heels. An Anglo-American committee set up in 1946 recommended rescinding the 'White Paper' to allow the immigration of a large number of Jews. Richard Crossman, a member of the committee, described how they had been appalled by the state of the survivors held in the camps and recommended urgent action.[11] But the British Labour government under Clement Attlee vacillated and only a trickle was allowed in. It feared that the rapid influx of 100,000 destitute Jews would cause chaos amongst the Palestinian Arabs and perversely recommended that Haganah, the army of the Jewish Agency, should be disbanded first to avoid bloodshed.

The British government's policy in 1945 was formulated by Foreign Secretary Ernest Bevin, who was strongly opposed to Jewish nationalism, even though the 1944 Labour Party conference had advocated a

Jewish state, and was supported by Attlee. Bevin was certainly regarded as anti-Semitic but it is also likely that a desire not to alienate the Arabs complicated his view. He thought of the Jews as clever propagandists, far too pushy, and the Arabs had to be protected from them.[12] The value of oil and the importance of the Suez Canal were further key factors for him. When the *Exodus*, a ship packed with more than 4,000 Jewish refugees, docked at Haifa, it was turned back by the British. Bevin ordered its return to France. When the refugees arrived a month later they refused to disembark, the French refused to use force and the refugees ended up back in German camps. Bevin was reviled across the world for this devastating action, yet he persisted in talking about a 'Jewish conspiracy' against him personally. He ignored the fact that while not all of the Arabs had been supportive during World War II, the Jews had fought in large numbers alongside Britain against the Germans.

The British position became increasingly untenable, costly and humiliating. Neither the Arabs nor the Jews were willing to tolerate the presence of the mandate and Britain risked alienating the USA, on whom it desperately relied for funds. It was spending £30–40 million a year it could ill afford to maintain the mandate and the thousands of troops it needed to keep order.

An embittered Bevin took on the cynical suggestion of an American diplomat that Truman's support reflected his wish to divert the Jews from New York. This aside did little to improve his reputation as an anti-Semite. It is true that America had also resisted Jewish immigration before the war with the US quota laws of 1924. At a conference in the French spa town of Evian, convened by Franklin D. Roosevelt back in 1938, when the plight of the Jews in Germany was becoming dire, only one of the thirty-two countries represented, the Dominican Republic, was willing to consider accepting Jewish refugees. Jews were welcome in very few places and it seemed that in a post-war world a Jewish state in Palestine would be a convenient way of easing its conscience.

It is easy to see why the idea was floated that it was the Holocaust that allowed Israel to come into being. However, this ignores the fact that virtually half the world's population of Jews were lost in the gas chambers and that there were almost too few of the cream of its youth to produce a viable state. If the war in Europe had continued for another year, and even more Jews lost, the creation of Israel would have been threatened.

Resolution 181 and Partition, 1947

In May 1947 the UN asked a Special Committee on Palestine (UNSCOP) to come up with proposals to break the impasse that was threatened as soon as Britain gave up the mandate. UNSCOP took evidence from all who were willing to give it and that included Jewish representation. Most, although not all, the Palestinians refused to co-operate on the grounds that they believed that it was illegitimate for the UN to accept League of Nations resolutions on Palestine. The committee, after visiting Palestine and the European camps, both of which shook them for different reasons, presented their observations to the UN General Assembly. These formed the basis of Resolution 181 and it was here that partition once again came to the fore.[13] Three separate areas were proposed: a Jewish state; an Arab state; and Jerusalem, including the holy sites of the Church of the Holy Sepulchre and Church of the Nativity plus Bethlehem. Jerusalem was to be administered separately in a 'corpus separatum' presumably to reflect Christian concerns about leaving this area to be controlled by Jews and Arabs.

Apart from Jerusalem, which accounted for 2 per cent of the whole, the Jewish state was to have 56 per cent of the land west of the Jordan River and the Arab 42 per cent, but the borders were drawn in a mysterious, and ultimately unworkable, way. The Jewish state was split in two by the strange proposal for Jerusalem with its long tail stretching to the coast at Jaffa. Most of the Jewish state was to be in the sparsely inhabited Negev desert and the rest comprised a coastal strip joined by a narrow isthmus to the Negev, while the Arab state was also divided with the prospect that it might become incorporated into Trans-Jordan. The proposed Jewish state would then contain a small majority of Jews (498,000 against 407,000 Arabs), while the Arab state would have about 735,000 Arabs and only 10,000 Jews.[14] Jerusalem was to have approximately equal numbers of Jews and Arabs.

While the vote on UNSCOP's report failed to reach the two-thirds majority needed, four days later, after huge lobbying efforts by the Jewish Agency staff in New York, it was passed by the General Assembly with a 72 per cent majority, well beyond the threshold.

It should have been clear that the proposed borders were both impracticable and indefensible. There had been much lobbying by Weizmann and the Jews and threats by the Arabs of the bloodshed that would follow, but a combination of pressure by the USA and a sympathetic recognition of the recent plight of the Jews in Europe carried the day. Although Britain abstained in the vote, Clement Attlee suggested that the Commonwealth countries might vote in favour, which they did. Recognising the problems that would follow, Britain was happy to hand over the administration of the deal to the UN.

The Jewish leadership accepted the resolution even though they understood that the extent of the land they were being offered had been much diminished and that they would face an immense problem in defending its borders. They were encouraged by the mention of a Jewish 'state' no less than twenty-seven times in the resolution. They accepted in the belief that this would be simply an interim position and despite the objections of the extremist groups Irgun and Lehi. The Arabs rejected the plan outright and because the resolution was agreed only by the General Assembly, and not the Security Council, its legitimacy was doubted.

The reasons why the plan did not go for approval to the Security Council then, where it could have been confirmed, are obscure. It may be that there was a reluctance to take this path because of the realisation that enforcement of the plan might have required military intervention to which the UN was unwilling or unable to commit. The Security Council did, however, finally accept Israel as a UN member in May 1949.

There were still several opportunities for the Zionists to lose their hard-fought position between the adoption of the resolution and the end of the mandate. The British government remained antipathetic, the Arabs were threatening oil embargoes, and anxiety was growing in the USA, where President Truman's advisors were urging caution and suggesting some type of trusteeship instead of partition. They feared that the Arabs would be alienated and dispatched into the arms of the Russians. They also saw that the Jews would be easily defeated by the massed Arab armies and they, the Americans, would be placed in a dilemma as to whether they should intervene. Of course none of that happened. The Americans also told the Zionists that they would not come to their aid if they were to be attacked by the Arabs. Fortunately for them, Weizmann was again active even though he had resigned from the Zionist leadership. By then the influence of America had overtaken that of Britain and its vibrant Jewish/Zionist leaders had demonstrated their position at a conference at the Biltmore Hotel in New York.

Weizmann met President Truman more than once and strongly made the Zionist case. It was he who probably ensured that the Negev should be included in the putative Jewish state. Truman remained a strong supporter of partition and that was decisive. If Roosevelt had still been alive there is some doubt as to whether he would have been so supportive since he had spent time talking to Ibn Saud in Arabia and subsequently became a less than enthusiastic friend of the Zionists. He equivocated about Israel's position and it is likely he would have taken the advice of his staff not to support the Zionists.[15] In any case the Americans did not come to the aid of Israel when it was being attacked in 1948. In her polemic against Israel, Alison Weir makes much of America's 'errors' in supporting the war against Hitler's Germany and in its support for Israel.[16] But her selective use of doubtful sources fails to convince that a succession of American Presidents were misled.

Despite the doubts, there was much celebration amongst the Jews across the world. Meanwhile in Palestine Arab mob violence, which had been simmering for years, broke out immediately. The civil war that followed in the dying days of the mandate began to make a mockery of the carefully constructed borders of Resolution 181. Then, when the British finally withdrew, with little preparation on the ground, a quite different set of borders emerged, as we will see in the next chapter.

Against this background it is not difficult to understand why the possibility of peaceful relations between Arab and Jew was off the agenda. The Arabs of Palestine viewed the invasion of their land as completely unacceptable while the Jews held firmly to the view that part of Palestine, now with the international legitimacy of a UN resolution, was their homeland by right of history and religion. These were the incompatible views that have bedevilled all efforts since then to reach a peaceful resolution.

CHAPTER 4

War, Armistice but Few Intimations of Peace

The 1948 War of Independence

THE CONFLICT BETWEEN ARABS and Jews of 1947 transformed from a civil war into the 'War of Independence', starting on the day Israel declared itself as a Jewish state, 14 May 1948.

In the build-up to that war, atrocities were mounting on both sides. Arab forces were besieging Jerusalem and more than 2,500 Jews were holed up in the Old City. Efforts to relieve them were frustrated by Arab troops firing from the villages lining the road from Tel Aviv. Irgun forces headed by Menachem Begin attacked the village of Deir Yassin, a serious gun fight followed and more than 100 villagers and militants were killed. Previous friendly relations between these villagers and the nearby orthodox Jewish community of Givat Shaul were blown apart in the conflict. But the repercussions caused even more devastation. Accusations of maltreatment of Palestinian civilians, including rape and beatings, that were reported in their media markedly accelerated the flight of many. And while much of the Palestinian news was shown to have little relationship to the truth this did little to quench the outrage within and without Israel. It may have also bolstered the desire of the Arab neighbouring countries to invade shortly thereafter. An ambush, four days later, on an Israeli medical convoy travelling to Hadassah Hospital on Mount Scopus, in which seventy-seven doctors, nurses and patients were killed, was regarded as a revenge attack. The massacre of Jews at Kfar Etzion on 13 May and then the murder of some and the evacuation of many more Arabs from Lydda in July were continuing examples of the devastating impact of the struggle. The international response to Israeli actions contrasts with the lack of interest in the French massacre in Algiers of more than a thousand occupants of the Setif and Guelma camps in 1945.

War

On 15 May the local Palestinian forces were joined by an armed invasion from Egypt, Jordan, Lebanon and Syria with support from Iraqi troops. The suggestion by Chomsky that Egypt, Syria and Jordan had approached the UN with a partition plan for Israel, but were rebuffed by the US, would have been news for the Israelis battling for survival. Hostilities became increasingly bitter, civilians suffered badly, many were killed and large numbers of Arabs were driven out as Israel fought for its existence. It has been suggested that many Palestinians fled on advice from Egypt and Syria that they would soon be allowed to return when the war was won but others have expressed doubt about the validity of this idea. One beacon of humanity in all of this mayhem was the plea from the Histradut trade union in Haifa to its Arab colleagues to stay and live alongside the Jews in that traditionally mixed city.

The war rapidly saw Israel's size reduced by the invading armies to a short, narrow strip along the Mediterranean Sea. Haifa was encircled in the north and towns within 30 kilometres of Tel Aviv had been lost in the south. Ben Gurion, by now Prime Minister, was at first being advised by his Chief of Staff that Israel's chance of survival was fifty–fifty.

After these initial losses, Israel slowly regained the initiative. On three occasions the UN called a truce; each lasted a few weeks, but they were used by both sides to re-arm and the war went on. Israel made better use of the cease-fires, organising its army, bringing in new recruits and weapons and launching concentrated thrusts in the north and south. In this way they were able to shape most of today's armistice lines.

The war finally ended after almost ten months in a series of armistices. The first was signed with Egypt on 24 February 1949, the second with Lebanon on 23 March, the third with Jordan on 3 April, and Syria finally signed on 20 July. It is worth noting that the armistice agreements specifically stated that the lines negotiated were not permanent and that final borders were to be negotiated at a later date. The armistice line in the east was not with the Palestinians but with Jordan. A resolution of the final border issue with the former is still awaited.

But, of course, an armistice is not a peace and Egyptian-trained Palestinian suicide troops (*fedayeen*) were encouraged to continue their attacks on Israeli villages. The Egyptians regarded the armistice as simply 'an interval in an unfinished war'.[1]

That Israel survived was due to a combination of factors. The absolute determination to fight to the death demonstrated by inspired military commanders, including Yitzhak Rabin, Moshe Dayan, Yigael Yadin and Yigal Alon, was critical, as was the fact that the entire population of Israel formed the fighting force. Israel's army, relatively small at the outset, was able to grow rapidly by immigration during the course of the war. In contrast the Arab armies constituted only a very small proportion of their countries' populations, and the existence of those countries was not threatened in the way that Israel's was. Furthermore the Arab states were poorly coordinated and taken up with rival thoughts about a division of the spoils after what they imagined would be a rapid victory. While their populations were incensed by Israel's presence in their midst, their leaderships were less concerned about the fate of the Palestinians than with their own separate plans for Palestinian territory. King Farouk in Egypt was desperate to expand his security interests into Palestine, as was his Syrian rival, President Shukri al-Quwwatli, with his long-term plan for a greater Syria. Both of them feared King Abdullah of Jordan's designs on Palestine while he in turn was anxious to avoid either of them gaining any ground next to his territory.[2]

Abdullah's role was critical since his army was the most disciplined and well trained but he had been double-dealing with the Arab League and the Jewish Agency. In secret discussions with the latter he had indicated that he would not invade Israel if he had the tacit approval for his annexation of the west bank of the Jordan. At the same time he was leading, and in part impeding, the Arab assault. This ambivalent and uncoordinated assault made it possible for the Israelis to halt the Arab advance and turn it back. A lack of any leadership amongst the Palestinians and the limited interest in their future amongst their Arab friends left them without any of the land promised in the UN Partition Plan.

By the end of the war, Israel had re-occupied the land originally proposed for it in the Negev and about 50 per cent of what was to have been Arab land, while Egypt occupied, but did not annex, the Gaza Strip. Abdullah's Trans-Jordan, having gained independence as Jordan in 1946, took over the West Bank, including the Old City of Jerusalem, where more than 1,500 Jews were driven out and many synagogues destroyed. The 'facts on the ground' of the post-1948 borders had overtaken Resolution 181.

The Swedish diplomat Folke Bernadotte, sent with a team of UN observers to mediate the truce, recorded that 'most of the Palestinian Arabs would be quite content to be incorporated in Transjordan'. Jordan and Egypt could have agreed to allow the formation of a Palestinian state in the West Bank and Gaza respectively but there was no appetite for them to do so even though the presence of Israel was a thorn in their side. In any event, Arab Palestine had disappeared into Jordan. It did not re-appear until twenty years later, in 1967, when Israel re-created it as it drove Jordan out of the West Bank.

Large numbers of Arabs had fled or were forcibly expelled from the new state during the war in 1948, while at the same time some 750,000 Jews were evicted from Arab countries around the Middle East. These, together with the European evacuees, flooded into Israel. The contrast between the Ashkenazi Europeans, many with their Western secularism and democratic idealism, and the more religious Middle Eastern Sephardim was striking and these contrasting backgrounds have had a continuing impact on their social and political behaviour. The 20 per cent of Israel's population that has remained Arab adds to this colourful, sometimes abrasive yet always fascinating, diversity of Israel's population.

Errors of Judgement

Mistakes and errors of judgement post 1948 were many and events were devastating for both Arab and Jew. The British had left precipitously, glad to be out of the fire, but with little or no preparation or handover for those who were left. The leaders of the Arab countries may have felt that they would soon throw the Jews into the sea. They were certainly better armed but as Israel's population grew, even though still outnumbered, they formed a more cohesive force than that which the Arabs could muster. The Arab recommendation to its citizens in Israel that they pack up and leave until the war was over was a serious miscalculation that played a part in the devastating refugee inheritance that followed. The Israeli leadership, recognising that their country would have great difficulty in becoming a Jewish state if Jews formed only a small majority, played its part in encouraging the Arab exodus, often by force.

And the war took a terrible toll on both sides. The Jews lost some 6,600 men and women, many the cream of their population and 1 per cent of their total. The Arab armies of Egypt, Syria and Jordan were not only humiliated but also lost innumerable personnel while the Palestinians suffered thousands of deaths.

Here were sown more seeds of the bitter conflict that have bedevilled negotiations.

UN Recognition

It is clear that Resolution 181 of the UN General Council, although not accepted by all the parties, triggered major consequences. It was never agreed in the form in which it was proposed but it is of interest that forty-one years later, in 1988, Yasser Arafat tried to accept it as a basis for the Palestinian state denied him first by Jordan and then by Israel. It did not escape notice that in belatedly accepting 181 he also tacitly accepted the existence of a separate state of Israel. He had no appetite, however, for a return of all Palestinian refugees from the surrounding Arab countries to his Palestine.

President Truman's recognition of Israel was rapidly followed by Stalin's, keen to support a socialist state in the Middle East. Britain took another eight months. Then finally, on 11 May 1949, the Security Council accepted Israel as a UN member by a narrow majority, seven for and five against. This seemingly auspicious day was also the one on which the USSR lifted its blockade of Berlin, with a temporary thawing of relations between the great powers.

Key individuals make the difference at historic moments and Chaim Weizmann presented Israel's case in any and every international forum. Without his influence, not least on President Truman, Israel's future may not have been assured. He worked his powers of persuasion to great effect at Lake Success, in the UN's new building on Long Island. He always emphasised the need for careful diplomacy in working with the British and later, the Americans. Yet despite his absolutely critical role in Israel's future it is remarkable how little he figures in the history of its early heroes. His brand of diplomacy became less valued as the baton was passed to those better versed in more aggressive armed resistance. Ben Gurion certainly believed that if the Jews were ever to remove the yoke of the British, more direct action was needed and Weizmann's pro-British views were no longer helpful. The two of them disagreed strongly and Weizmann mentions Ben Gurion only once, and Begin not at all, in his autobiography. Israel was extremely fortunate in having Weizmann's diplomacy and Ben Gurion's aggression at the right time and in that order. He remains one of the three towering figures responsible for the birth of Israel, alongside Herzl and Ben Gurion, and I, as a Mancunian like Weizmann, cannot help believe that it is regrettable that his critical role has been air-brushed out of Israel's popular history.

Unreliable Friends

International politics are rarely conducive to reliable friendships. While Stalin appreciated the socialism of early Israel and denounced initial Arab attacks, a short while later, after the 1948 war, he blocked every attempt to criticise the Arab states while encouraging Security Council condemnation of Israel's actions. Before and during the war Israel had strongly depended on Czechoslovakia, assisted by France, for a clandestine but vital supply of arms but after the war the Czechs began to supply huge amounts of arms to the Egyptians instead. King Abdullah I had secret meetings with the Jewish Agency in which he agreed not to attack Israel but that did not prevent him from invading with his Arab allies in 1948. Even the USA, Israel's early supporter, put up an arms embargo during the war.

Such is the unreliability of friends, a lesson that Israel was quick to learn.

CHAPTER 5

At the United Nations

IN DECEMBER 1948, WHILE the war continued, the UN General Assembly adopted Resolution 194 in an effort to define what a final settlement should look like. It included proposals for resolving the Palestinian refugee problem and the establishment of an international zone around Jerusalem. A conciliation committee, set up at the same time, proved to be a damp squib. The Arab states rejected it out of hand, Israel opposed most of the resolution's articles and the war continued.

In trying to solve the refugee problems, however, more confusion was introduced and, as is so often the case, the exact meaning of words became and remains the subject of debate. Article 11 of Resolution 194 has been increasingly interpreted as a basis for the right of return of Palestinian refugees.[1] Since then the UN General Assembly has re-affirmed this resolution every year, perhaps forgetting that all the relevant Arab states had voted against it and rejected it outright when it was proposed. Israel on the other hand points out that the right of return applies only to those 'wishing to live in peace with their neighbours' and only then at some unspecified date. The resolution also 'instructs the Conciliation Commission to facilitate the repatriation, resettlement and economic and social rehabilitation of the refugees etc'. We will return later to the inclusion of the word 'resettlement' in this instruction.

Despite the differences of opinion, they did not prevent Israel being admitted as a member of the UN in May 1949 under Resolution 273. Note was taken of explanations given by Israel about the implementation of Resolutions 181 and 194 and the UN avoided a confrontation about a lack of commitment by Israel to any particular actions or timeframe.

The Lausanne Conference and the Failure of the First Tentative Peace Proposals

This conference, following in May 1949, was one of those rare occasions when both the Arab and the Israeli delegates seemed to accept a joint protocol, albeit with many reservations. Set up by the UN Palestine Conciliation Commission, it included representation from Israel and an Arab High Committee, including Egypt, Lebanon, Jordan and Syria. It got off to a poor start as the Arabs flatly refused to sit in the same room with the Israelis and there was much to-ing and fro-ing between the separated parties by the Commission. The basic positions of the two regimes could not have been further apart. The Arabs concentrated on the right of return of the Palestinian refugees as a first step while the Israelis were not willing to consider this unless it was part of a wider peace deal. The Arabs wanted nothing to do with any wider deal without a prior settlement of the refugee issue. Catch-22. There was pressure from the US on Israel to return to the 1947 UN Partition Plan borders and on Jordan to return Jerusalem to international administration. Neither party was willing to give way. Under more pressure Israel offered to see the return of 100,000 refugees with certain strict conditions. The Arabs refused because they considered this too small a proportion of the overall number of refugees and the offer was soon withdrawn. An offer by Israel to take over the Gaza Strip with all its refugees was rebuffed by the Arab states, believing it to be just another attempt by Israel to annex further territory. Israel wanted to negotiate with each of the Arab states individually and to settle differences between each of them in complete packages rather than piecemeal. Neither of these approaches was acceptable to the Arab representatives. Despite the American pressure, Israel felt that as the winner in the war it should not be asked to sue for peace and that it was those who had lost who should be doing so. It stuck rigidly to its line and while it signed the protocol it failed to commit itself to the borders that were being proposed or to a number, or timeline, for return of refugees. The whole tortuous process is spelt out in Neil Caplan's monograph on Lausanne.[2]

Despite signatures on documents the Lausanne Conference achieved little and simply cemented the positions reached at the end of the war.

Intimations of Peace with Jordan

Of the Arab leaders only King Abdullah I of Jordan was keen to sign a peace treaty with Israel, not least because he wanted Israel's support for his annexation of the West Bank. The US also favoured an enlarged Jordan into which Palestinian Arabs might be incorporated. But Arabs who try to negotiate with Israel tend to come to a sticky end, as we will see.

There were many lessons to be learnt. Israel began to understand that it could not rely on others to come to its aid and had to be self-reliant. It knew too that it could not afford to take threats against it less than seriously. The Arabs accepted, at least until 1967, that wars often have unexpected consequences and should not be embarked upon unless there is a clear idea of their limitations and what it is they hope to achieve. And both sides learnt that ambiguity in the wording of protocols and agreements allows each side to selectively quote sentences and paragraphs to its own advantage, leading to problems of interpretation that persist thereafter. Ambiguity does at least allow each side to claim to be a winner.

The lessons of the Lausanne Conference and for those who

promoted UN Resolutions 181 and 194 were how far apart the Arabs and Jews were and how much further there was to travel if the gap was to be bridged. The Jews had waited centuries for their opportunity and had risked everything to achieve it. They were never going to give up what they had gained so painfully and with such sacrifice. The Palestinians on the other hand could not abide the idea that their land, villages and houses had been forcibly taken from them by immigrants. They were going to continue to fight to remove them. There was a long way to go if these differences were to be overcome, but there was no shortage of efforts to achieve a peace deal, as the next chapters will show.

CHAPTER 6

More Wars and Abortive Peace Proposals

1956 and 1967

THE YEARS FROM 1948 to 1967 saw no signs of a thaw between Israel and its neighbours. It is true that there were a number of secretive approaches to exchange refugees for territory – from Husni al-Za'im, President of Syria, who offered to take several hundred thousand refugees in exchange for control of half the Sea of Galilee; from King Abdullah of Jordan, for a swathe of land to the Mediterranean; and from King Farouk of Egypt, for control of all the Negev desert – but they were unrealistic. Unilateral concessions were not on Israel's agenda and in any case the position of these leaders was fragile. All of them were either executed, assassinated or deposed shortly thereafter.

Egypt in particular took a strongly belligerent stance. From 1952 it was led by Jamal Abdal Nasser, who took on the self-proclaimed role of leader of the Arab nations. With the largest army, accumulating huge amounts of modern weapons from Czechoslovakia, and with strong support from the USSR his confidence grew. He saw little need to sign any peace treaties with an Israel that he repeatedly promised to destroy in his many rants to his parliament.

There were several efforts to bring the parties together. In December 1952 Abba Eban had made a proposal at the UN for a peace initiative, without any preconditions. Although this covered all the areas of contention, including return of refugees, borders and Jerusalem, it was rejected out of hand by Colonel Nasser. Similarly an initiative by the US led by Robert Anderson, who spent eight weeks shuttling between Jerusalem and Cairo, came to nought. David Ben Gurion had direct if inconclusive discussions with him but Nasser refused even to consider face to face meetings. Britain too tried to intervene when the unlikely figure of Ernest Bevin had secret discussions in London with Israeli and Egyptian emissaries, but neither party was interested in any Bevin-inspired plans. In Israel's case this was because it could not trust a man with his history of anti-Israel activities. His efforts to persuade the US that Israel would be just another communist state in the Middle East and Britain's abstention in the UN vote on partition were recent memories while the turning back of the *Exodus* with its load of Holocaust survivors cast a long shadow over Israel–Britain relationships. In any case, Nasser summarily rejected Bevin's approach. All efforts fell on stony ground in Egypt. Nasser found the idea of peace with an enemy that had humiliated his country anathema. His reaction was dominated by an unquenchable desire for revenge and reprisal, a difficult psychological state from which to retreat. His vision of pan-Arabism, with himself as its leader, was a strong motivator for him and the Palestinian cause gave a greater legitimacy to his quest.

The one exception to the universal Arab antipathy to Israel was King Abdullah I of Jordan, who was anxious to complete a peace deal with Israel. He was the only Arab leader to have accepted the 1947 UN Partition Plan and could see a situation in which the West Bank and East Jerusalem would remain part of Jordan with Israel occupying most of the remainder of Palestine. A draft agreement had even been drawn up in secret negotiations but this had to be put on ice when the Arab League, led by Egypt, resolved to expel any member that signed a deal with Israel. Britain too was cautioning against such an agreement. Abdullah withdrew but that did not prevent him being assassinated as he went to pray at the Al-Aqsa Mosque in Jerusalem on 20 July 1951. This was four days after a Lebanese emissary, the former

Prime Minister Riad Bey Al Solh, had in turn been assassinated in Amman for a number of internal Lebanese disagreements but also because of a suspicion that he was secretly plotting with Abdullah for a separate peace deal between Israel and Lebanon.

It is against this background that Israel was made painfully aware that the Arab states were not the least bit interested in making peace. Nasser was more keen on eliminating Israel and at the same time taking over the Negev, opening a route to Jordan and Iraq to expand his sphere of influence. Soviet support gave him the confidence to repulse US and Western blandishments and the Arab–Israel conflict took on a much wider significance as the Middle East became a key part of the cold war and a dangerous interface between Russia and the West.

The Suez Canal Unhappy 'Adventure', 1956

Nasser's growing confidence led him to overreach and, when he decided to nationalise the Suez Canal, Britain and France reacted with anger and concern. France took the initiative because of its anxiety about the role Egypt was playing in stirring up unrest in Algiers and, ever the pragmatist, made common cause with Israel. Although Israel was not primarily concerned about the canal, from which it had been denied access for years, it felt increasingly threatened by Egypt's build-up of arms and aggressive rhetoric. It was suspicious that Egypt was near to starting a war with it. And Britain was dragged into this peculiar alliance because of its fears about access to passage through the canal.

Britain, France and Israel embarked on the ill-fated 'Suez Crisis' talks in 1956. Nasser had previously sought funding from the US and Britain to build a dam at Aswan as a way of bringing much-needed irrigation to the Nile valley. He was turned down by an angry John Foster Dulles, Secretary of State, who had learnt that Egypt was also in negotiation with the Russians. Nasser was incensed and, on 26 July 1956, nationalised the French–British-owned Suez Canal. The Americans were upset but it was the French and British who were more directly concerned. Public opinion in France was strongly in favour of action against Egypt especially when an Egyptian boat-load of arms heading for the Algerian opposition was intercepted by the French.

'Operation Musketeer' was hatched in meetings held in strict secrecy in France. Israel was to invade Egypt and head for, but not reach, the Suez Canal. Within twelve hours, Britain and France would then enter the war to 'protect' their interests in the canal. Three written documents outlining the agreement were produced. The British copy was immediately destroyed, the French copy was 'disappeared' (it re-appeared only in 1996), and the Israeli copy, placed in Ben Gurion's pocket at the time, was retained. Despite all this secrecy the agreement was soon revealed, much to the anger and dismay of the British Parliament and Cabinet as well as the public, while President Eisenhower was incandescent. Coming immediately before the US elections this Egyptian adventure caused him great embarrassment.

Israel advanced much further than anyone expected, at least in part because of delays in the British and French invasions. Israel's aim had been to remove the bases of the Egyptian-trained *fedayeen*, who had been very effective in killing several hundred Israelis in raids from Gaza. They were successful in this as well as opening access to the Red Sea through the Straits of Tiran, which had been closed to Israeli shipping for many years. They captured more than 6,000 Egyptian troops as well as considerable amounts of arms as they advanced towards the canal. It was, however, at great personal cost with over 600 Israeli combatant lives lost in the conflict.

But it was the political fall-out that was especially dramatic.

Political Damage for All

In Britain the Prime Minister, Anthony Eden, resigned in disgrace. He had sponsored the plan in secret, leaving his government and the public completely in the dark, and against the will of his ally in the US. France too suffered as its Prime Minister, Guy Mollet, also had to stand down, while Nasser's reputation as an invincible, all-powerful leader of Arab nationalism was damaged.

Israel, while making some military and strategic gains, placed itself in an extremely vulnerable international position. Censured by the US and the UN, it was threatened by Russia and at the same time French and British support was withering away as they too felt the wrath of the great powers. Russia was threatening to wipe Israel off the map if it did not withdraw from the Sinai Peninsula and even menaced Europe with missiles it may or may not have had. Russia, of course, was not unhappy for international attention to be diverted to the Middle East as Soviet tanks rolled into Budapest in the brutal suppression of popular uprisings in Hungary. For Israel to lose American support, although it was not very strong at the time, at the same moment as earning the wrath of Russia was not a happy experience and its fears were not assuaged by UN General Assembly resolutions. It had managed to avoid Security Council censure because of British and French vetoes (they could hardly do otherwise), but the Assembly's voice was strong in condemnation. Conor Cruise O'Brien described the UN's minatory resolutions as 'the modern counterpart of medieval excommunication'.[1] These resolutions contrasted with UN silence on Russia's Hungarian venture.

However, Israel did manage to salvage something from the mess, largely because of the remarkable work of Abba Eban in America and at the UN. A Cambridge graduate of considerable and sometimes over-powering intellect, he was never fully accepted within Israel where earthier characteristics were prized over intellectual prowess in politicians. Not much change there then. In contrast, he was highly prized in America and at the UN, where he was enormously successful in gaining support for Israel. His speeches at the UN were models of clarity and erudition and he became popular, successful and widely regarded as Israel's most effective advocate. After a fallow political period on his return to Israel, he eventually became its Foreign Minister; more of that later.

He used his considerable diplomatic skills to modify the demand at the UN for withdrawal from the Sinai to one in which withdrawal was accompanied with Israel's replacement by a UN international emergency force to prevent Egyptian troops returning. That was accepted and it was followed by a period of eleven years of peace along that front until Egypt evicted the UN force in 1967.

Perhaps most important of all was the agreement that the Straits of Tiran were to remain open to all international shipping including Israel's. The reason that it was so vital to Israel's interest was not only access to the sea but more significantly the need to make it clear that these were international waters that had been denied to a nation state without any international reaction. Even more importantly and largely as a result of Eban's activities, a statement approved by the United States was read out by Golda Meir at the General Assembly that was to have very long term consequences. The statement made it clear that any armed attack on Israeli flag-flying ships sailing through the Gulf of Aqaba 'will be regarded by Israel as an attack entitling it to exercise its inherent right of self defence'. This was to have profound implications when Israel went to war in 1967. The remarkable rescue of Israel's position at the UN was largely due to the persuasive diplomatic skills of Abba Eban. His efforts were likened, by O'Brien, to those of Talleyrand at the 1815 Congress of Vienna, where France came out virtually unscathed despite its defeat in the Napoleonic Wars.[2]

Relations between France and Israel had been improving well before the Suez adventure, largely due to the diplomatic efforts of Shimon Peres, then director of the Defence Ministry. A month before Nasser's ill-fated canal-nationalising bombshell, a large arms deal had been struck between France and Israel after Moshe Dayan and Peres presented their case. Both, incidentally, were awarded the Légion d'Honneur, Peres a year after Suez, as their reward.

Israel had done nothing to rescue its reputation in the Arab world through its ill-fated liaison with the two declining colonial powers. But it had managed to gain something important internationally, the opening of the Straits of Tiran, as well as a supply of desperately needed arms from its new ally, France, and a reduction of the threat posed by the 'suicide' *fedayeen* in Gaza. Furthermore, Nasser's military capability had been badly damaged, at least for the time being. But Egypt's seething humiliation increased its need for retribution and peace was moved even further off the agenda.

Eleven Years of Uneasy Stand-Off

With no signs of a thaw between 1956 and 1967 both sides concentrated on rebuilding their arms stocks. The Russians began to increase their supply to Egypt and its allies while Israel had to depend on clandestine supplies from France and to a lesser extent from Britain and Germany. A number of Arab countries severed diplomatic relations with Germany when news of its support for Israel emerged. The USA under Eisenhower had not been obviously supportive but when John Kennedy became President in 1960 he spoke of his willingness to come to Israel's aid if it was invaded. This turned out to be an empty promise in due course and Germany also remained 'neutral' during the 1967 and 1973 wars.

With the exception of the Shah of Iran, who recognised Israel in 1960 (that remained true until the revolution of 1979 when Ayatollah Khomeini came to power), in the rest of the Middle East antipathy to the very idea of peace was unyielding. Before and after this period, violence was meted out to those who ventured along the path of peace. The assassination of Abdullah of Jordan was not a lone event. Fauze al-Husseini, the nephew and opponent of Grand Mufti Husseini, was killed off in 1947, as were Said Hamami, Palestinian diplomat and peace negotiator, and Issam Sartawi, Fatah peace negotiator in 1983 and, most notably, Anwar Sadat in 1981. Not much encouragement there for anyone interested in peace. The Arabs were not alone in such disruptive activities and the assassination of Yitzhak Rabin by a religious extremist in Israel much later, in 1995, cut short any softening of Israeli attitudes then.

CHAPTER 7

The 1967 War

THERE WAS LITTLE ARAB appetite for another war during the eleven years leading up to 1967 although there were occasional skirmishes testing the unstable truce. Syrian and Lebanese efforts to cut off Israel's water flowing through the river Jordan were aborted by Israeli action in 1963 but Syria was reluctant to respond militarily without an Egypt that was not quite ready. That was to come with a vengeance in 1967. This war left a very long shadow and the consequences remain to plague both Israel and the Palestinians. Yet it was the result of a mixture of malicious and false Russian rumours and Egyptian and Jordanian miscalculations.

Egypt started an aggressive build-up of troops in the Sinai in 1967 and told the UN emergency force to leave the area, in contravention of UN agreements made in 1957. It increasingly used the pretext given by Soviet misinformation that Israel was building up its forces for an invasion of Syria in the north. Although he soon knew that these rumours were baseless, it suited Nasser's purpose to continue his preparation for a war with Israel, particularly as he had managed to extricate himself from his protracted war in the Yemen. But its progress was hastened when the Straits of Tiran were blockaded to Israeli shipping once again. It is sometimes suggested that, despite Egypt's obvious preparations for war, it was Israel that started it. Perhaps it is forgotten that the blockade of the Straits of Tiran had already been accepted by the UN as an act of war.

King Hussein of Jordan was in a difficult position. His relationship with Nasser was poor but if he stood out against him and the war were won he would face the prospect of an Egyptian takeover of his country. If the war were lost, as it was, and he did not join in he would be blamed for the result and suffer the wrath of his population. In the event he placed his forces under Egyptian direction and when war began, believing Russian propaganda, he began shelling West Jerusalem and occupying the no-man's land. This turned out to be a fateful error. If he had not succumbed to the temptation to enter the war, albeit at great risk to his life, the West Bank might have become part of his greater Jordan and Palestinian Arabs citizens of his country. One can speculate what might have happened thereafter but it seems likely that a separate Palestinian nationalism would not have had as much traction later as it did in 1994 under Arafat's evolving Palestinian Liberation Organisation (PLO).

The appeals of Israel's Prime Minister, Levi Eshkol, to Nasser to avoid a war went unheeded and the UN and the USA were powerless to intervene. President Johnson's harsh words to Nasser had no impact and the inevitability of war became a reality.

The war, well described in several excellent accounts,[1] was short and decisive. Egypt's air force was destroyed on the ground and those of Syria and Jordan both in the air and on the ground. With little capacity for air support Egypt was unable to prevent Israel from taking over the Sinai desert again or from taking Sharm el-Sheikh and opening the Gulf of Aqaba to its ships. Syria lost the Golan Heights and Jordan the West Bank and Jerusalem. Cease-fires were agreed with Egypt within four days and with Syria in six. But the devastating defeat by Israel and the depth of Arab humiliation again simply prepared the ground for further war.

When the war ended Israel was again reminded that it was on its own. The ineffectiveness of the UN, the USSR's use of the veto in the Security Council and its role in stirring Arab discontent together with the severely limited international support provided the usual lessons. However, despite the sorely felt loss of life, morale in Israel was high.

Victory was also deemed by some as due to divine intervention and fostered feelings that the cradle of the Jewish nation in the West Bank, where biblical sites from the First and Second Temple periods could be found in abundance, had now been returned to its rightful owners. Here were sown the seeds of the settler movement. For the first time since 1948 the Palestinians, who hitherto had been divided under Jordanian, Egyptian and Israeli rule, were now united under one of them.

And now Israel was in a strong enough position to be able to offer something in exchange for a peace treaty; and this it did, at least initially. But here too Israeli hubris caused problems.

Resolution 242

In November 1967, some five months after the end of the war, the UN Security Council unanimously adopted Resolution 242, the wording of which has been debated ever since. It includes the following:

> The Security Council ... Affirms that the fulfilment of Charter principles requires the establishment of a just and lasting peace in the Middle East which should include the application of both the following principles:
>
> (i) Withdrawal of Israel armed forces from territories occupied in the recent conflict;
> (ii) Termination of all claims or states of belligerency and respect for and acknowledgment of the sovereignty, territorial integrity and political independence of every State in the area and their right to live in peace within secure and recognized boundaries free from threats or acts of force.[2]

This resolution is the basis of all peace proposals since then but remains open to interpretation. It is clear that both principles quoted above have to be adhered to and each is locked into the other. Uncertainty was introduced by the absence of the single word 'the' before 'territories', leaving it open as to what 'territories' should be withdrawn from. Was it all territories or only some territories? The Arab nations have insisted that it means all of the territories occupied, and the French version of the resolution includes the word '*des*' before '*territoires occupés*' to muddy the water still further. However it is the English version that was voted on and although there is room for some disagreement there seems little doubt that the omission was deliberate. After much debate the idea that there should be room for some negotiation about the exact siting of defensible borders between the parties was accepted. Lord Caradon, the UK representative largely responsible for drafting the resolution, stated as much and this has been reiterated by many of those most closely involved at the time.[3] Although it was clearly the intention that the great majority of the land occupied in the 1967 war should be returned, the position and nature of the pre-1967 'borders', known as the 'Green Line', were accepted as simply the cease-fire or armistice line when troops stopped fighting at the end of the 1948 war. It was never a rational agreed border that was 'secure and recognised' despite suggestions to the contrary. It had also been recognised in the original armistice agreements that this cease-fire line was just that and not an accepted border. Insistence on its exact location, when negotiations occur now, fails to take account of its origins. Those who drafted Resolution 242 clearly understood that final borders would have to be left for negotiation and agreement by both parties. That remains the case today.

Much has also been made of the inadmissibility of the occupation of territories by war but it is relevant that this resolution was written under Chapter VI of the UN Charter and not the more stringent Chapter VII, which deals with the results of wars of aggression. In this case Israel gained ground in a defensive war waged to threaten its existence. A Chapter VI resolution provides for a negotiated withdrawal while one drawn up under Chapter VII would provoke an obligatory withdrawal with force if necessary.

The importance of this distinction is clear if it is understood that any attacking nation would suffer no consequences from its aggression since it would be guaranteed by the UN to have its land returned to it should it be defeated. Many at the time, including several leading Israeli figures as well as President Johnson, envisaged Jordan taking back the West Bank in any peace deal. On these grounds Chapter VI was clearly more relevant in Israel's defensive case. Although Israel did indeed initiate the war it did so only when it was inevitable and Egypt and Syria's intentions were absolutely clear, and the fact that Egypt had stopped the passage of Israeli ships through the Straits of Tiran was in any case a *casus belli* accepted by the UN after the war of 1956. There is no doubt too that the Arab nations' intention was to annihilate Israel; many in Egypt, Syria and Iraq repeatedly stated as much well before Israel occupied any of the territories now so hotly disputed. However, none of this stopped Arab and Soviet leaders presenting the war as due to an Israeli act of aggression. The UN, at least, understood the case very well in plumping for a Chapter VI resolution.

It is noteworthy that Palestine is not mentioned in Resolution 242 and the nearest it gets to 'Palestinians' is in reference to a settlement of the important question of refugees. Even here the type of refugee is not defined and is taken by some to include the Jewish refugees who had fled from Arab countries in almost equal numbers to the Arabs fleeing Israel. However, the plight of the two sets of refugees was strikingly different; one set were kept in camps and not allowed to integrate in most of the countries to which they fled while the others automatically became full citizens of Israel.

Peace Offerings, Missed Opportunities and Costly Errors of Judgement

Immediately following the 1967 war, discussions in the Eshkol-led Israeli Cabinet were not triumphalist since they were well aware of the long-term instability of their gains. They were faced with the dilemma of ruling over newly conquered lands or offering full citizenship to the Palestinians and becoming a bi-national state. The exception was the offer of full Israeli citizenship to Palestinians living in East Jerusalem and the Druze living in the Golan Heights, although only a minority in either place accepted the offer. The Palestinians of East Jerusalem are now residents of Israel but not citizens. A bi-national state was a very unwelcome proposition since it would have eroded Israel's essentially Jewish status, and if it offered to give back conquered lands how could it ensure its safety without a peace treaty? These have continued to be serious questions and show why it was so important for Israel to include peace treaties in any negotiations for territorial returns. This then led to offers of 'land for peace' being made within ten days of the war ending and well before Resolution 242.

Prime Minister Eshkol and Abba Eban were amongst the more forward-looking and realistic leaders of Israel and Eshkol's Cabinet resolved to offer the Golan Heights and the Sinai in exchange for peace treaties with Syria and Egypt respectively. A plan to hand over the West Bank to Jordan was also mooted but this proved to be anathema to Menachem Begin, then a member of Eshkol's emergency unity government.

The Arab League's Three Noes

In any event these early tentative proposals were met with outright rejection by the Arab nations and by September, that is before Resolution 242, the Arab League had met in Khartoum and issued their infamous 'three noes'. Transmitting their message to the United States, since they were not talking to Israel, they stated that there would be no recognition of Israel, no negotiation and no peace. In case that was not clear enough there were many public statements by leading Arab figures that a Jewish state was unthinkable in Islamic terms, that holy war had been declared, that all the Jews would be massacred and that anyone who felt otherwise would be accursed until the Day of

Judgement. Not a promising basis on which to begin negotiations on Resolution 242.

Abba Eban said that this was the first time that a country that had won a war had had to sue for peace only to have it rejected by those who had lost. However, the Arab Congress in Khartoum also saw a change in attitude to and by President Nasser, whose power and position in the Arab world had been eroded, and this had profound implications for later negotiations, as we will see.

President Johnson was also early in putting peace plans forward. Within two weeks of the cease-fire he had presented his five-point plan to the Soviet Premier, Alexei Kosygin, at a meeting arranged at Glassboro, New Jersey, to discuss broader East–West relationships. Anxious about the Vietnam War and a need to encourage détente he proposed a plan that leant towards the Egyptian position of withdrawal before negotiation in an effort to placate the Russians. That was not to be the end of US pressure on the Israelis but this plan also bit the dust as neither Egypt nor Israel were in any position to consider it. Nor did King Hussein or the PLO accept, and Salah Jadid, who had taken over a leadership role in Syria in a military coup in 1966, rejected all proposals out of hand.

Jordan, Egypt and Israel, however, entered into separate discussions on the resolution with Gunnar Jarring, the UN envoy appointed to oversee the resolution's proposals. Egypt and Jordan were interested only in Israel's return to the pre-1967 borders without a peace deal while Israel accepted on condition that a suitable peace deal would be struck before withdrawal. That is, both parties would take an interest in the resolution but only if one of its parts was accomplished before the other; unfortunately they each wanted a different part first.

Eban's Nine-Point Plan, 1968

The last effort by Eshkol to reach an agreement before he died was laid out in a speech given by his Foreign Minister, Abba Eban, to the

UN General Assembly in October 1968. In the catalogue of missed opportunities that abound in the Middle East, the offers in his nine-point plan must rank high. It is worth quoting the points he raised.[4]

After stating that Israel 'has accepted the Security Council's Resolution for the establishment of a just and lasting peace and declared its readiness to negotiate agreements on all the principles mentioned therein', he said that 'past disappointment should not lead to present despair' and 'a new effort be made in the coming weeks to cooperate with Ambassador Jarring'.

He then set out his nine-point plan:

- The establishment of peace … to follow the cease-fire to be a just and lasting peace duly negotiated.
- Secure and recognised boundaries within the framework of peace, the cease-fire lines to be replaced by permanent, secure and recognised boundaries.
- Security agreements, with a pledge of mutual non-aggression.
- An open frontier, with freedom of movement, intermingling in peaceful contact and commerce. Included were free port facilities for Jordan on Israel's Mediterranean coast and mutual access to places of religious and historic associations.
- Freedom of navigation in international waterways.
- Provision for refugees. Included was 'a conference of Middle Eastern States to be convened', joint refugee integration and rehabilitation commissions and an interim measure to intensify and accelerate action 'to widen the uniting of families scheme, and to process "hardship cases" among refugees who had crossed to the East Bank during the June 1967 fighting'.
- Provision for Jerusalem. 'Israel does not seek to exercise unilateral jurisdiction in the Holy Places of Christianity and Islam. We are willing in each case to work out a status to give effect to their universal character … Our policy is that Christian and Moslem Holy Places should come under the responsibility of those who hold them in reverence.'

- Acknowledgement and recognition of sovereignty, integrity and right to national life.
- Regional cooperation.

He went on to say: 'Lest Arab Governments be tempted out of sheer routine to rush into impulsive rejection, let me suggest that tragedy is not what men suffer but what they miss ... In the long run, nations can prosper only by recognising what their common interest demands.' The speech was well received at the UN but unhappily for all sides Nasser was unwilling to consider the possibility of entering into any negotiation with Israel and the opportunity was lost.

Israel is often accused of intransigence but note what the British Ambassador to Israel, Sir Ernest John Ward Barnes, had to say when he wrote a confidential letter to his Foreign Office in November 1971.[5] After saying that the Israelis were often exasperating, he went on to say 'On the basic issue, first it is not Israel who is denying the Arab's right to exist. Nor was it Israel who attacked the Arabs in the first place when the British Mandate was withdrawn.' And 'It is certainly a truism to say that if Israel lost a war, she would not, unlike the opposition, live to fight another.' He also stated that their intransigence was 'more apparent than real'.

It is noteworthy that at this time efforts to negotiate were pursued between Israel and surrounding Arab nations but not with the Palestinians or PLO. Although Nasser continued to pay lip service to the needs of the Palestinians, after Khartoum he focused his attentions much more on the need to remove Israel from occupying Egyptian land in the Sinai. His pan-Arab leadership role had been irretrievably damaged and this concentrated his mind on his own domestic needs.

It was this important change in strategy that laid the foundations for later peace negotiations but it is perhaps not too surprising that Israel failed to understand its significance as Nasser stepped up his belligerency. His sense of humiliation and the need for retribution saw him reneging on the cease-fire in March 1969.

More Belligerency

Soon increasing shell-fire across the Suez Canal and a rise in terrorist attacks within Israel by Egyptian-funded Palestinian terrorists were taking a heavy toll. A 'war of attrition' was in full swing and UN envoy Jarring shuttled backwards and forwards between Jerusalem, Cairo and Amman to little effect. In the face of Nasser's intransigence, positions began to harden in Israel. Eshkol died in February 1969 and Golda Meir was elected leader, rather to her surprise but partly because there was a desire to keep her strong and feared rival Moshe Dayan out of the running.

She was seventy-one by the time she was elected and she was tired, unwell and ready to retire. She hesitated at first but accepted the honour and went on to become Israel's first and only female Prime Minister. The reasons why she was promoted are easy to see in retrospect. She had had an impeccable ten year career as Foreign Secretary and as Minister of Labour before that. She was one of the signatories of the Declaration of Independence and recognised by Ben Gurion as 'the best man in the Government', a description she disliked, suggesting that no man would like to be described as the best woman in anything. She was a no-nonsense person, strong willed, straight talking and spoken of as the grandmother of the Jewish people. Certainly she was formidable with a fierce moral assurance; Nixon described her as 'an elemental force of nature'. But she was far from cold and detached. Her warmth and humanity were obvious and her hatred of war and the impact equally on both Arab and Jewish mothers of the death of sons in battle weighed heavily on her. 'When peace comes perhaps we will forgive Arabs for killing our sons but harder to forgive them for forcing us to kill their sons.'

The 1973, Yom Kippur, war tested her more than most as we will see.

The continuing attacks across the canal provoked her government into retaliation and soon this escalated into deep air raids within Egypt. The Israeli response was harsh and unremitting and Egypt's population suffered badly. Nasser turned again to Russia for arms and was rewarded with a massive influx of sophisticated weaponry. It suited the Soviets to strengthen their southern flank by appealing to the Arabs and they dramatically increased the number of their 'advisors' and officers stationed in Egypt. These, together with several squadrons of Soviet aircraft now stationed there, began to have an impact on American policy towards Israel.

It is here that the story turns complicated and dangerous, with far-reaching consequences as both the Israeli and American governments became bedevilled by disputes within their own administrations.

Damaging Squabbles in the US and Israeli Administrations

US Middle East policy was now, in 1969, dominated by President Nixon's National Security Advisor, Henry Kissinger, while the State Department, headed by William Rogers, became increasingly sidelined. On the Israeli side, Abba Eban, now Foreign Minister, was being ignored by Golda Meir, who instead turned to her US Ambassador, Yitzhak Rabin. Rabin provided a channel to Kissinger, thus bypassing both America's Rogers and Israel's Eban.

Henry Kissinger was the most powerful Secretary of State ever wielded by America. His heavy, thick-set figure and even heavier deep German accent made him an easily recognisable figure on the world stage. Responsible for much of President Nixon's foreign policy during his period as Secretary of State from 1969 to 1977, he was directly involved in remarkable international events. The end of the Vietnam War, détente with Russia and rapprochement with China were examples of his commitment to realpolitik, and he expended enormous personal energy in the Middle East. Intellectually superior to most mortals, as he readily admitted, he strongly divided opinion. Lauded by many as the most successful of operators in world affairs, he was also capable of raising strong opposition. He was accused of 'crimes against humanity' for his roles in fomenting unrest in south-east Asia and South America and an offer of a post as Professor at Columbia University was withdrawn after student protests and a media campaign. He was awarded a Nobel Peace Prize but wanted to return it, failed to attend the ceremony and gave the money to charity. Despite the controversy surrounding him, it is difficult now not to appreciate his enormous achievements and his advice continues to be called for, not least most recently by President Trump. His revealing remark to Golda Meir, when she was Israel's Foreign Minister, that he was an American first and a Jew only second was followed by her response that she was pleased, because in Hebrew one reads from left to right. His Jewishness made Nixon try unsuccessfully to keep him out of Israeli negotiations. We now come to his role in the Middle East, a role again not short of controversy.

The Kissinger–Rabin axis encouraged aggressive action against Egypt and Meir believed that this advice came directly from Nixon. She was powerfully supported by her Defence Minister, Moshe Dayan, and blithely carried on with her destructive actions in Egypt.

Personal relations between Kissinger and Rogers were fraught and when the latter put forward his peace plan in December 1969 Rabin signalled to Meir, what he felt was Kissinger's view, that not too much notice needed to be taken of it. This Meir was happy to accept since she felt that the Rogers Plan leant too far to the Egyptian position of withdrawal before negotiation. Rogers revised his peace plans and when he put them forward in June 1970 the Israeli Cabinet was split in its response. As so often in Israeli politics a mixture of democracy and strong personalities interfered with its ability to reach an agreed position. Meir decided to press her Cabinet to accept the plan and to re-visit Resolution 242 (and 'withdrawal from territories'). Dayan played his usual game of a mixture of support and opposition but while he finally agreed to stay with his Prime Minister, Menachem Begin immediately resigned. This is the same Begin who, seven years later as Prime Minister, agreed to the same terms, with even more concessions, at the Camp David peace talks. It is now just a little ironic to recognise that Israel, after so vehemently resisting the presence of Egyptian troops anywhere in the Sinai, by 2014 had welcomed them there in the fight against militant Islamic groups.

But back in 1970 Nasser remained firm and the increasing Russian build-up in Egypt was beginning to tell on the American administration. The need to avoid a confrontation with the Soviets and to protect the American oil interests was becoming more urgent and the final straw was the shooting down of five Russian aircraft west of the Suez Canal by Israeli planes on one day in June 1970. America applied heavy pressure on the Israelis, who agreed to a cease-fire the following day and re-affirmed their acceptance of Resolution 242. A stand-off between the great powers was avoided for the time being. Golda Meir was finally brought to accept that the US might be slow to come to her aid if Russia was tempted to take a more personal interest in Israel's affairs.

In this Chapter the major concern has been the relationship between Israel and Egypt. An agreement would never have been reached with Nasser who completely rejected Israel's right to exist in the Middle East. Only with a change of leadership in an Arab state was a rapprochement possible. The Palestinians were used as a pawn in Egypt's game but never achieved any traction of their own until the rise of Yasser Arafat and the PLO. There are signs now that the pragmatic Sunni Arab states may be losing patience with the Palestinian leadership for holding back on direct negotiations with Israel. They sense that peace with them is being held back by Palestinian reticence.

CHAPTER 8

The Palestinians

THERE SHOULD BE LITTLE doubt that Israel needs a peace with all its neighbours. Its continuing existence is dependent on it. The peace deal with Egypt, long sought by Israel but rebuffed by Nasser, only became a reality when Egypt's new leader, Anwar Sadat, accepted Israel's existence and knew that peace was a more productive option than war. Peace with the Palestinians has never quite reached that position. For many years they lacked any cohesive voice or leadership, relying instead on other Arab nations that were not always wedded to their cause. Even when a more distinctive Palestinian resistance emerged there was no possibility that its leadership would accept Israel's presence in the Middle East. Not only would they not accept a division of the land, the two-state solution of Resolution 242, they wanted Israel removed completely. They did not have a negotiating position, just no negotiation with the 'Zionist Entity'. Their attitude then was quite unlike that of the Jews when they were pressing for a Jewish homeland. Whatever was offered was accepted. This left open to them the prospect for future negotiation. The homeland envisioned in the Balfour Declaration was whittled down from a land that incorporated present-day Jordan to one that was first limited by the river Jordan and finally to the sliver of land along the Mediterranean and the desert in the 1947 Partition Plan. The Israelis accepted each in turn, albeit reluctantly, but lived in hope of further change. Some Palestinians went along with it but most did not. They wanted all or nothing for far too long. They were, of course, encouraged in this attitude by other Arab states and indeed Yasser Arafat was long fearful of suffering a fate similar to the one that eventually overtook Sadat if he softened his stance.

The development of Palestinian identity and the continuing conflict is intimately bound up with the position of the refugees and it is worthwhile here examining how their plight has influenced attitudes to Israel.

Palestinian Refugees

When large numbers of the indigenous Palestinian population were expelled or fled in 1948 their refugee status created one of the most lasting and resistant barriers to peace in the Middle East. Estimates of between 500,000 and one million fled or were forcibly evicted and the majority of them were kept in camps, many of which persist more than sixty-five years later in surrounding countries. Only in Jordan were some allowed to assimilate.

After the war of independence several NGOs and aid groups were rapidly deployed to deal with the immediate humanitarian crisis. The most prominent was that set up by the American Friends Service Committee (AFSC), a Quaker organisation which had already been awarded the Nobel Peace Prize in 1947 for many years of remarkable aid work around the world. They were soon faced with the longer-term problems of repatriation and/or re-settlement once the immediate crisis had been improved.[1] They had little difficulty with the 750,000 Jewish refugees but the Palestinian problems had just begun. Firstly, trying to understand the numbers of refugees posed questions about who should be counted. Were the Bedouin who had been moved from part of their land to be counted? And what about the admittedly small numbers of migrant workers who had simply spent some time temporarily in Palestine? Or local residents in Gaza, Syria or Lebanon now overwhelmed by Palestinians? The AFSC tried hard to deal with that and with the problem of double counting, as children ran round the back from tent to tent, that increased the funding requests that followed.[2]

However, the major difficulty was the politicisation of their work. After immediate humanitarian aid their efforts were aimed primarily at education and vocational training, leading to self-sufficiency and possible integration into the society where the refugees then found themselves. The AFSC fancifully believed that a mixture of repatriation to Israel for some and re-settlement in Arab countries for others could be achieved. The refugees themselves and the Arab nations had other ideas. The refugees adamantly refused to consider anything other than a return for all of them to their original homes. Re-settlement was not on their agenda and they were wedded to the concept of 'rights of return', using resistance as the route to achieve this aim. The idea of accepting work in Arab host countries would mean abandoning their claims for return and in any case Palestinians were not allowed to work in most professions in Lebanon and Syria.

Nor would the host countries consider accepting the refugees even with blandishments in the form of financial aid from the UN and USA. They much preferred the option of taking their slice of the AFSC aid and using the refugees as a rod to beat the back of Israel. Tentative Syrian offers were lost as the multiple coups removed a series of temporary leaders while Egypt flatly refused to accept the refugees in Gaza as citizens. It did agree to offer education for them but according to Alwin Holtz of the AFSC 'the kids are learning reading, writing and bombing tactics'.[3] Israel's offer at Lausanne to take on the refugees in Gaza was rejected by Egypt, which viewed it as an expansionist ploy.

The AFSC, having completed their emergency tasks and failed in their efforts at rehabilitation, were very pleased to hand over to the new UN body, UNRWA (United Relief and Works Agency for Palestine). In December 1950 UNRWA was tasked by UN Resolution 393 with the objective of re-integrating the refugees by either repatriation or re-settlement 'for when international assistance is no longer required'.[4] This temporary measure is now in its sixty-eighth year.

A major mistake was the setting up of UNRWA as an arm's-length body and outside administrative control by the UN Secretariat. It thus became self-perpetuating and has never been able to move the Arab states or the refugees on from their initial resistance. The end result is that UNRWA has become the largest employer of Palestinian refugees; it is largely run by them and that has undoubtedly helped perpetuate their refugee status. This permanent welfare system has led to a humanitarian trap and the refugees now find themselves in an impossible position in the nutcracker formed by the stand-off between Israel and the Arabs. Israel is willing to accept the repatriation of only very limited numbers because of a fear of being overwhelmed and the Arab host countries will not move on re-settlement while UNRWA continues to maintain the status quo. But keeping them in limbo in other Arab countries, as I fear that UNRWA has succeeded in doing, has only damaged their prospects. And the tragedy is that the original Foreign Office and State Department documents at the time clearly envisaged re-settlement of refugees in Syria, Jordan, Lebanon and Iraq. The original refugees have now multiplied through high birth rates and their humanitarian needs are increasingly used by the PLO to denigrate Israel in the international community.

The refugees' tragedy was compounded for years by a lack of leadership or any representative body but that did not prevent their plight being used by the Arab nations as an asset in their propaganda war against Israel.

Yasser Arafat

Arafat was born into a middle-class family in 1929 in Cairo, not in Palestine as he later claimed. Given a series of names in the Arabic tradition, he later dropped them all in favour of Yasser. He was sent to Jerusalem to live with an uncle after the death of his mother and spent four years there before returning to Cairo in 1937 to continue his education.[5]

He had not been radicalised by having suffered the expulsions of 1948, as had the erstwhile rivals to his leadership George Habash and Khalil al-Wazir, later his colleagues. He nevertheless embraced the Palestinian cause and took on a leadership role at university with alacrity. He helped form the Palestinian Student League, becoming its first president, and made efforts to fight in Gaza and in the 1956 war.

Meanwhile a number of disparate resistance groups had been formed, largely sponsored by Arab states to whom they were answerable. Arafat much preferred to see an independent Palestinian resistance movement that was free of the shackles of other nations. Politically astute and very persuasive in Arabic (his English was poor), he gathered some like-minded colleagues and, in about 1959, formed his Fatah (a reverse acronym for 'Palestinian National Liberation Movement' and an ancient Arabic word meaning 'opening' or 'conquest' and by implication 'opening by conquest of a land for Islam').

Throughout the 1960s he faced many difficulties in establishing himself and his movement. Based in Syria, he was arrested and sentenced to death on one occasion after one of his rivals died in suspicious circumstances. He was later pardoned but was expelled from Syria. He then based himself largely in Jordan and continued leading terrorist incursions into Israel. It was here that he managed to rescue his reputation at the battle of Karameh in March 1968. The IDF had launched an attack on this centre of repeated incursions into Israel and managed to demolish most of the infrastructure there. The strong resistance put up by Arafat's Fatah troops, who inflicted heavy Israeli casualties, converted a defeat into a victory in Palestinian eyes. Arafat was the hero, at least for the moment.

By 1964 when the Arab League agreed to the formation of the Palestinian National Council and its executive arm, the PLO, the Palestinians gained some legitimacy. Their own voice was being heard and a variety of factions with their separate anti-Israel activities came together under the PLO umbrella with Fatah as the dominant party. Under Arafat's leadership of Fatah (and, from 1968, of the PLO), the

Palestinians gained an increasingly independent voice. And what they said was that they were committed to the 'liberation' of Palestine by any means possible, including terrorism.

The Palestinian Liberation Organisation

The initial PLO draft constitution spoke of the 'liberation of their country' while their later covenant (July 1968) clarified this as a 'national duty'.[6] Article 9 says, 'Armed struggle is the only way to liberate Palestine' and Article 10, 'Commando action constitutes the nucleus of the Palestinian popular liberation war.'

But it is Article 15 that seeks the end of Israel: 'The liberation of Palestine ... aims at the elimination of Zionism in Palestine.' That is the English translation but what the original Arabic states is 'the liquidation of the Zionist Presence', a common Arabic euphemism for the state of Israel.

The covenant goes on: 'The Partition of Palestine in 1947 and the establishment of the State of Israel are entirely illegal, regardless of the passage of time' (Article 19) and 'The liberation of Palestine will destroy the Zionist and imperialist presence' (Article 22). And then there is the remarkable Article 24 that describes 'the Palestinian people [as] believ[ing] in the principles of justice, freedom, sovereignty, self-determination, human dignity, and in the right of all people to exercise them'. Except the Jews of course!

There's not much room here, then, to doubt the aim of the PLO was to get rid of Israel.

Arafat made some efforts to downplay this message at various times over the next few years, as we will see later. He produced a '10 Point Plan' in 1974 and although this again saw no place for Israel, he encountered much opposition in his own camp, never entirely cohesive, because it seemed to be a softening of attitude.

It is clear from the PLO Covenant that Resolution 242, and the

Partition Plan, were anathema to Arafat and it was not until twenty years later, in 1988, that he tentatively accepted the idea of a two-state solution, by which time he was holed up in Tunis, broke and broken. Only then did he tacitly accept Israel's right to exist, albeit with the proviso of a right of return for all refugees and with Jerusalem as capital of his Palestine. Then, in 1993 as part of the Oslo Accords, he accepted the idea of rescinding the PLO Covenant and in 1996 it was finally nullified.

Meanwhile, Arafat played a careful game of allowing Palestinian freedom of religious belief while maintaining a secular outlook. He avoided both the extremes of jihad on the one hand and the outright communism of some groups beneath the PLO umbrella on the other. In this way he managed, at least at first, to retain the support of the other Arab nations.

In Nasser's Egypt, efforts to develop a pan-Arabic position were bolstered by common cause with the Palestinians – liberation of Palestine, return of refugees and destruction of Israel – and Arafat was almost entirely dependent on that support. It was only after the 1967 war and with the demise of Nasser's pan-Arabism that Arafat understood that the prime objective of Arab states, especially Egypt, had shifted towards recovery of their own lost territories and away from an emphasis on Palestine. Not that this was explicit but Arafat clearly worried that a peace might be struck, between Israel and Egypt, without a deal on Palestine. He was right, of course, because that is what eventually happened at Camp David in 1979. But back then it was becoming obvious to him that he had to be more self-sufficient if he was to liberate his land. He became more reliant on Syria, having lost the support of both Jordan and Egypt, but President Assad kept him on a tight rein. Arafat, ever an opportunist, then turned to a disparate mixture of extreme groups for support.

The PLO became the spear-head of the war of attrition that was being waged from Gaza, the West Bank and Lebanon but the Israeli response was taking its toll on the populations there. It then went through a series of enforced moves as its host nations found its presence increasingly uncomfortable. Initially based mainly in Jordan, it not only terrorised the Israelis, but it was also busily engaged against the Jordanians, who were trying to curtail its activities.

King Hussein was embarrassed even further by the Palestinians as they turned against him. He was severely threatened by an assassination attempt followed by the hijacking of three civilian airliners, blown up at Dawson's Field, in the desert east of Amman, by George Habash's Popular Front for the Liberation of Palestine (PFLP). But when the PFLP, in a final act of desperation, seized the Intercontinental Hotel in Amman and took all the foreigners hostage, including the many journalists staying there, threatening to kill them unless Hussein stopped his army's assaults on the Palestinians, it was just too much. Syria then entered the fray when it invaded Jordan from the north ostensibly in support of the Palestinians but as a convenient cover to expand their sphere of influence. That was aborted when Hussein sought aid and Israel, at US urging, mobilised its forces nearby.

Hussein had had enough and sent his army to eradicate the PLO with devastating effect. Several thousand Palestinians, civilians and militants alike, were killed. The lack of a UN response to this slaughter contrasts strongly with the condemnation heaped on Israel for somewhat less action against Palestinians. Indeed many PLO fighters fled to Israel rather than fall into the hands of the army.

This was the PLO's darkest moment, their 'Black September' of 1970, when they were evicted from Jordan. They moved to Lebanon, where they continued their attacks on Israeli targets in Galilee and on Jewish targets around the world. And as an act of revenge against the Jordanians they assassinated Wasfi al-Tal, Jordan's Prime Minister, in November 1971. They were hardly welcomed in Lebanon and soon became a thorn in the side of the large Christian population. We will leave them there for the moment and return to them later.

CHAPTER 9

Anwar Sadat Takes Over in Egypt, 1971

DRAMATIC CHANGES IN LEADING personalities and attitudes on both sides were occurring. In September 1970 Nasser had died in Egypt and Anwar Sadat took his place while in Israel Golda Meir was already in office, having succeeded Levi Eshkol on his death. It is one of the many tragedies in the Middle East that when one side loses a hawkish leader, the other gains one. With Eshkol as Prime Minister efforts to reach a deal were continued but his successor was a much more hard-line leader. While in Egypt Nasser's rejectionist stance was transformed by Sadat who was initially thought of as a harmless transitional figure, but then played a much braver, cleverer and more far-sighted role.

What happened next does not redound well on the Israeli leadership. Sadat, less strident than his predecessor, made a remarkable speech to his parliament early in 1971. Here he laid out his ideas about the conditions for a possible peace negotiation. To have made such a speech was incredibly brave although the groundwork had been laid when Nasser decided to limit his immediate ambitions to the liberation of the Sinai. The offer even to talk about engaging with Israel was remarkable but it was completely ignored by the Israelis. They made the mistake of favouring the advice of Kissinger and Rabin in Washington while ignoring that of Rogers and his plan. The tragedy of that missed opportunity was played out in the inexorable march to the 1973 war.

The consequences of that war for Egypt, Syria and Jordan were bad enough but the impact on Israel, even though it won, was devastating.

The sad fact is that the peace deal hammered out at Camp David in 1979 was probably there for the taking in 1971 but the mood in Israel had become one of invincibility. They regarded the Arab military as a spent force, they miscalculated the Russian arms build-up in Egypt and Syria and they grossly underestimated President Sadat, as did many in the international community. But Sadat was becoming recognised as a highly intelligent and effective pragmatist, at least by the Americans, with whom he had opened discussions. Keen to see Israel out of the Sinai and to rebuild civilian life along a re-opened Suez Canal, he made a number of proposals that fitted well with the Rogers Plan of June 1970. The problem for Israel was the need to agree to withdraw in the absence of any clear commitment to a time scale for a peace deal and to what such a deal might include.

While Meir's Foreign Office were advising her to take Sadat's words seriously she preferred to listen to Kissinger, who was not exerting pressure for her to do so, and Israel persisted in dragging its heels. Furthermore it sent completely the wrong signals when Moshe Dayan gave a speech at Masada in which he described Israel as having complete authority over the whole of the Sinai up to the Suez Canal. The setting up of an Israeli settlement at Yamit and at a small number of other sites in occupied Sinai was the final straw.

Sadat was left with two alternatives: accept Israeli occupation of Egyptian land and face the prospect of a huge uprising by his population, the ire of other Arab nations and the distinct possibility of assassination; or stand and fight. Conor Cruise O'Brien suggests the possibility that Kissinger, with whom Sadat had built a good relationship, gave him some encouragement to go to war.[1] Did Kissinger want to shake Israel out of its complacency? Certainly Machiavellian intrigue was never entirely beyond Kissinger's capacity but it seems unlikely that he would have willed the end result. He certainly gave the impression that he was as surprised as many that Sadat attacked in such an effective way in 1973. It is also the case that the US had noted Sadat's increasing independence from Russia when he expelled some of its senior officers and purged his government of pro-Russian members. America no longer needed Russia to negotiate with Egypt and it would have been very unhappy to see Sadat fall.

More Peace Proposals

There had been other plans for peace before this time. There was the Rogers Plan of October 1969, as well as proposals put forward later by a four-power conference, with America, Russia, Britain and France as members, but they seemed to Israel to be veering too far towards Nasser's position of full withdrawal without a peace agreement and without any direct negotiation. Neither plan was in any case accepted by the Arab nations and pressure on Israel from Washington was variable. When Israel offered to come to the aid of Jordan to repel the Syrian invasion intended to support the PLO in 1970, America showed its gratitude by reducing any pressure it may have had on Jerusalem.

This was the background leading to the 1973 war, a war that put paid to Israeli self-confidence and fundamentally changed its attitude from one of invincibility to one of vulnerability and anxiety. This whole sorry episode is spelt out in Conor Cruise O'Brien's book *The Siege*, and Israel's unhappy part in it is accepted by at least three of its past ambassadors to the UK, Gideon Rafael,[2] Yehuda Avner[3] and Moshe Raviv.[4]

Thus from 1967 to 1973 the so-called peace process swung from one extreme to the other: outright rejection by the Arab nations of any direct negotiation with Israel and no agreement to even contemplate peace in 1967, followed by Israel's tragic failure to recognise the possibility of peace talks that Sadat opened up in 1971. Internal government squabbles in Washington and Jerusalem did not help and the on–off pressures exerted by America on Israel complicated matters still further. It seemed almost inevitable that another war would follow, but when it did it caught the Israelis completely off guard.

At the outbreak of the war, as Israel's future appeared more uncertain, appeals for arms became more urgent and America responded rather late in the day. The fact that it was Egypt and Syria that started the war did nothing to inhibit the UN General Assembly from chastising Israel. The European and non-aligned nations not only refrained from supporting Israel; they actively obstructed American efforts under the threat of Arab oil embargoes. Britain, for example, refused even to allow US air bases in the UK to be used to re-fuel supply planes. Gideon Rafael painted this episode as follows: 'Oil has the singular quality of not only moving the wheels of transport and industry but also removing the scruples of morality.'[5] If ever there was doubt about the power of oil to exert a malign influence on governments it has been dispelled in remarkable detail in Leif Wenar's recent book, *Blood Oil*.

1973: War and Peace

The die was cast for the Yom Kippur War. In retrospect its inevitability was obvious but the Israeli government and the military were taken completely off guard. The impact on the population was devastating and Israel's well-rehearsed self-confidence was shattered. The fall-out left a scar that has still not healed.

It is likely that neither Egypt nor Syria expected to be able to win the war. Their aims were to regain some of the land lost in the 1967 war and to engage the international community in their efforts to break Israel's status quo mentality. As we saw earlier, it has been suggested that Kissinger had encouraged Sadat to start the war for just that end, to shake Israel out of its complacency. That seems unlikely but if it is true it was a cynical and costly manipulation by a superpower. It has always been the case that for the Arab nations the loss of a war with Israel was not a threat to their existence, but for Israel the loss of a war would mean the end of the state and probably the Jews in the Middle East.

The simultaneous attack by Egypt and Syria on Yom Kippur, 6 October 1973, left Egyptian troops reaching beyond the Suez Canal and into the Sinai, while the Syrians re-occupied some of the Golan Heights. Eventually Israeli troops pushed them both back but only after they had lost almost 3,000 soldiers and vast amounts of arms. Egyptian forces retreated behind the canal while some were surrounded and cut off as Israel advanced to a position 101 kilometres from Cairo. In Syria they came within 50 kilometres of Damascus.

As in the three previous wars it was joint US and Soviet pressure, exerted through the UN Security Council, that eventually led to a cease-fire. In the initial stages, while Israel's enemies were winning, Russia delayed its efforts. But once Israel became the dominant force, and especially when it had crossed the Suez Canal in the south and was advancing on Damascus in the north, the Kremlin called Kissinger for urgent meetings and a cease-fire was hastily agreed and pressed on their warring allies.

There were many lessons to be learnt by Israel and some of these came out in the judicial inquiry set up after the war under the President of the Israeli Supreme Court, Simon Agranat.[6] Intelligence failures and lack of preparation by military and civil authorities were foremost. Several senior military heads were made to fall while the politicians, including Dayan, who held much of the responsibility, were excluded from the judicial review but not from the ire of the public. It was inevitable that Golda Meir would have to resign and in 1974 Yitzhak Rabin was elected for his first period as Prime Minister.

CHAPTER 10

Rabin, Begin and Sadat

A COMPLEX CHARACTER, YITZHAK Rabin had commanded the entire Israeli Army by the age of forty-two. He had led the assault in the 1967 war and before that had been involved in the notorious expulsion of Palestinians from Lydda.

Known for his hawkish views as an army general and then ambassador to the US, he now began the process of earning his reputation as a peace maker. He became Prime Minister in June 1974 and in a conversation recorded during this, his first term of office by Shlomo Avineri, the director general at the Ministry of Foreign Affairs, he set out the principles on which a future peace might be achieved.[1] He clearly saw that Israel could not hold on to the West Bank and Gaza. The millions of Palestinians living there could not be ruled against their will and in any case it would not be acceptable to a democratic Israel. Privately he opposed settlements and wanted to see Israel's eventual withdrawal. But all this would have to wait. It was too soon for him and for Israel's traumatised population to accept and too soon also for the Arab countries. The Arabs would view withdrawal as proof that they should renew their aggression in light of their recent success. For any territorial concessions American support would be vital and both Arabs and Israelis were only just becoming convinced that Israel was a permanent feature of the Middle East.

Rabin combined a hawkish public stance with a pragmatic dovish longer-term policy.

A rather more significant lesson was learnt by the Arabs, whose pride had been improved. They had shown in 1973 that Israel was not invincible and even though Israel won the battle in the end, the Arabs could cause considerable damage and, at least initially, make many gains. Israel was shaken, and this increased the Arab sense of legitimacy and confidence. It encouraged Sadat to move further on bargaining and compromise. The fact that the Arabs could hold their heads up ensured that they could enter a negotiation as a partner, rather than as a supplicant, and it is likely that this was one factor leading to the Egypt–Israel peace treaty. Kissinger's activities did eventually bear fruit and with Sadat the prospects for peace with Egypt were immeasurably improved. A peace deal was finally struck six years after the war in 1979, rather longer than the three or four years that Rabin had envisaged. And by then Israel's Prime Minister was Menachem Begin.

The war itself caused mayhem in Israel initially and a terrible loss of personnel on both sides. After the war the UN went into action and America, again in the shape of Henry Kissinger, went into overdrive.

Post-War Moves

UN Security Council Resolution 338 promoted the cease-fire and implementation of Resolution 242. Israel accepted Resolution 338 and made concessions that, if made in 1971, might have avoided the war altogether. The Geneva Conference, led by the USSR and the USA, followed shortly thereafter and a disengagement was agreed with Egypt in January 1974, and with Syria in the following May. A buffer zone under UN control was set up along the Suez Canal as Israeli forces withdrew and Egyptian troops fell back.

There is little doubt that relationships between the Palestinians and Israel on the one hand and the Arab nations on the other deteriorated markedly during this time. The massacre of Israeli athletes at the Munich Olympics in 1972 by the 'Black September' terrorist group of the PLO was the nadir in a continuing terrorist campaign. By now Egypt wanted little to do with the Palestinians, King Hussein had expelled them from Jordan and only Syria and Iraq were fostering their cause against Israel.

It is against this background that the softening of attitudes between Egypt and Israel was particularly interesting. Kissinger beavered away with a willing Anwar Sadat and to some extent the resulting peace was the happy result of a misunderstanding.

Intimations of Peace with Egypt

The idea of peace was in the air and, although it was still some way off, it should be noted that no shots have been fired between Israel and Egypt since February 1974.

The 1973 war gave Sadat an opportunity to negotiate a deal that would give him back the Sinai Desert (in which he was successful) and get something for the Palestinians (in which he was not). He grasped it with both hands.

Kissinger immediately embarked on his shuttle diplomacy. His aim was to seek firstly a disengagement by a cautious step-by-step approach, and he succeeded in persuading both governments to accept proposals from him that they may not have accepted from each other. Kissinger's efforts with Syria were more troublesome and while disengagement agreements were reached in the end, a peace has never been achieved.

It is worth considering why it was possible to achieve peace with one but never with the other. Perhaps it is because Sadat valued the return of the Sinai and an improvement in his country's reputation and economy more than Hafez al-Assad regarded the return of the Golan Heights. More importantly, Assad had territorial ambitions that included a Syrian hegemony over Lebanon, Jordan and Palestine. An independent Palestine was not on his agenda and indeed he had imprisoned Yasser Arafat for a while until the Arab League persuaded him otherwise. He also knew that his plans for a greater Syria were never going to go down well in Israel. I explore the prolonged and ultimately unsuccessful negotiations with Syria in Chapter 22.

In 1977 the political chess-board changed yet again as Jimmy Carter became President in America while, in Israel, Menachem Begin was elected Prime Minister. Rabin had resigned following the revelation that his wife had maintained an illegal bank account in America long after he had returned from his role as ambassador. His successor, a highly intelligent, politically astute, but much more inflexible right-wing figure, was to play a key role in Israel's future.

Sadat in Israel

Anwar Sadat's capacity for surprise was undiminished. Shortly after Begin came to power Sadat dramatically discarded a set speech to his National Assembly to speak of his willingness 'to go to the ends of the earth for peace', even to Jerusalem to debate the possibility in Israel's Knesset.[2] Many, but not all, in Israel were surprised by this bombshell but so astounded was Sadat's audience, which included Yasser Arafat, that they simply applauded.

When Sadat flew to Israel some ten days later, Mordechai Gur, Begin's chief of staff, who had been kept in the dark, was certain it was a ruse and expected gun-fire from the plane as it landed. Instead Sadat was greeted by cheering crowds of children waving Israeli and Egyptian flags. He was enveloped in a warm embrace as he visited Yad Vashem, the Al-Aqsa Mosque and the Church of the Holy Sepulchre. In the Arab world, meanwhile, he was branded a traitor and his Foreign Minister resigned. Sadat had placed himself in an extremely vulnerable position.

Of course it was not an entirely spur-of-the-moment event. Cease-fire agreements had been reached and Sadat had renounced the use of force, had re-opened the Suez Canal and was busily rebuilding his cities in the Canal Zone. Begin had clearly stated in his inaugural address to the Knesset that 'our prime concern is the prevention of a new war' and 'I call upon King Hussein, President Sadat and President Assad to meet with me … to discuss the establishment of true peace between their countries and Israel'. And there had been much clandestine and indirect contact between Israel and Egypt. Begin had followed Rabin in engaging the support of Nicolae Ceauşescu in Romania and the King of Morocco as intermediaries, and the Iranian Shah and the Indian Prime Minister had also been helpful.

But much the most significant, and certainly the most theatrical, contact occurred when Moshe Dayan travelled twice in disguise to Morocco. 'Pressed upon my skull was the mane of a beatnik; my upper lip was adorned with the moustache of a dandy; and on the bridge of my nose rested large dark sunglasses.'[3] He was dressed in this disguise simply to leave Israel to meet King Hassan of Morocco on the first occasion but on the second he again donned his wig, false moustache and dark glasses on his way from America to meet Sadat's Deputy Prime Minister, Hassan Tuhami. It is here that Dayan is said to have given assurances that were either not agreed at home, or misunderstood, which encouraged Sadat in his peace initiative.

Tuhami stated that Sadat's stipulated condition for direct talks between him and Begin were predicated on the agreement by Israel to vacate all Arab lands occupied in the 1967 war, including the West Bank and Gaza. Dayan himself in his account of the meeting, however, says nothing of having given such an assurance, only that he would take the message back for the idea to be included in any future peace negotiations.[4] He felt that Tuhami was rather a stiff man, lacking in humour and somewhat aloof, but Shimon Peres's account of this meeting suggests that Tuhami told him of his very warm feelings for Dayan.[5] But whatever was said by Dayan, or understood by Tuhami, by the time Sadat spoke to his Cairo parliament about his willingness to go to Jerusalem, it was no longer a surprise to Begin's inner circle.

Begin responded with an immediate invitation, via American

ambassadors, for Sadat to come as soon as possible and, within forty-eight hours, had broadcast directly to the Egyptian public in English. 'We wish you well ... Let us say to one another and let it be a silent oath by both peoples ... no more wars, no more bloodshed and no more threats.'[6]

Sadat also spoke to the Knesset in English, in a stumbling but electrifying manner.[7] Full of biblical allusions, he was listened to with respect as he spoke of his deeply felt desire for peace despite being uncompromising in his demands that Israel should withdraw from all the lands conquered in 1967. But it was the fact that Sadat had made this historic visit rather than the content of his speech that was of such consequence. The content, uncomfortable as it was for Israel, certainly did not assuage the anger of the Arab world. Begin, wisely ignoring the verbal message, calmly re-stated Israel's case and, in concentrating instead on the fact of the historic visit, welcomed Sadat's speech and responded by stating his equally strong desire for peace and a wish to be invited to Cairo.[8]

Begin also included the statement that he wanted 'to also invite genuine spokesmen of the Palestinian people to come and hold talks with us on our common future, on guaranteeing human freedom, social justice, peace and mutual respect'. It was in the different interpretations of what he intended by those words, and what Sadat understood, where a gap emerged.

That Begin and Sadat formed a bond should not be too surprising. They had both been involved in terrorism in their pasts and both had been imprisoned for their sins. Sadat had been implicated in a number of assassinations and, in an effort to remove the yoke of British rule, had sided with the Germans in World War II. Begin had been jailed by the Soviets, had headed the Irgun and had also been active against the British. A common bond of sorts.

It was now time for President Carter to intervene.

CHAPTER 11

President Carter and Camp David

AMERICAN PRESIDENT JIMMY CARTER had been paying increasing attention to the Middle East. He began to invest enormous personal effort in this, the key part of his foreign policy, at a time when his domestic standing was on the wane.

During his first year as President in 1977, he pressed both parties to produce their peace proposals for the conference he hoped to re-convene in Geneva. His idea was to have it jointly chaired by the Americans and Russians and attended by all the Arab countries, including the PLO, and Israel. Begin spoke of a Geneva meeting in his response to Sadat, but he was unhappy about sitting down with this combination of opponents. Sadat too did not want to be encumbered by a Syria that had its own expansionist plans for the Middle East. And in the USA there was dismay at the thought of working so closely with the Russians. This combination of obstacles ensured that the idea never got off the ground.

Meanwhile Israel and the Egyptians were beavering away at their own plans. Begin had presented his cabinet with a 'Framework for the Peace-Making Process between Israel and Its Neighbours', which included withdrawal from the Sinai and moves in the Golan Heights. But his sticking point was the exclusion of the West Bank and Gaza, which Sadat had demanded for negotiations. Here was the nub of the problems that had to be decided at Camp David. That an agreement was reached there depended almost entirely on Jimmy Carter's persistence and persuasive powers. Carter was also exerting more pressure on Israel about its settlement policy, which continued to be a serious bone of contention throughout negotiations thereafter.

It is worth exploring here why what seemed to be a rational and reasonable approach to a comprehensive peace agreement between Israel and all its Arab neighbours, including the Palestinians, was so elusive then as now. Carter's policy was heavily dependent on the Brookings Institution's report of 1975, largely written by his National Security Advisor, Zbigniew Brzezinski.[1] It talked of a 'comprehensive process' that included a fair and enduring settlement, territorial integrity of all parties, security and boundaries, peace, and Palestinian self-determination, all to be achieved in stages. The US would not be involved in negotiations but would offer inducements and give impetus to the process. Unfortunately this idea of a comprehensive set of agreements failed to take account of the realities of Middle Eastern rivalries and factions. The impossibility of agreement by all the parties on the Arab side, leaving aside any Israeli intransigence, was ignored. When it became clear that this strategy was not working it was replaced by one in which a peace treaty with one country, Egypt in the first instance, would be followed by some sort of ripple effect in which treaties with others would fall in to place; the 'concentric circle' strategy of Brzezinski. Again, Middle East realities intervened. Instead of welcoming what the Americans thought of as a first step by Egypt, both Syria and the PLO vehemently rejected it, closely followed by King Hussein of Jordan. Any deal with Israel was seen as a betrayal and the idea that an agreement between Egypt and Israel might be linked to a comprehensive peace process was soon destroyed.

Efforts by Carter in 1977 to get the PLO on board were frustrated. Despite his blandishments he could not persuade them to accept Resolution 242, which would have required them to recognise Israel. It is also the case that Assad in Syria would not have given his approval while he held the PLO in his grasp. Even later, when a US-inspired effort to modify the wording of Resolution 242 to make it more acceptable to the PLO was being mooted at the UN, it was aborted because of strong opposition from Syria, Egypt and the PLO itself. The latter simply wanted the whole resolution to be lost.

Nevertheless this idea of a comprehensive process is what motivated the Carter administration in 1977. They were taken aback by Sadat's own peace move in travelling to Jerusalem, and this would not be the first time that a local initiative was more productive than a US initiative. The Americans did, of course, welcome it and were to prove absolutely vital in ensuring that this initial step was successfully followed through.

The Rocky Path to the Summit

As always, however, the path to Camp David was far from straightforward. Events intervened after the sweetness and light of late 1977 in which Sadat spoke in the Knesset and an agreement to set up two committees, military and political, was reached at a further meeting between Sadat and Begin in Ismailia. Apart from these two types of committee there was little agreement between the parties on any substantive issues and the committees themselves soon fell into abeyance.

Although Begin was pragmatic about returning the Sinai and Golan Heights in exchange for peace, his ideas for the West Bank went only so far as some sort of administrative autonomy for the Palestinians while security would remain with Israel. Although that idea was rejected by the PLO then, it turned out to be not too dissimilar from both the Interim Agreement of the Oslo Accords in 1995 and the current position in the West Bank. Begin's view that sovereignty for the Palestinians was not open for discussion left a gap between him and Sadat that seemed unbridgeable. However, other significant developments intervened.

In 1978 Yasser Arafat's Fatah mounted an attack on an Israeli bus on the Haifa–Tel Aviv coast road in which thirty-seven civilians were slaughtered and eighty-two others wounded. Begin was incandescent and any ideas that the newly formed Israeli 'Peace Now' movement may have had were immediately quashed. Israel retaliated and, in an effort to remove the PLO from southern Lebanon, began a military operation that saw Israeli troops advance to the river Litani, where they remained until a UN force took over from them a few weeks later. It is noteworthy that Syria did not come to the aid of a PLO that they were almost as anxious as Israel to see held in check.

It is little wonder that Carter's peace efforts were being frustrated. Nor did it help his position with the Israelis when he promoted UN Resolution 425, which called for Israel's withdrawal from Lebanon without mentioning the PLO's takeover of the south of that country or the immediate cause of the invasion – the terrorist attack on the coast road.

But it was Israel's continuing build-up of the Sinai settlements at Yamit and elsewhere, led by Agriculture Minister Ariel Sharon, that created even more dismay, and not only for Sadat. Carter was enraged by these Israeli actions and only strong American pressure aborted their further development. It is likely that Begin's resistance to including settlement withdrawal from the Sinai in a peace deal with Egypt was prompted by a fear that this would give encouragement to those seeking withdrawal elsewhere; a rather insubstantial argument. Defence Minister Ezer Weizman was prompted to point out the folly of allowing an isolated settlement to derail progress on a potentially momentous peace deal. This, then, was one of those many inauspicious moments for a peace negotiation that had much chance of success.

Meanwhile Sadat had been cementing relations around the world. He received invitations to visit the Pope in the Vatican and to repair relations with the Shah of Iran. The Shah even tried to oil the wheels for an Israeli withdrawal from the Sinai by offering them free Iranian oil in exchange for the loss of the oil fields they had developed there. It was in America, however, where Sadat was made most welcome when he visited in February 1978. Carter formed a good opinion of him and greeted him warmly. Not so Begin, who received a frosty reception when he arrived a month later to try to placate Carter's anger over the settlement issue. Unsurprisingly, Carter was unable to move Begin on the idea of a comprehensive peace deal but was forced to recognise that at least here was a strong man capable of delivering.

The 'Two Frameworks' Proposal

Carter was attracted by the report Cyrus Vance, his Secretary of State, gave him of discussions he had had with Moshe Dayan and Muhammad Kemal, Sadat's Foreign Minister, at Leeds Castle in the UK in July 1978. Here the idea of two 'frameworks' for peace, with different time scales, was floated. Dayan, the architect of the contentious Yamit settlement, had already raised this possibility with Vance at a meeting in April.

The 'two frameworks' idea would allow details to be filled in over time and the time scales for the two parts might be staggered to allow at least some agreements to be reached before others. The framework for an Israel–Egypt deal could go ahead first while peace arrangements with the Palestinians would follow after a five-year interim period of 'autonomy', at the end of which negotiations for independence could resume. Dayan persuaded Begin that this offered the best, and probably the only possible, way of breaking the deadlock. For the first time it opened the prospect of disassociating peace with Egypt from a resolution of the Palestinian problems. Although Sadat had repeatedly insisted upon a comprehensive deal, this line might give him what he most wanted, namely a return of all of the Sinai.

Carter, desperate though he was for a comprehensive solution, also accepted that postponing the Palestinian framework might be the best that could be achieved then. He was also facing mid-term elections in November and desperately needed a success in the Middle East, so eventually he took on the idea of two types of agreement. He knew also that Israel's government was secure and contained the formidable trio of Begin, Dayan and Weizman, who, together with the legal expertise of Attorney General Aharon Barak, would later form the Camp David negotiating team.

Carter's Persistence

The fact that a deal was struck in September 1978 was due to President Carter's unrelenting efforts. He staked his reputation on success at a time when his domestic standing was far from high. He ignored his closest advisors who were warning him of the huge risks he was taking in pressing so hard.

July 1978 saw Carter's invitation to Begin and Sadat to Camp David. Both accepted immediately. Carter's earlier, much broader, Geneva conference idea was now well and truly dead. Talks began on 5 September and lasted thirteen days.[2]

Despite the cosy isolation of Camp David, free from any media, there was little informal contact between the Egyptians and Israelis with the exception of Ezer Weizman, who, having been amongst the most hawkish of military men, became the most dovish. He formed a good relationship with Sadat but it was Carter, investing enormous personal effort, that kept the parties talking.

The relationships of the two leaders with their own respective teams could not have been more different. Sadat was clearly anxious to reach a deal that would give him back the Sinai while his team were desperate for him not do so in the absence of a comprehensive settlement. The opposite was true of Begin, who gave every impression of resistance to an agreement while both Weizman and Dayan were much more conciliatory.

It took the whole of those thirteen days to reach an accord and there was much reason for despair. There were serious threats of a walk-out, first from Sadat and then from Begin, prevented on one occasion by Carter standing physically in the way as one or other tried to leave the room. Day four saw the Egyptians about to leave while on day six the Israelis were busily looking at El Al flight times. Sadat had his bags packed again on day eleven. It is possible that the threats of ending the talks were simply to gain a better negotiating position. If so they were very risky bluffs.

There was much fear in Sadat's camp that he was giving too much away in not being strong enough on the future for the Palestinians. He had already lost a number of his supporters. One of his officials had died of a heart attack during his trip to Jerusalem, two Foreign Ministers had resigned in quick succession before Camp David while their replacement, Kemal, fearfully stepped down immediately before the Accord was signed.

The linkage between a peace agreement with Egypt, which both parties desperately wanted, and a withdrawal by Israel from all the lands occupied in the 1967 war remained the overarching problem and it was only bypassed by their eventual separation into the two agreements. The immediate sticking point for Begin on the specific peace deal with Egypt was the withdrawal of all settlements from the Sinai that Sadat demanded. Apart from what he took to be a security risk in leaving the Sinai completely he had an intense distaste for the idea that Jews could not settle where they liked and worried that withdrawal here would provide a precedent for withdrawal from the West Bank. He was also being asked to give up three air bases and oil fields in the Sinai, but although these were of practical and economic importance they were less emotive for him.

The impasse was finally broken on day twelve by some inspired manoeuvring. Aharon Barak, who later went on to become Israel's Supreme Court president, provided the minute attention to the legal wording that was critical. It was agreed to adopt the 'two framework' proposal, one on the Sinai and the other on the Palestinian questions, the latter to be put off for the moment. Begin finally consented to the withdrawal of the Sinai settlements after he had the telephoned reassurance of Ariel Sharon that there was no strategic security reason to maintain them there; but even then he agreed only to put it to his Knesset for approval. The idea of sovereignty for the Palestinians was never envisaged by Begin but he did agree to the inclusion in the 'Framework for Peace' of the words 'The solution … must also recognise the legitimate rights of the Palestinian people and their just requirements'.[3] He was the first Israeli Prime Minister to have spoken of 'legitimate rights'. However, instead of the twelve months that was envisaged for even an autonomous administration on the West Bank, it took another fourteen years for the Oslo Accords to put it into effect.

The Camp David Accord was signed the next day. It included free movement of Israeli shipping through the Straits of Tiran and the Suez Canal, the phased withdrawal from the Sinai and the start of normal relations with the exchange of ambassadors.

Whatever Begin's negotiating position had been at Camp David, he used all his political skills and powers of persuasion to push the conditions of the Accord through a seven hour Cabinet meeting and then through the Knesset in two marathon sessions. These debates were characterised by what has been described as Israel's 'vibrant' democracy. Immediately Begin rose to speak, a member of the Knesset, Geulah Cohen, an extreme right-wing member of Likud, started shouting abuse and demanded that Begin should resign. She was eventually removed from the chamber but that did not stop a constant level of heckling that would make the UK House of Commons sound like a hushed London club. The agreement signed at Camp David was finally passed by a large majority.

Begin's achievement here belies the impression that he was rigidly unyielding on the need for peace that is sometimes given by Lawrence Wright.[4] But he knew full well that he was being asked to give up land, a stable asset, for a peace that could be overturned at any time. He had already, in 1977, spoken in his post-election inauguration speech about his strong desire to negotiate peace with Syria, Jordan and Egypt (although refusing to talk to the PLO), and he had overcome resistance in his Cabinet and military with their gloomy predictions, to welcome

Sadat's visit to Jerusalem. And he had immediately responded to Sadat's message with a broadcast to the Egyptian public about his desire for peace.

There can be little doubt that despite his negotiating tactics at Camp David he was desperate for peace. Begin was the most ideological of Israel's Prime Ministers and his motivation stemmed almost entirely from his experience of the Holocaust. Above all he was determined that nothing would be allowed to threaten the Jews or Israel ever again. 'We, the generation of the Holocaust … swore an oath of allegiance: never again shall we endanger our people; never again will our wives and children – whom it is our duty to defend … – be put in the devastating range of enemy fire,' he said in his response to Sadat's speech to the Knesset. It is clear where he was coming from, but he also said, 'Although we differ we do not rule out negotiation on any subject – everything will be negotiable.'

A wily negotiator he may have been but he certainly gave an impression of intransigence to Carter that coloured the President's views of Israel. It was not improved later when the fate of the Palestinians went into limbo and Begin expanded his West Bank settlement programme. However, Carter seems to have downplayed the fact that it was the PLO that continued to refuse to accept Resolution 242 and it was they who had immediately rejected Begin's acceptance of the loosely worded Camp David agreement on Palestinian administrative autonomy.

The peace treaty with Egypt was finally signed on the White House lawn on 26 March 1979, but not without significant hiccups on the way.

Aftermath of Camp David

The immediate response in the Arab nations was one of extreme hostility to Egypt. They and the PLO summarily rejected the idea of administrative autonomy for the Palestinians. Begin was far from displeased with this rejection.

The peace agreement was condemned at a series of Arab summits in 1978, and with no sign that any other state would follow Egypt's example, the fond idea that the Americans had had of a comprehensive settlement was blown out of the water. No 'concentric circles' of agreements or 'ripple effects' were in view. Those who thought that the signing of the Accord in September 1978 would be followed seamlessly by a peace treaty faced a rude awakening. True, the Israeli government had given its backing to what it thought had been agreed. Unfortunately there were several other unresolved issues, some backtracking and a number of new complicating factors.

In Iran the Shah, Mohammad Reza Pahlavi, had been deposed and the fundamentalist regime of Ayatollah Khomeini had taken over. Egypt (and Israel) had lost one of its few Middle East supporters at a time when the Baghdad Arab summit had ejected Egypt from membership of the Arab League. This left Sadat desperate to see if he could find anything in his agreements with Israel to placate his Arab neighbours. He and the Americans were pressing Israel to yield further concessions for the Palestinians after their agreed period of autonomy. Sadat was clearly also under heavy pressure internally, as well as regionally, as he seemed to be selling the Arabs short.

Begin too was at the worse end of internal political dissent, largely from his own party, which thought that he was giving too much away. Israel was also worried about pre-existing treaties between Egypt and the other Arab nations that obliged them to come to each other's aid if they were attacked. Would Egypt, for example, respond to a skirmish in the Golan by coming to the military aid of Syria? What was the legal position of these treaties vis-à-vis a new peace treaty with Israel? This was not a trivial concern and it now needed to be resolved. What is more, Israel was faced with a huge bill that it could barely afford in evacuating the Sinai. Would the Americans help fund the replacement air-fields that were to be left? And would Egypt guarantee to provide oil on which Israel now relied from the Sinai?

All these questions bedevilled the lead-up to the signing of the peace treaty, and at times it looked to Moshe Dayan, who chronicled these manoeuvrings, as though the treaty would be lost. In the midst of all this Begin and Sadat were awarded the Nobel Peace Prize! But it took a personal visit by President Carter to Cairo and Jerusalem to push the parties into an agreement to resolve all these issues. The treaty between Egypt and Israel was finally signed at the White House on 26 March 1979.

Despite the isolation of Egypt by the rest of the Arab world the Camp David peace initiative has survived for over thirty-seven years in the face of assassinations, changes of leadership, wars, coups d'état, the 'Arab Spring' and the turmoil in much of the wider Middle East. But peace with Egypt did not mean reconciliation of mind-sets. The often virulently anti-Israel and anti-Semitic stance of the Egyptian media and public has failed to dislodge the peace, probably because the Egyptian leadership, especially the military, understand as much as Israel the considerable advantages of not being at war. For most of the time since then it has been a 'cold peace' that characterised relations although now there is a softening of attitudes as President Sisi tries to bring the Israelis and Palestinians together.

The painful withdrawal of the 7,000 settlers in Yamit, Ophira and the isolated agricultural settlements was accomplished by firm pressure from the IDF over the next couple of years and all of the Sinai was handed over to Egypt by 1982. Meanwhile the Arab League had moved their offices out of Cairo and into Tunis and most of the Arab states severed diplomatic relations with Egypt. Their embassies in Cairo only re-opened some six years later and the League finally returned in 1989.

Sadat's Assassination

On 6 October 1981, the annual celebrations of the successful Egyptian crossing of the Suez Canal witnessed the assassination of Anwar Sadat. He sat on a platform overlooking the huge parade, stood to take a salute, or to meet his end straight on, when a group of armed Muslim militants flung themselves at the platform. A grenade was thrown but did not explode and it was left to Lieutenant Khalid Islambouli to fire multiple shots into Sadat's body.

Islambouli had been recruited by Salafi Islamic extremists and while the ultimate reason behind the attack might have been the peace treaty with Israel, there had been much unrest in Egypt since 1979. The economy was failing badly and Sadat had taken severe action in suppressing both Muslim fundamentalist uprisings and earlier assassination attempts. His unpopularity leading up to his death was based as much on these factors as on the Israeli deal.

Hosni Mubarak had been Sadat's Vice-President and immediately took over as President. He continued Sadat's policies but by then the PLO had lost the support of its major ally, Egypt.

There were important lessons to be learnt from these momentous events of the 1970s.

The most obvious was the emergence of a far-sighted leader of an Arab state courageous enough to stake everything for a peace. And it took a strong, Israeli leader with a stable government capable of overcoming resistance at home. It is the case that we do not now have Palestinian leaders capable of such actions, while we have an Israeli leader hidebound by his right-wing coalition. We await change.

We can also take away from this episode the critical importance of locally inspired initiatives between the parties directly concerned, coupled with unwavering American pressure and unswerving presidential involvement once the direction of travel is determined. Both are essential components. It remains quite uncertain whether President Trump will be cast in the necessary mould.

We can now turn to the impact of these events on the question of an agreement with the Palestinians.

CHAPTER 12

The PLO and War in Lebanon

BY 1971 THE PLO was ensconced in Lebanon, where it was hardly welcome, and began making life difficult for the large number of Christians living there. The country was already mired in a raging civil war and the PLO created even more havoc. In 1976, in retaliation for a massacre at Karantina, the PLO murdered almost 700 Christians in the town of Damour and drove the remainder out. Their treatment of Christians was remembered with terrifying results when, several years later, a Christian militia committed a brutal revenge in the form of the Shatila and Sabra camp massacres (see below).

The terrorist attack on Israel's coastal road in 1978 described earlier and the harsh Israeli response in southern Lebanon did little to improve the position. It was fortunate that this Israeli adventure into Lebanon did not derail the Camp David talks later in the year. After Camp David the PLO, having lost its major supporter in Egypt, as well as Jordan, relied more on a mixture of various extremist groups for its aid. Assad in Syria was an ambivalent supporter and indeed shunned Arafat, backing opposition Palestinian groups and leaders. He was happy to use the PLO as a proxy weapon against Israel, but held it firmly in his grasp.

Despite all these tribulations Arafat was gaining regional and international recognition for the PLO. He had been accepted as the sole legitimate representative of the Palestinian people at the Arab League Summit in 1974. This was also the year that the UN General Assembly granted the PLO observer status. Arafat was skilful in presenting terrorism as 'freedom fighting' and himself as an advocate of peace. The makeup of the General Assembly was changing and now included large numbers of Third World and radical countries, amongst which Arafat was gathering a ready audience. His leadership of the PLO was becoming increasingly legitimised and his speech to the General Assembly in 1974 had been a masterpiece of prolonged obfuscation, lasting several hours and accompanied by a flamboyant display of the symbols of a peace-loving man, an olive branch in his hand and a closed gun holster at his waist. His condemnation of Israel was, however, uncompromising and meanwhile terrorist attacks continued.

This was the position from which the PLO would have to row back if they were ever going to accept the existence of an Israel. They eventually did so only when they were isolated and weakened in Tunis but with a continuing resistance to the idea that Israel could be accepted as a national Jewish state.

The Inevitability of War in Lebanon

The influence of what became known as the first Israel–Lebanon War on the PLO's relations with Israel and other Arab states deserves comment. The PLO presence in Lebanon was a continuing provocation as it masterminded repeated terrorist raids into Israel and elsewhere. That Israel would respond was increasingly obvious to the Americans, who in the shape of Secretary of State Alexander Haig urged only modest restraint. The US was anxious only for Israel to wait until it had completely vacated the Sinai as agreed at Camp David. Syria too did not appear entirely averse to Israeli actions in Lebanon so long as they did not threaten Syrian interests or stray into Syrian territory. Damascus was in any case distracted by its own problems. Alienated from Egypt and hostile to both Jordan and Iraq, Assad was concerned that his own minority Alawite sect was under threat from a growing Muslim fundamentalist insurgency. No doubt Sadat's assassination was playing on his mind when in 1982 he exterminated about 20,000 Muslims in a vicious attack on his fourth largest city, Hama. That action certainly discouraged others in Syria and was accompanied by hardly a peep of condemnation from the UN.

Meanwhile, preparations in Israel were well in hand to try to remove the PLO, the long-running sore, from Lebanon. In reality no government could long tolerate the constant rocket attacks into Galilee and acts of terror around the world. Israel's espoused aim was to eliminate the PLO and develop peaceful relations with certain groups in Lebanon. Only an excuse was needed to trigger an invasion. The attack on a Viennese synagogue and the assassination of an Israeli diplomat in Paris the previous year were remembered but Israel was held back by an argument that these were insufficient indicators of a violation of the cease-fire across the Lebanese border brokered by the Americans. But in 1982, it was the attempted assassination of the Israeli ambassador, Shlomo Argov, in London on 3 June that provoked Begin into a frenzy of retaliation against the PLO. The impact of the fateful war in Lebanon is discussed in the next section but in one respect it was successful in that it drove Arafat and the PLO out of the country and on to Tunis, where they festered for the next six years. We will leave them there for the moment.

Lebanese Wars and Adventures in Iraq

The invasion of Lebanon in 1982 had disastrous consequences that were as damaging to Israel and its international relations as they were to Lebanon and the PLO. The constant PLO provocation of Israel could not long be tolerated. Although there was a US-brokered cease-fire in operation along the Lebanese border the Israelis appeared to have been given the green light to attack the PLO stronghold and it mattered little to them by then that the responsibility for the assassination attempt on Argov had been laid at the door of Abu Nidal, an enemy of Arafat and head of a rival faction.

It was the extent of the invasion, up to and into Beirut, and the time it took for Israel to withdraw that proved so damaging. The original plan was for a 48-hour incursion to remove the PLO, to limit the ground covered to 40 kilometres from the border, not to involve any action against Syria and to try to engage the Maronite Christian leadership in a peace treaty. That they failed in all of these aspirations can be attributed largely to Israel's Minister of Defence, Ariel Sharon, and to the generals and commanders in the army. Sharon was the proverbial loose cannon and was said to have misled the Prime Minister and the Cabinet. He pressed the troops to enter not only the Christian quarter of Beirut, where they were welcomed by the relieved Maronite community, but later West Beirut, where they were not. The elimination of Syrian anti-aircraft missile batteries moving into eastern Lebanon and the downing of a large number of Syrian planes widened the conflict so that when the PLO did eventually vacate Beirut the Syrians were waiting for a suitable moment to return.

Israel had had relationships established across the border with Maronite and Druze communities in a narrow 'Security Belt' established after Operation Litani in 1978. Many residents worked in northern Israel at that time and sought help from Israel against the PLO. Begin and Sharon were keen to build on this friendship and the most likely prospect lay with the militant Christian Phalangists, headed by Bashir Gemayel. In August 1982 he was rapidly elected President, but before he could sign a peace treaty, and within three weeks he and the peace were dead. A devastating bomb killed him and many others and it is widely assumed that the Syrians were responsible.

The Phalangists, already dangerously enraged by their treatment at the hands of the PLO, were incensed by Gemayel's assassination and took a terrible revenge two days later. They were more than ready to level the balance sheet of the earlier slaughter of Christians by the PLO and invaded the Shatila and Sabra refugee camps. There, they massacred over 800 Palestinians while the IDF apparently stood by. This act caused revulsion around the world, nowhere more so than in Israel itself. Demonstrations in Tel Aviv and outside the Prime Minister's home continued throughout the year. A judicial inquiry into the Palestinian massacre resulted in Sharon's dismissal from the Foreign Ministry, since he had ultimate responsibility for the inaction of the IDF, and several senior officers were relieved of their command. Begin's position became increasingly untenable as the continuing occupation in Lebanon caused growing casualties and enormous resentment amongst Israelis. A toxic mix of rival Christian factions, Shia Muslims and Palestinians was never going to provide any suitable Lebanese partner for the peace that Sharon had fondly imagined might be possible.

The Syrians took advantage of the disintegration of Lebanon and tightened their grip even further during the 1980s. Assad installed a puppet regime later still in 1991 while the world was distracted by events in the Gulf. As the war went on thousands of mostly Palestinians but also some Lebanese were being killed, as were hundreds of Israeli troops, while relationships with America were becoming stressed. Public resentment continued to rise and Begin became ill, increasingly withdrawn until he resigned in August 1983. His success in negotiating a peace with Egypt was forgotten as he became mired in southern Lebanon. The situation there continued to fester long after Israel withdrew to the buffer zone in 1983.

Hezbollah

Now a new belligerent force, Hezbollah, emerged and became entrenched in the villages in and around the narrow buffer ostensibly policed by UN forces and the Southern Lebanese Army. Hezbollah was repeatedly sniping at Israeli positions, killing soldiers and firing rockets into Israel, and Israel found it difficult not to respond. Later, in 1996, 'Operation Grapes of Wrath' would cause much damage and loss of life deep in Lebanon. The now mainly Muslim population, already much depleted of its Christians and Druze, who had left in droves, lost any of the fondness for Israel that had been apparent in the 1970s when visits across the border by Christians for work or shopping were not uncommon. As we will see, Ehud Barak's complete withdrawal from the security buffer zone in 2000 left Hezbollah in place, with its strong Syrian backing, to succeed the PLO as a thorn in Israel's side.

Iraq's Nuclear Ambitions Aborted, 1981

By 1982 Begin's domestic position in Israel had become weak but in sending a mission to destroy Iraq's Osiraq nuclear reactor in 1981, three weeks before the new parliamentary elections, he no doubt helped tip the balance in his favour at home. He was re-elected, albeit with a very small majority, but it is too cynical a view to suggest that this was a sudden election ploy. The Israeli government had been watching with growing apprehension the build-up of Saddam Hussein's nuclear programme for at least three years. Begin had chaired many high-level security meetings to discuss their options during this time. It became increasingly the view that a nuclear-armed Iraq would not hesitate to launch an attack against Israel and time was of the essence. Begin's decision to remove this threat was taken in full consultation with his Cabinet and, at least towards the end, with the opposition parties.

The attack was successfully accomplished by a small number of jet fighters flying below the radars of Jordan and Iraq and was completed within a very few minutes. There was widespread condemnation across the Arab world but they could not completely hide an underlying sense of relief as Saddam Hussein's wings were clipped. Syria and Egypt in particular had a less than equivocal attitude to a limitation being placed on Saddam's ambitions.

The UN Security Council condemned the attack and the US administration of President Reagan cancelled the transfer of a consignment of F-16 fighter planes that Israel had bought. The Americans seemed to forget their antipathy to Israel's actions when twenty years later President Bush and Britain's Prime Minister Blair attacked Iraq on rather weaker evidence of a stash of weapons of mass destruction. Iraq with a nuclear capability in 1981 would have had disastrous consequences for the rest of the Middle East and would certainly have made the West more wary of interfering after the invasion of Kuwait in 1991. They now have reason to be grateful to Israel.

CHAPTER 13

More Lost Opportunities

ONE OF THE TRAGEDIES of Israeli–Palestinian relations has been the lack of a coincidence between a leader committed to negotiation on one side with a similarly motivated one on the other. As a result opportunities for peace have been lost by one side or the other.

In 1982–3 the prospects for a peace deal with the Palestinians were much improved. The PLO and Yasser Arafat had been weakened and driven out to Tunis. The Syrians were also in a weakened position and conceivably more willing to reach an agreement on the Golan. Jordan under King Hussein was interested in taking a bigger role with the Palestinians, while in the West Bank support for organised terrorism was at a low ebb. This was a time when a greater effort by an Israeli leader to press for at least an increase in the level of autonomy for West Bank Palestinians and a halt to settlement building might have had a significant impact, although this is pure speculation of course.

When Yitzhak Shamir took over as Prime Minister after Begin's resignation, his policies were even more intransigent. There followed a period in which there was much jockeying for positions within Israel and between Israel and the Palestinians. Settlement building continued apace as Shamir tightened his hold on the West Bank, giving little room for thoughts about how Israel was going to deal with 1.3 million Palestinians then under its jurisdiction but who were not its citizens.

The election of 1984 produced no outright majority for either Likud or Labour and in a peculiar deal Shamir and Shimon Peres took turns of twenty-four months each as leader. Israel's so-called 'unity government' was hidebound by a 5:5 split in the National Security Cabinet between Labour and Likud but it was during Peres's period as leader that Israel finally withdrew to the 12-mile security zone in southern Lebanon in 1985, three years after the two-day adventure originally imagined. There is no doubt that Israel could not have simply stood by as the PLO continued to wage a war of terror within and without Israel. But in successfully removing the immediate local threat they compounded their problems by going beyond this objective and continuing the war for too long. The Israeli people well understood the errors of judgement made by their leaders in Lebanon and felt badly let down.

UN forces moved in but not before Hezbollah started to become established. Initially a creation of revolutionary Iran, Hezbollah soon took on the mantle of a suppressed Shiite minority in Lebanon as the PLO was ousted. This emboldened Shiite organisation has as its stated objective the elimination of Israel and is now widely recognised as a terrorist organisation. No suggestion here of peace, and the UN security force has been powerless to prevent its activities. And it was strongly supported by Iran and Syria with a ready supply of missiles and sophisticated weapons. It is now the case that Hezbollah is the much stronger partner in its relationship with a Syria that has become increasingly reliant on its support.

Frustrated Peace Efforts

The Peres–Shamir premiership was dysfunctional. The two men rarely agreed on how to further peace negotiations although the Palestinians were still far from ready to accept Israel's existence. During Peres's administration he held several meetings with King Hussein about the prospects for peace with Jordan. Hussein, anxious to avoid a confrontation with Syria and the PLO, insisted on an international conference involving both of those parties. While Peres was a little sympathetic, both Shamir and President Reagan objected strongly to the inclusion of a PLO that had been branded a terrorist organisation. George Shultz, Reagan's Secretary of State, set to work to try to find Palestinian representatives who had no connection with the PLO, to little avail.

La ronde continued in Israel and Shamir took over the leadership from Peres in 1986. Initially he resisted efforts to agree to an international conference but by 1987 he seemed to have acquiesced to a proposal that emerged from a meeting between Peres and Hussein at Lord Mishcon's home in London.[1] This, the so-called Peres–Hussein London Agreement, envisaged a UN-led conference, including Syria, Lebanon and Jordan but without the PLO, to take forward a peace deal along the lines of Resolutions 242 and 338. But reference to 242 was anathema to the Palestinians, with whom Hussein was losing his patience. This time it was he who turned down the proposal. He knew that his position at home, where the majority of the population was Palestinian, was not strong enough to do a deal with Israel without Palestinian support.

Shamir too was firmly against a deal that he thought would involve Israel giving up any land for peace. In fact he was not too unhappy with the then status quo. There is little doubt that the lessons of the Holocaust were as live an issue for him as they had been for Begin. He had lost many of his family then and had been a member of Irgun and the Stern Gang, an extreme militant group, later labelled a terrorist organisation, in the resistance against the British mandate. He regarded the loss of an inch of land now as the beginning of the end for the Israel for whose birth he had fought so hard.

Hussein was not the only one to lose patience. Shultz lost his with the divided Israeli government, where clear decisions were hard to come by as Peres and Shamir took completely opposing positions. Hussein could not move forward without the PLO and Shamir and Peres would not move forward with them. A formula in which non-PLO-affiliated Palestinians would form part of the Jordanian contingent got nowhere.

A variety of proposals floated by the Americans to try to break the deadlock, including an international conference, to satisfy Hussein, but one in which all the negotiations would take place between the two main parties, to satisfy the Israelis, also failed to get off the ground.

Peres was the first to suggest evacuation from Gaza to allow the PLO to return from Tunis. He thought that it might be an initial step to be followed by discussions about the fate of the West Bank. That too was soon shot down by a Likud government that included Ariel Sharon, who, much later as Prime Minister, took up that idea and unilaterally removed Israeli settlements from Gaza. It was that particular Sharon-initiated precedent that has had a number of unfortunate and unintended consequences.

Intifada

The result of the failure to move the peace forward was disastrous. Frustration amongst the Palestinian population boiled over as they saw that nothing was being achieved for them either by other Arab leaders or by the PLO.

The ostensible reason for the intifada that followed was a car crash in which four Palestinians from Gaza were killed. But tensions were already at bursting point as disillusion and despondency at the failure to gain self-government took over. The intifada was as unexpected by the PLO leadership as by Israel. Many Israelis were killed or injured and even more Palestinians were lost as Israel clamped down with a heavy hand. It continued for about eighteen months and then slowly died out over the next few years, by which time Israel had lost even more of its international reputation, which had already been badly damaged in the Shatila and Sabra massacres. Here again we have an example of lost opportunities when first Shamir and then Hussein turned down the possibility of a deal that, six years later, they agreed to, but not before the devastating consequences of the intifada had intervened.

However, two potentially positive outcomes emerged. Israel was made more aware that it could not go on simply ignoring its precarious relationship with the Palestinians. And the PLO was brought to realise that it might have to think about compromise. The intifada had been an uprising from the street and only later did Arafat step in to try and take advantage of it. As it was dawning on many in Israel that they could not continue to assume that Jordan would take a lead for the Palestinians, let alone take them under Jordanian rule, so Arafat began to realise that terrorist attacks alone were not going to deliver his ultimate aims. Meanwhile another, even more militant and uncompromising, organisation was born in Gaza.

Hamas

Hamas (its name is an acronym that stands for 'Islamic Resistance Movement') arrived on the scene in 1988 as a more fundamentalist rival to the PLO. Hamas, initiated by Sheikh Ahmed Yassin, was never going to recognise Israel. Formed as the Palestinian branch of the Muslim Brotherhood, it merged with the Jordanian wing of the Brotherhood in the West Bank. Its *raison d'être*, as set out in its charter, was to remove Israel from the map of the Middle East. It soon took on the terrorist technique, copied from Hezbollah, of suicide bombing in its war against Israel.

At the same time, after forty years of unyielding opposition to the 'Zionist Entity', the PLO began to inch towards the possibility of tolerating Israel's existence. Yasser Arafat was about to lay out proposals for a deal with Israel at the Palestinian National Council in Algiers. Here he demonstrated his capacity for intrigue when Bassam Abu Sharif, his right-hand man, drafted a note for him in which a compromise deal might be put forward. Arafat refused to acknowledge even the existence of such a note until he had taken soundings around Europe and until he was clear that he had sufficient support within the PLO for such a move.[2] He shrewdly understood that within his own group there was strong opposition to any deals with Israel and it was only in November that there was reluctant acceptance of the principles. He then announced that he would engage in an international conference on the basis that he would renounce violence, accept Israel's right to live in peace, and agree to UN Resolutions 242 and 338. This was conditional on an agreement that an independent state of Palestine would be set up in the West Bank and Gaza with Jerusalem as its capital. The rejection of terrorism in a press statement in Geneva was enough for President Reagan to accept the PLO as an organisation with which America could negotiate, albeit indirectly. But in Israel, Shamir dismissed Arafat's words as so much hot air and could not believe he would act on them.

As Arafat appeared to be moving towards compromise, in words if not actions, Shamir was moving in the opposite direction and he felt justified as the intifada continued. When Arafat failed to condemn the boat-loads of terrorists intercepted on their way to attack a crowded Israeli beach, the Americans also suspended relations. The Palestinian cause was not helped later, in 1991, when, picking the wrong side, they strongly supported Saddam Hussein's raid on Kuwait.

Despite the unyielding opposition of Shamir's government to talks with the PLO and despite Arafat's untrustworthiness, the seeds had been sown for the Oslo agreement of four years later. George Shultz had spent an enormous amount of energy and time in trying to get a peace deal between Israel and Jordan. He had journeyed backwards and forwards to the Middle East but was ultimately frustrated by the intransigence of Shamir just as Hussein was by the PLO. The intifada had shaken things up on both sides.

Distractions Elsewhere

Elsewhere in the Middle East events were distracting attention. Two in particular were alarming: 'Irangate' and Saddam Hussein's attack on Kuwait.

The Iran–Iraq War was causing a devastating loss of life on both sides. Iraq had developed chemical weapons and long-range missiles and these, together with its continuing efforts to develop nuclear arms, left Israel feeling seriously threatened. It entered into a clandestine compact with senior members of President Reagan's administration to supply American arms to Iran as part of a deal whereby Iran and Hezbollah would release US hostages. It suited the Israelis to be 'middle-men' since in arming Iran they believed they were helping maintain a balance with the then more feared Iraq. But supplying arms to Iran was illegal and when news of the deal leaked it created havoc in the USA. Israel was also castigated for its role but it was the Americans who bore the brunt of the backlash in the West. In the Middle East, trust in Israel, never high, was eroded further as it was shown to be interfering in Arab affairs.

The PLO and the Palestinians, for their part, had their reputation sullied in the Iraqi raid on Kuwait. They came out strongly in favour of Saddam and in doing so they lost ground with America. They also lost support in Saudi Arabia, Jordan and Syria, and thousands of Palestinians were expelled from the Gulf states.

The constantly shifting sands across the wider Middle East always have a bearing on how local Israeli–Palestinian relations wax and wane. The Palestinians were well aware that their Arab neighbours were rather more interested in their own problems than in Palestinian well-being. However, Arafat felt that any sign that he might move too far in the direction of conciliation with Israel would be unpopular with his Arab supporters and endanger his own life. Nor did the continued existence of camps for Palestinian refugees for fifty years in Lebanon and Syria speak too highly of much sympathy for their plight. While many refugees had moved to the West and other Arab states, it is the case that the Palestinians in the West Bank and Gaza were not always in concert with the exiled PLO leadership in Tunisia and were more open to discussion about practical day-to-day matters. Israel too recognised that the PLO was a beleaguered pawn in the wider game being played and was constantly on guard against much wider threats.

The Iraqi invasion of Kuwait and the subsequent war in which America and its allies invaded Iraq had a number of repercussions for the Israeli–Palestinian dispute. Firstly UN resolutions calling on Saddam Hussein to withdraw from Kuwait were used by Arab nations as rods to beat Israel's back. Why should such resolutions not be equally applied to Israel? Israel's response, that the land it had occupied was the result of defensive, not aggressive, wars, and that it remained ostensibly open to the prospect of 'land for peace', did not deter its critics.

More significantly, the Gulf War action against Saddam was supported not only by the UN but also by many of the other Arab nations, including Syria, Egypt and Saudi Arabia, and America's role in the Middle East was considerably enhanced. The Arab nations also recognised that the USSR under Gorbachov had weakened its military support for them after he proposed glasnost in 1986. This too did much to increase their regard for America's influence in the region.

All this encouraged James Baker, President Bush's Secretary of State, to strengthen his resolve to deal with Arab–Israeli differences. Israel, in restraining itself from responding to Saddam's Scud missile attack during the Gulf War, had earned American support, while in contrast the PLO was weakened by its picking the wrong side. Neither did the cheers of delight in the West Bank as the Scud missiles rained down on Israel endear the Palestinians too much to Israel or America.

This is the unlikely position from which it became possible to take some sluggish steps towards peace between Israel and the Palestinians.

PART II

Introduction: Inching towards Peace

AFTER THE FALTERING STEPS of 1988 the first time that the Palestinians and Israelis officially accepted each other's existence was in 1993 with the signing of what became known as the Oslo Accords. During the twenty-four years since then the mood has oscillated between elation and despair, between high optimism and deep pessimism. In 2016, they were at one of the lowest points in their relationship, although subtle signs for optimism emerged from time to time. Too many in Israel are convinced that the Palestinians will never accept Israel as a Jewish state, or even as a distinct entity, while Palestinians see Israel's settlement policy as an indicator of its intention to take over the whole West Bank. These are not necessarily the views of the majority on each side but that is barely recognised in the common rhetoric.

Abraham Lincoln said, 'I don't like that man; I must get to know him better.' The lack of understanding of the other is alarming and efforts to get to know the other's view have been severely constrained. The idea of compromise with the other side has come very hard and now the position is fraught after years of failure. Many Palestinians and Israelis have never met a civilian in the opposite camp personally and have little understanding of them as people. When you only meet a terrorist or a soldier in fully armed regalia it is easy to demonise the other and the media find it easy to drum up ill-feeling. So much of the hatred has been driven by ignorance and fear.

Nor can Israel or the Palestinians ignore the current strife in the rest of the Middle East. While 2016 saw Islamic State being constrained and contained it was far from defeated or deterred. Iraq remains a broken country and King Abdullah II in Jordan continues to cast worried glances across his borders at Syria and Iraq. Bashar al-Assad in Syria has begun to re-assert himself, albeit in a reduced power base, and only with Iranian and Russian support. The deal on nuclear weapons has allowed Iran back into the commercial world while maintaining an extremely belligerent stance against Israel and the West. Iran's continuing development of long-range missiles armed with potentially devastating war-heads coupled with repeated threats of Israel's demise hardly speak for a regime searching for peace. Hezbollah, currently distracted in fighting rebel forces in Syria, is still managing to build a vast array of missiles aimed at Israel. The build-up of Al Qaeda and other unsavoury groups on Israel's northern border with Syria is uncomfortable for both Israel and the Palestinians. And in the south, the presence of IS and the Muslim Brotherhood in the Sinai Desert, where they are finding ready recruits amongst the Bedouin, is giving little reason for joy. Nor are the multiple tunnels still being built under Israel's border by Hamas in Gaza viewed with any equanimity.

It is hardly surprising then that these threatening forces surrounding Israel are now making it more than cautious in its dealings with the Palestinians. The prospect of Palestine as another Arab state on its long-vulnerable eastern border is difficult to contemplate in the absence of adequate security arrangements and no one seems likely to be able to give that sort of assurance under the conditions currently prevailing across the wider Middle East.

Leaving aside the many advantages of a peace deal and a two-state solution for Israel and the Palestinians themselves, there are two schools of thought about what might be the response in the wider Middle East to such a peace agreement. In one, the deal would be welcomed and Iran, Hezbollah, Hamas and Syria would cease their antipathy to Israel and drop their threatening behaviour. That would require a suspension of all rational thought. The second view sees that the reason for their antagonistic behaviour is nothing to do with the Palestinians and everything to do with their ultimate aim to see Israel and the Jews out of the Middle East. That is the inevitable conclusion if any of the repeated statements by the Iranian, Hezbollah and Hamas leaderships are to be believed. Indeed they are unlikely to deal kindly with a Palestinian Authority that made peace with their bitter foe. Hamas has already made clear to Mahmoud Abbas that it will not support a unity government that would consider negotiating with Israel. The propensity for one Muslim extreme group to act mercilessly against another weighs heavily on anyone who does not conform to their beliefs.

Given all these circumstances, it is hard to think that a peace between Israel and the Palestinians would not unleash a backlash by these extremists against both of them. But there is an alternative view. Now, a number of more pragmatic Arab leaders have dropped their antipathy to Israel and say they are ready to make peace if only the conflict between Israel and the Palestinians is resolved. Their publics are clearly not so favourably disposed but the leadership is more realistic about the potential advantages of a peace dividend in new commercial and security activities. Egyptian and Jordanian leaders have long been in favour of an Israeli–Palestinian rapprochement, and Saudi Arabia and the Gulf states have put forward peace proposals via the Arab League in the past. They now have an added reason to see a strong Israel at peace with its neighbour as they face common enemies. There is a growing need for security collaboration and intelligence sharing between these nations as they deal with IS in its various guises in the Yemen and Sinai Desert and the major threat emanating from Iran. Turkey, after some years of stand-off, has made moves to reconcile its differences with Israel as it too has suffered a series of devastating terrorist attacks and its relationship with Russia has cooled. And just as Israel faces the prospect of extremist forces on its border with Syria, so Turkey too suffers from a toxic mix of IS and rebel Kurds active against it as well as each other along its border with Syria.

It might be thought then that it would take a brave, some might say foolhardy, Israeli or Palestinian leader to begin talks now. Although Benjamin Netanyahu has spoken repeatedly of his willingness to go anywhere at any time to engage in negotiations 'without pre-conditions' it is doubtful whether he would have been able to persuade the right-wing of his Cabinet to make many concessions and, in the wake of a serious outbreak of violence in 2015–16, he would have had even more difficulty in taking the public with him. Imagine a UK government faced with a regular barrage of terrorist attacks being willing to make concessions to the perpetrators of the attacks when the public had become so incensed that they demanded punishment rather than appeasement for the attackers. Netanyahu's democratic mandate would be sorely stretched but it is conceivable that President Sisi's recent offer to host a meeting with Mahmoud Abbas could strengthen his position in negotiations.

On the Palestinian side, any leader would have to be willing to accept the risk to life and limb for him and his family. The elderly and now very unpopular Abbas is unlikely to be that man. And his initial response to the Sisi initiative has not been promising.

Clearly the time does not appear auspicious for a resolution of the differences between Israelis and Palestinians. And yet, and yet… despite this gloomy picture there are opportunities arising now that could be grasped. There have been occasions in the last twenty years when brave and forward-looking leaders have been found even during equally inauspicious times. It is the current parlous position that makes it even more important to re-examine what made peace seem possible and so near at times and what it was that prevented its achievement. Rabin, Peres, Barak and Olmert made brave efforts and even Sharon, after years of abrasive behaviour, became more dovish in his later years and in his withdrawal from Gaza. On the Palestinian side there have been times when Arafat and more recently Abbas seemed to be veering towards peace only for them to be blown off course, sometimes by Hamas, by Syria or by their own people but too often because of their reticence to sign a deal that was short of their maximal position.

What lessons might be learnt from these efforts to reach a resolution and why were they snatched away by events? Are there any other positions that might be adopted other than the usually cited one-state and two-state solutions? It is on these questions that I focus in the second part of this book, covering recent history.

CHAPTER 14

Tentative Steps towards Oslo

IT WAS ONLY IN the 1990s that the first signs of a more optimistic thaw in Israeli–Palestinian relationships emerged. Until then there was no prospect that the Palestinian side, led by Yasser Arafat, would contemplate reaching a compromise with the Israelis. In 1988 the first signs of change in Arafat's rhetoric had occurred. By then George Bush the Elder was America's President and James Baker his Secretary of State. The next three years saw the fall of the Soviet Union, the Gulf War and the first intifada in Gaza and the West Bank. Arafat, weakened and isolated in Tunis, was showing signs that he might acknowledge Israel's existence. Any signals were dismissed by Israel then and even during the early 1990s efforts to bring the various parties together for talks were stymied by Yitzhak Shamir and Arafat.

Shamir was opposed to an international meeting that was again being mooted, this time by the US, if it would include Arab states and Russia, who he felt would gang up against Israel, while the inclusion of the PLO could not be countenanced. Arafat, on the other hand, would not join such a meeting without the prior agreement that it would lead to permanent statehood with Jerusalem as the capital of his Palestine.

Despite this, Baker redoubled his efforts to set up the meeting and was eventually successful, after eight separate visits to the region, in convincing all parties to gather in Madrid in October 1991. Israel, still under Shamir, finally agreed to join on condition that the PLO did not attend and that the Palestinians were to be represented by residents in the West Bank who had no connection with the PLO. They were to be part of a joint Jordanian–Palestinian delegation but in practice they secretly and not so secretly reported directly to Arafat in Tunis. Arafat agreed since he had fallen out of favour with his major funding Arab states after having backed Saddam Hussein earlier that year. Israel also stipulated that, while the conference was to be international and shared regional problems such as water and environmental issues could be discussed in plenary meetings, all the significant negotiations concerning peace were to be conducted bilaterally between Israel and each Arab state separately.

Meetings between the delegation of Israel and those of Syria, Jordan–Palestine and Lebanon were able to be held separately on several occasions in Washington and Moscow but none produced any obvious advance towards peace. The bilateral negotiations slowly faded out and by 1993 they were overtaken by the secretly developing Oslo Accords. But they were significant, not only because Israel was able to sit round the table with representatives of states that had hitherto failed to recognise its existence, but also because they had raised hopes that a solution might someday be achieved. The fact that a number of other Middle East countries had developed diplomatic relations with Israel was a bonus.

It was, however, at Oslo where the heavy lifting was done and by then Shamir had been ousted as Prime Minister in the 1992 elections. More conciliatory policies were adopted as Rabin returned to office and his Labour government took over.

The Norwegian Connection

By 1993 the PLO had recognised that it could not defeat Israel by terrorism nor could it rely on any other Arab state to do it for them. Israel, under Rabin, was also becoming painfully aware that it could no longer rule over the increasing number of Palestinians in the West

Bank and Gaza, deny them autonomy and yet remain a democratic, liberal society. Rabin had admitted as much during his first period as Prime Minister in 1974 to 1977,[1] and now he had the added stimulus for a compromise in the strategic threat posed by Iran.

An opportunity arose when a visiting Norwegian academic, Terje Rød-Larsen, met Yossi Beilin in Israel and raised with him the possibility of a secret 'back channel' meeting with the Palestinians in Oslo.[2] Beilin had been made Deputy Foreign Minister to Shimon Peres, who had himself been appointed by Rabin as Foreign Minister. Trust between Rabin and Peres, both Labour politicians, had long been at rock bottom and Rabin put strict limits on the roles Peres could play. He was to be prevented from involving himself in any peace negotiations or in dealings with the USA; these roles were to remain with Rabin.

All this left Peres's deputy, Beilin, in a difficult position. He had, however, long been in regular secret meetings with a number of prominent Palestinian intellectuals in an effort to tease out the parameters of a final status. By the time Rød-Larsen approached him he had a keen understanding of the position of the Palestinians and what their demands and needs were likely to be. Through the Economic Cooperation Foundation, a think tank he had set up, he was also well aware of the economic problems of a future Palestinian state.

Rød-Larsen was the director of the FAFO Research Centre, an organisation examining the social and economic position of populations around the world, and was now working in Gaza. He had strong connections with the Norwegian government and its involvement was to prove critical in due course. He had recently met Faisal Husseini of the PLO and Ahmed Ali Mohammed Qurei (Abu Alaa), Arafat's economic advisor, who had encouraged him to approach Beilin. Husseini was despairing of the progress being made at the talks in Washington and was desperate to seek alternative approaches.

Here then was an opportunity for Beilin but he was immediately faced with two dilemmas. Direct talks with the PLO were prohibited for Israelis. Beilin had managed to persuade the Labour Party to rescind that law but had to wait until January 1993, for the Knesset to finally put it to rest. More significantly he, as Peres's deputy, could not be seen to be involved in direct negotiations, secret or otherwise, with the Palestinians under the prohibitions imposed by Rabin. He had to step carefully in the war zone between Rabin and Peres and came up with a solution that provided him with sufficient cover.

He sent two non-government colleagues whom he trusted, Yair Hirschfeld, an academic from Haifa University, and Ron Pundak, one of Hirschfeld's earlier students, to Oslo. Both were well versed in Israeli–Palestinian affairs and Beilin was now able to deny his own involvement should he be challenged. He only revealed what he was up to much later.

On the Palestinian side Abu Alaa led his small team at the first meeting in January 1993 at Sarpsborg, a city just north of Oslo. They made rapid progress as it later emerged that Arafat and the PLO were increasingly desperate to gain some immediate improvement on their parlous position in Tunis. The Israelis were impressed by these signs of commitment and by the second meeting in February a draft proposal had been drawn up. The third meeting in March provided both with a sufficiently worked-up plan for it to be presented for approval to a PLO that had already had considerable input, and to the Israeli leadership, which had not.

By February Beilin could no longer keep the meetings secret from Peres and had to tiptoe round and present him with the emerging proposals. Angry at first, Peres eventually came round and he in turn was faced with the delicate task of telling Rabin, who was less than enthusiastic. Eventually Rabin agreed to allow the discussions in Oslo to continue. Despite the hesitancies, and only after Peres had held prolonged telephone discussions with Arafat, by August 1993 Abu Alaa and Shimon Peres were able to secretly sign an agreed position paper. Neither side had yet fully recognised the other but that did not deter them. This whole tortuous process of negotiation with its periods of optimism and despair is spelt out in Beilin's account, *Touching Peace.*

What the Accords Say

The Oslo Accords had much in common with the Camp David Accords of fifteen years earlier. Prime Minister Begin had then agreed with President Sadat that the Palestinians should be given limited autonomy in the West Bank and Gaza coupled with the prospect of negotiations for a final formal status. Begin was far from sold on the idea and, when the PLO and the rest of the Arab world rejected the proposal out of hand, he heaved a sigh of relief. If they had accepted it then instead of in 1993 much of the pain of the intervening years might have been avoided. While Begin, and Shamir who followed him, might have resisted offering statehood to the PLO, it is feasible that by the time Rabin came into office he would have been able to move much more quickly to final status negotiations without the need for secret Oslo meetings and the like.

The initial Oslo Accord was simply an outline set of proposals, lacking in much detail and avoiding such difficult questions as the status of Jerusalem, borders and refugees. Its title, 'Declaration of Principles on Interim Self-Government Arrangements',[3] shortened to 'Self-Government Arrangements', is an indication of its limits. But it was the first agreement reached between Israel and the Palestinians and it showed very clearly that while American involvement is indispensable they do not have the monopoly on initiating peace negotiations. Indeed it demonstrated that it requires the two main parties themselves to agree first to what they might find acceptable. It seemed that Arafat had been able to accept a compromise only when he was faced with the dire consequences of not doing so.

The agreed agenda included the Israeli withdrawal from Gaza to begin within two months and to be completed within four. Arafat and the PLO together with his police force would then move in. Responsibility for five areas of activity would be taken on by the Palestinians: education, health, social welfare, direct taxation and tourism. Most importantly the prospect of negotiation on the final status to begin within two years, left vague at this stage, was dangled before Arafat.

Despite the agreement, Rabin was not keen on the idea of an independent Palestinian state. His focus on security certainly made him cautious and the idea of a Jordanian–Palestinian confederation was more attractive to him, an idea to which Arafat seemed not entirely averse.

Over the next few months intensive discussions took place in which President Mubarak of Egypt played a valuable role. In his discussions with Peres the idea arose that Jericho in the West Bank should be part of the deal to encourage Arafat, who feared that an agreement limiting his newly acquired state to Gaza would leave him stranded without much else. Arafat also suspected that Jordan, Syria and Lebanon might well feel themselves absolved from further responsibility for the Palestinians, whatever deal was struck, leaving them free to reach peace deals of their own with Israel.

The Impact of Oslo

Although the Oslo Accords had not set out to be a formal treaty, they were the most significant development in Israeli–Palestinian relations up to that time and most of what was accepted has remained in place. The misfortune is that while they were regarded then as simply an interim first step in a process they have remained the only significant step.

It was, however, the first occasion when Israel and the PLO recognised each other's existence and were willing to talk about a possible resolution of their differences. The fact that they ultimately failed in achieving a sustainable peace should not detract from the remarkable acceptance that the other side also has a view that has to be taken into account. The Oslo process served many purposes and has been the basis of every peace initiative since that time.

While one or two senior Americans knew that the meetings were being held they had no input into, nor knowledge of, the ideas being discussed. But now was the moment when it became important to involve them. Warren Christopher, Secretary of State in the new Clinton administration, was informed, and knowing that the Washington meetings were going nowhere and that a quick win for his President would be invaluable, he immediately accepted the Oslo agreements as something he could take on. For Israel and the Palestinians too there were advantages in making the agreement appear to be an American inspiration.

Of course there were voices raised against the legitimacy of the Accords. Based largely on assumptions about what may or may not have been written in missing documents, Hilde Waage, a Norwegian historian, accused the Norwegian facilitators of hoodwinking the Palestinians and of being in the pocket of the Israelis and the Americans.[4] This hardly seems credible when it is clear that the Americans were barely aware of how the meetings were developing, the Norwegian facilitators had no input into the substance of the agreements and Arafat was kept fully informed, and involved, throughout.

Neither Rabin nor Arafat was entirely comfortable with the agreements being hatched out in Norway and both knew that they would have a hard time persuading their own people that they were not leading them into danger. There was certainly little trust on either side. They had been implacable enemies for over twenty-five years and had difficulty moving on from the picture of a 'Gang of Murderers' (the PLO) on the one hand and of the 'Zionist Cabal, Stooge of World Imperialism' (Israel) on the other. Swallowing their hatred was no easy task.

The balance was finally tipped when Arafat sent a long, nine-paragraph letter to Rabin in which he renounced violence and agreed to remove the vow in the Palestine National Charter to destroy Israel and to accept UN Resolution 242. Rabin, despite an understandable scepticism, replied briefly, giving in a single paragraph his acceptance of the PLO as a representative of the Palestinians and as a negotiating partner. Even then the letters left open several questions. Arafat did not commit to a time scale for when he would modify the PLO Covenant.

It would require acceptance by the Palestinian National Council and that did not happen until several years later. Subtle as these issues may sound now, at the time these and many other details made the difference between success and failure.

Even at the last moment, in Washington, there was nearly a failure to agree to signatures being placed on paper as Arafat threatened to walk out. He had acted in a similar way previously when it came to signing the Interim Agreement in Cairo, either showing a lack of faith or trust, or perhaps demonstrating to his people that he had fought to the last. But for now the stage was set. Four days after the exchange of letters, only nine months after the first Oslo meetings, Clinton invited Arafat and Rabin to sign the Accords at the White House. Until then the PLO was not acceptable in America but Clinton had been able to invite Arafat after his letter to Rabin.

At first Rabin was reluctant to appear in public with Arafat and thought of sending Peres in his place. He was eventually persuaded to go to Washington but only if he would not be expected to embrace, much less kiss, Arafat. In the event, on 13 December 1993, Peres signed for Israel and Husseini for the PLO. Then, after an elaborately orchestrated *pas de trois*, Rabin and Arafat shook hands with Clinton standing between them to prevent any further signs of affection. That is the picture that the media spread around the world. Rabin made a remarkable speech on the White House Lawn that set out his vision for a peace and included the fateful phrase 'enough of blood and tears. Enough.'[5]

After the signing of the Accords Beilin immediately started urging Rabin to move rapidly to a final status position for the Palestinians while there was some momentum. Rabin, although not hidebound by his predecessor's idea that Judea and Samaria were inviolable parts of biblical Israel, remained concerned about security. These concerns were not allayed by the heightened level of terrorist attacks from Hamas, which was anxious to derail the agreements. Rabin preferred a cautious approach because of a fear that it would be difficult to row back if efforts to quicken the pace failed. He was also exploring the possibility of peace with Assad in Syria and was weighing up which of the two negotiations to pursue first; not both together. (The Syrian track is dealt with further in Chapter 22.)

There followed a series of agreements between December 1993 and September 1995 culminating in the Oslo II Accord, or Taba, formally termed the 'Interim Agreement on the West Bank and the Gaza Strip'.[6] Incorporated in it was a series of other negotiations including the 'Protocol on Economic Relations' or 'Paris Agreement' of April 1994, the 'Cairo Agreement' of May 1994, arising from the Peres–Mubarak discussions on Jericho, the 'Agreement on Preparatory Transfer of Powers and Responsibilities between Israel and the PLO' of August 1994, and the 'Protocol on Further Transfer of Powers and Responsibilities' of August 1995, all suggesting a considerable degree of goodwill. But there was no overt discussion of the more sensitive issues that had yet to be faced. There were, however, more secret 'back channel' discussions that went much further, as we will see.

Hammered out and signed off at Taba in Egypt, the Accord was signed formally a few days later, on 28 September 1995, by Rabin and Arafat in a low-key affair at the White House in the presence of Clinton and representatives of the EU, Russia, Norway and Egypt. Jordan, which had recently signed a peace deal with Israel, was also represented.

After a preamble full of good intentions, including acknowledgement of Resolutions 242 and 338, the Oslo II Accord incorporated all the previous agreements. In 300 pages, thirty-one articles and nine maps, it provided for the establishment of the 'Palestinian Interim Self-Government Authority' and a 'Palestinian Council'. Brave words about reducing violence and increasing collaboration for the common good and economic cooperation were included. And Rabin and Peres had been pressing Clinton to provide much needed economic aid to the Palestinians as they took up their new responsibilities.

It was here that the West Bank, the nascent Palestinian state, was divided into the three sections that have been the cause of unrest since that time. Area A was to come under the complete control of the future

Palestinian Authority, Area B was to be under joint Palestinian civil and Israeli security control while Area C, the largest area, was to be under Israeli military control without Palestinian involvement, ostensibly for security reasons. The 60 per cent of the West Bank in Area C has remained a significant cause of resentment amongst the Palestinians and takes up much more land than the 2–3 per cent that the Israeli settlements occupy. At the time, of course, this division of the West Bank was being propounded as a temporary solution while 'permanent status' negotiations got under way. These were supposed to start within two years and be completed in five. During that time the little problems of future borders, refugees, security and the status of Jerusalem were to be solved.

However, the mood amongst the majority of the public in Israel and amongst the Palestinians was buoyant as peace seemed almost within their grasp even though what had been agreed amounted to no more than a recognition of each other and much less than a complete resolution of their differences. Even then there were problems that almost prevented further progress. Acts of terror, as we will see, almost derailed the agreements before, finally, Arafat entered Gaza in triumph in a fleet of Mercedes in October 1995.

By then a peace treaty between Israel and Jordan had been struck in October 1994 and long-standing warm relations between King Hussein and Rabin were revealed. The King, who had been anxious to make peace, had had to hold back until an agreement between Israel and the Palestinians could be established (see Chapter 16).

More Secret Discussions

During 1994 Yossi Beilin had been holding quiet, unrecorded discussions with like-minded colleagues on what a future final status for an independent Palestine might look like and what essential conditions Israel would impose.[7] Many of these ideas, although not immediately practicable, became valuable in discussions that were to follow with

PLO representatives, this time in Stockholm. The Swedish Foreign Minister, Margaretha af Ugglas, proposed that a further back channel might be useful to begin fleshing out what a permanent status might include. Sweden, home of the Nobel Prize, had felt side-lined by the earlier Norwegian initiative in Oslo.

Secret meetings began in September 1994 once again with the Israeli pair of academics, Hirschfeld and Pundak, and their Palestinian counterparts, Ahmed Khalidi and Hussein Agha. Over the following several months they were able to hammer out many areas of agreement while leaving the more difficult ones still open. Agreement on borders and refugees left open the position of Jerusalem and the status of settlements. These were thorny issues but the shape of a future final status agreement was beginning to be clarified. By November of 1995 the outline was sufficiently clear for it to come out of hiding and to be presented to the leadership in Israel and the PLO.

Rabin echoed David Ben Gurion's comments on the 1939 White Paper when he said, '[We will] fight terror as if there is no peace and implement the peace process as if there is no terror.' How sadly optimistic that turned out to be. During the whole time that secret and strenuous efforts were being made to try to find a peaceful resolution, extremists on both sides were determined to undermine any progress being made. That was the moment when Rabin, whose mandate was already beginning to be eroded, was assassinated and negotiations were fatally wounded.

Much cynicism has now overtaken initial optimism and many on both sides now believe that Oslo was a hopelessly misplaced error. The reasons are not difficult to discern. The accords promised too much that could not be delivered and the aftermath soon sapped all enthusiasm. Trust by both sides was eroded further, leaving many feeling nothing was achieved and that peace has been put back. For any future negotiations it will be vital for there to be sufficient trust to be generated by confidence-building measures and in a greater understanding of the other side's position, before tackling the major sources of disagreement.

CHAPTER 15

How Extremists Began to Win the Future

IN FEBRUARY 1994 THERE had been a turn for the worse as terrorism once again almost derailed all that was being attempted. In the next six months weekly attacks by Hamas killed more than twenty Israelis and were followed by severe retaliatory actions. Buses exploded in Tel Aviv and suicide bombers killed twenty-three soldiers in Israel. Then during Ramadan a firebrand, far-right Israeli extremist, Baruch Goldstein, entered the Ibrahim Mosque in Hebron at 5 a.m. and opened fire on worshipping Muslims. Twenty-nine Palestinians were killed and hundreds injured. Born in New York, he had qualified as a doctor albeit one who had been censured for refusing to treat Arabs, and for which he had been detained by the military police. A devotee of the far-right politician Meir Kahane, he may have been tipped over by the death of an Israeli father and son a week before.

The perverse celebration of Goldstein's 'achievements' by right-wing extremists in Hebron and elsewhere brought home to Rabin the size of the battle that had to be fought within Israel itself. That was a battle that brought Israel to the edge of civil war later and led to his assassination in 1995.

Rabin immediately outlawed the extremist groups Kach and Kahane Chai but this did nothing to placate the Palestinians, who stopped the peace process dead. Arafat suspended his moves to Gaza. More terrorist attacks followed and Israel tried to close its borders.

Some 60,000 Palestinians who had been working in Israel lost their jobs and relations with Arafat were severely stretched. In the year after Oslo there were more Israeli and Palestinian deaths than for many of the years before.

But all was not lost.

Opportunities and Threats

The prospects for Palestinian autonomy grew as Gaza and Jericho were finally handed over. Israel's position in the international community improved, as did its economy, and Yossi Beilin continued to press Rabin to move quickly to final status negotiations, although without much success. But mistrust was running high and signs that Arafat was playing a double game began to emerge. The slow progress in talks was allowing opponents on both sides to mobilise. The rise of Hamas and Islamic Jihad was causing alarm amongst the proponents of peace in Israel while Arafat stood by.

It was in this situation that a month after the Oslo Accords were signed, Arafat, Rabin and Peres were awarded the Nobel Peace Prize. This was just the moment when the ominous rumblings of discontent within Israel began to shake its foundations. When Rabin presented his Knesset with the outline of what had been agreed at the signing in Washington he was heckled so loudly that he could hardly be heard, but in the end, the Interim Agreement was endorsed by sixty-one votes to fifty-nine.

While the majority of the public favoured the emerging two-state solution provided it brought security, the minority included a sub-set of extremist groups who were determined, well organised and vehemently opposed. Opposition to even the limited autonomy offered to the Palestinians was growing and Benjamin Netanyahu, leader of the Likud opposition party, did little to dampen the mood when he addressed a huge anti-Rabin rally in Jerusalem. Hundreds of angry demonstrators invaded Hebron while death threats were increasingly being made against Rabin. He was depicted as a traitor to the Jews and a threat to their possession of all the Holy Land. Rabbinic authority was invoked and there were indeed rabbis who were prepared to endorse the idea that the death sentence could be pronounced on Jews thought to threaten Jewish rights to their land.

The curse placed on Rabin and the crowds in Hebron chanting 'Death to Rabin' made it seem inevitable that an attempt would be made on his life. He, however, resisted all efforts to take precautions and would not accept the idea of protective clothing in public. He reluctantly agreed to travel in an armoured Cadillac which, as it turned out, served as a clear indicator of his whereabouts.

There were none keener to see Rabin dead than a young student, Yigal Amir, from the coastal town of Herzliya. He was driven by a desperate religious belief in a biblical Israel that included Judea and Samaria. He saw Rabin as about to destroy that dream and had been plotting for a couple of years with his brother to kill him.[1] He finally had his chance when the Prime Minister came to address a cheering crowd of over 100,000 at a peace rally in Kings of Israel Square in Tel Aviv. After a rousing reception, an elated Rabin descended the steps and walked towards his Cadillac, easily recognisable behind the platform. Security must have been lax because no one paid any attention to Amir, who had been standing idly by for an hour or more not far from the car that he knew was shortly to be taking Rabin away.

Quickly taking out his gun from his belt, Amir walked unheeded up to Rabin and shot him three times in the back.

Rabin died on the way to the hospital but it is now clear that his death was probably avoidable. A more alert security detail and a less foolhardy approach by Rabin to wearing a bullet-proof vest and history might have been different.

Israel and Palestine have been repeatedly bedevilled by misfortunes that have influenced the course of peace. The decision by Shimon Peres, who succeeded Rabin after his assassination, not to go for immediate elections when he was in a strong position allowed the right wing to gain momentum and disengagement was put on hold. Then later Ariel Sharon's stroke, suffered after he had withdrawn settlements from Gaza and was contemplating further withdrawals from the West Bank, and later still the indictment of Ehud Olmert that cut short the important discussions he was holding with Mahmoud Abbas are unhappy examples of misfortunes that got in the way.

This is not the whole picture of course. It is far from clear that Rabin would have been able to go much further with an Arafat who was somewhat slippery and his own public was restive about the lack of any security dividend as Hamas rockets rained down. Similarly Peres may not have got much further for the same reasons while Olmert was faced with a very insecure Abbas who was reticent about making any compromises.

Shimon Peres Takes Over – Temporarily, 1995

Israel went into deep mourning on Rabin's death, or at least the vast majority did. In Hebron there were those who cheered and celebrated Yigal Amir's achievement while he himself felt completely justified and has never shown the least signs of remorse. At the funeral the United States was represented by a large number of individuals including President Clinton and two previous Presidents, Carter and Bush, as well as three Secretaries of State, and eighteen senators. Prince Charles and Prime Minister John Major represented Britain together with Tony Blair, then Leader of the Opposition. King Hussein of Jordan and President Mubarak of Egypt were present along with senior representatives of eighty-one nations including Oman, Lebanon and Qatar. The significant absence of President Assad boded ill for the future and his failure to send any words of condolence to Rabin's widow, Leah, won him few friends in Israel or America. In contrast, Yasser Arafat visited Leah at home to offer his condolences.

Against an unstable background Shimon Peres took on the premiership. It was, paradoxically, the single most opportune moment when it might have been possible to negotiate an acceptable resolution of Israel's differences with the Palestinians. Arafat, ensconced in Gaza and Jericho, was desperate to see progress towards a fully independent state across the whole of the West Bank although he was tardy in tempering the rise of Hamas. And in Israel the right wing was in retreat, while Benjamin Netanyahu was deeply unpopular. Peres's left-wing party had the strong support of other parties and this was just the moment to try to condition public attitudes.

Peres could have called an immediate election that would have given him a further four years in which to negotiate a settlement. Instead, he decided to wait out the six months remaining in Rabin's premiership. He probably felt that an election called immediately after the assassination might have been divisive and he could have been criticised for winning, as was likely, on the back of a wave of sympathy rather than for his own attributes. Peres had failed to earn the public's respect, partly because he had not served in the army, a sine qua non for full acceptance. The fact that he had been made the first director general of Israel's Ministry of Defence by Ben Gurion and had been responsible for developing Israel's defence policy did little to diminish this injustice. Perhaps his vital role in securing a deal on nuclear technology with France had been forgotten too.

Immediately after taking on the premiership he began weighing up the prospects of a separate peace with Syria. He reasoned that if he could achieve a quick success there it would be a significant step towards a major change in Israel's position in the Middle East and, not unreasonably, it would bolster his election prospects. These concerns probably caused him to hesitate but it turned out to be a grave error because it gave time for his many opponents to build their offensive. Assad in Syria proved too resistant and by the time Yossi Beilin presented Peres with his Stockholm documents outlining a way forward on the final status arrangements with the Palestinians it was too late.

In the Middle East 'situations' change rapidly and Israel's public were soon persuaded by a series of vicious attacks by Hamas, which Arafat did little to curtail, that peace with the Palestinians was not an immediate option. Peres called elections in May 1996 but he was defeated by Netanyahu, who played the security card for all it was worth. Only he could ensure the safety of Israeli citizens, or so he said, and the idea of a peaceful Palestinian state as an immediate neighbour was a figment of the left's imagination. That result saw the end of serious negotiations, at least until it became obvious that no one, not even Netanyahu, could guarantee Israel's security. But for then, progress from Oslo was dead.

One Small Step Forward, One Large Step Back

Oslo created a number of opportunities and although ultimately it has been regarded by many as a failure there were successes too. For the first time in over twenty-five years it allowed Israel and the Palestinians to overcome their otherwise implacable enmity for a while. They were able to meet and to discuss their differences, and it even allowed their leaders to shake hands. Considering their long-term belligerency this was a remarkable achievement. Oslo gave the Palestinians the opportunity to return from exile in Tunis and gain an, admittedly small, foothold in Gaza and the West Bank. It was the beginning of Palestinian autonomy and an opportunity for self-government.

Unfortunately it was overinterpreted by the Israeli and Palestinian publics as a peace treaty when it was merely an interim arrangement pending further discussion; more a recognition of each other's existence than a substantive agreement. It was supposed to provide an atmosphere of trust and ability to compromise. In fact it showed the opposite and the five-year timetable it envisaged proved illusory. Important, even vital, though it was, far too much was expected of it. It was greeted with an exaggerated enthusiasm that had no chance of being sustained when it became clear that the lowering of Israel's defences envisaged did not bring the security hoped for.

As a bridging arrangement Oslo differed from peace treaties that Israel had struck with Egypt and Jordan. With Jordan, peace had been on the agenda for many years and in Egypt's case the return of the Sinai had none of the biblical connotations of Judea or Samaria. And in any case peace with a sovereign state is quite a different matter from a resolution with a stateless people. In both the former cases the leaderships had been meeting for some time and had formed a reasonable working relationship, Sadat with Begin and Hussein with Rabin. In the Palestinian case Arafat and Rabin had hardly met when they found themselves awkwardly shaking hands at the White House, well before they could even begin to trust each other. But perhaps the most significant difference was the intractable nature of the problems that were left to be negotiated later.

Admittedly the parties had come some way before that. Arafat had dropped his demands that interim negotiations could only go ahead when there was an already agreed position on the status of Jerusalem as his capital and on refugees. In dropping this pre-condition he adopted the approach of Weizmann and the Zionists when they accepted an offer that was much less than satisfactory to them in the 1947 Partition Plan. They did so in the belief that they might be able to work for a better arrangement once they had their state, and Arafat knew that he was in too weak a position, sitting in Tunisian exile, to set such terms. Israel under Rabin had also recognised that ruling over increasing numbers of West Bank Palestinians was not a viable option for a democratic state in the long run. And it was losing international goodwill.

A major problem centred on the instability of the interim arrangements. Opponents in both camps were ready to prevent any progress. The opinion of many in the PLO camp was that too much was being sacrificed for too little gain, and in Israel the silent majority understood that security was being lost in exchange for too much while the right wing wanted nothing to do with the idea of a Palestinian state sitting in their biblical land. Then there was Hamas, with its chilling charter calling for the elimination of the 'Zionist Entity', and the growing threat of Hezbollah. Even these limited agreements were always going to be susceptible to upset by the toxic mix of fear and extremism.

The slow pace of progress on final status agreements provided just the conditions in which extremists were able to destroy the best-laid plans, as they did. Even in the absence of these negative forces the conflicting positions on Jerusalem, borders, refugees, settlements and security have remained almost impossible to overcome.

What Was Learnt?

So were Oslo and Stockholm complete wastes of time? Was nothing learnt? That would be too harsh a judgement. While many topics on which agreement was reached seem no longer relevant in the changed circumstances of today, a number of important clues to how it might be possible to develop future peace plans can be discerned. Much can be said, for example, for meetings held in secret and away from the glare of the media and an expectant public; a safe haven where opposing and off-the-wall views can be explored without fear of being shot down. Most of what came out of the Oslo meetings would not have been feasible without the secrecy that was so well kept.

There is another sort of lesson too. It has to be recognised that there is often a gulf between what the clear evidence suggests should be a particular course of action and what politicians can accept as practical and achievable. Isaiah Berlin in one of his remarkable essays describes the nature of this mismatch.[2] What seems like a crystal clear set of reasonable proposals to rational negotiating teams in closed rooms is never easily sold to a sceptical politician who has to seek public approval for his actions. For example, in internal Israeli discussions in 1995 about the security arrangements that might be necessary along the river Jordan, much was made of the need to station troops there.

However, the hard-headed ex-Chiefs of Staff and security expert participants came out strongly against this idea. They pointed out that at that time troops stationed there would be in an exposed position and with little capacity to provide much early warning of an attack from Iraq. They were drawn to the fact that Jordan and the Palestinian state together would provide a much more effective 500-kilometre early warning barrier. This proved to be an idea too far for the politicians. They would have a hard time convincing the Israeli public that security measures on the river Jordan should be minimal and in any case it is unlikely that such ideas would have much traction now in the changed circumstances in the Middle East.

So the second lesson is that while seemingly logical advice from experts is always vital, whether that advice can be transcribed into action is dependent on many factors that are not always susceptible to rational argument.

Lesson three is that in any future negotiations attention should be paid to the content of agreements reached previously. Can any of the steps that were taken then be built upon now or do the wheels have to be constantly re-invented? Documentation of negotiations then is an invaluable resource now. A collective memory is invaluable.

Finally, reliance on other parties to help negotiations does not necessarily produce results. Only the parties directly concerned can reach solutions acceptable to both. Seen in this light, recent appeals by the PLO for international recognition without negotiating with Israel are likely to fail.

CHAPTER 16

Peace with Jordan but Not with Syria

IT WAS ALWAYS GOING to be possible to make peace with Jordan. King Hussein and his grandfather, Abdullah I, before him had made friendly overtures to Israel over the years since the days of the mandate. President Hafez al-Assad of Syria on the other hand had been at the forefront in an Arab desire to remove Israel from the map of the Middle East. Syria and Jordan started from two different positions. Jordan had been formed at almost the same time as Israel out of pre-existing Syrian and Mesopotamian land. The Syrians, on the other hand, saw their own state being carved up to form these new countries. They had long wanted to correct this injustice as they saw it and had dreamt of re-taking Jordan, Lebanon and Palestine. Assad's immediate concern, however, was with recovering the Golan Heights. He had an intense dislike of Yasser Arafat personally and only used the Palestinians as a means to his own ends.

King Hussein saw things differently although he was certainly cautious in his approaches to Israel. As a child he saw his grandfather assassinated at the Al-Aqsa Mosque in 1951 after reaching out to Israel, and this must have played on his mind. He had secretly agreed not to attack Israel before the 1967 war and only went back on that promise when it was clear he would otherwise have been placed in an impossible position. If Israel had lost the war and he had not joined in Jordan would have been the next to be attacked. If it had won, as it did, he would have been open to blame. These considerations did not prevent him from holding back in the 1973 war. While he lost the West Bank in 1967 he clearly preferred Israel to Syria as his neighbour. Instead of Israeli occupation he would have been faced with Syrian annexation.

On a number of occasions the idea was mooted of a combined Jordanian–Palestinian state incorporating the West Bank under Jordanian rule. Jordan had, after all, run the West Bank for twenty years from 1948 to 1967. The proposal had come up in Israel more than once and was the subject of the agreement reached between Peres and Hussein in the London meeting described in Chapter 13, but it was scotched by Yitzhak Shamir, the PLO dragged its heels and Hussein lost his patience. The idea had been favoured by the Americans and, after Oslo, even Arafat and the PLO were not repelled by it. By then Hussein was again interested but anxious about the prospects of ruling a vastly increased Palestinian population. The idea of a confederacy with Jordan has not entirely faded and the PLO does not reject the idea provided that it has its independent state first.

As early as 1960 Hussein had entered into secret discussions with the Israelis and had shown himself to be a far-sighted leader. By the 1970s he had begun to allow the exchange of intelligence and goods with Israel and secretly developed more friendly relations despite his own Palestinian majority population. Sadat's peace initiative in 1978 gave him some encouragement but he was in a weaker position than the Egyptian and was not anxious to make any moves towards peace in the absence of a resolution to the Palestinian questions.

When Rabin came into office in 1992 Hussein formed a personal bond with him and progress with the Palestinians made it inevitable that an agreement would be reached. He received encouragement from President Mubarak of Egypt while Assad was characteristically less than supportive.

It was, however, the proposal to offer the PLO a foothold in the West Bank at Jericho after the Oslo Accords that prompted him into action. He saw this for what it was, the beginnings of a Palestinian state in the whole of the West Bank and while this allowed him to move on peace with Israel, it caused him some anxiety too. He preferred a stable Israel on his border, and the ready access to the Holy Mount that it provided, to a Palestinian state. But once he had decided to move ahead he did so quickly, announcing his intentions to make peace with Israel to his parliament. He had already met Rabin in secret in London and agreed the outline of a peace agreement. He caught the Americans completely unaware, causing not a little panic as they felt they were being side-lined. After many frantic calls between the Jordanians, the Israelis and Dennis Ross, who was leading the negotiations for the American administration, a formula was agreed for a choreographed series of meetings.[1] In the first, the Jordanian and Israeli negotiating teams would meet at their border on 19 July 1994; the second was to be held in Jordan in a trilateral session, including American representation, the following day; the third and final meeting would be held four days later in Washington with all the fanfare the Americans could offer. While the Jordanians and Israelis tried hard to keep their own private negotiations away from the Americans they yielded to the pressure and reluctantly let them in on their plans. Hussein was persuaded that he needed the US administration's stamp of approval if they were to encourage Congress to agree the economic bail-out Jordan desperately needed. In the end the White House meeting was only the beginning of the peace process although it rejoiced under the title 'The Washington Declaration'.

The treaty itself was not signed until 26 October, by the two countries' Prime Ministers, Rabin and Abdulsalam al-Majali of Jordan. This time the ceremony took place in the Negev desert at Arava, just north of Eilat and Aqaba. President Clinton flew to the Middle East for the ceremony in recognition of the significance of local labours and went on to address the Knesset and the Jordanian Parliament. Land and water disputes were settled, agreements on tourism and trade were reached and an arrangement whereby Jordan would be given responsibility for overseeing the holy places on the Dome of the

Rock in Jerusalem followed. Assad was furious and Hezbollah greeted the treaty with a salvo of rockets into northern Israel.

One novel idea that gained ground in these talks was that of land swaps. Jordan agreed to accept alternative land in lieu of some of the land being farmed by Israel. The concept is one that has returned to the table in dealings between Israel and the Palestinians.

This was the third occasion when a negotiation was successfully initiated locally. As with Sadat's move and then Oslo, the influence of the United States was vital in seeing it fulfilled. But in each case the negotiations arose when the time was ripe and regional leadership was strong enough, brave enough and far sighted enough to be willing to take the necessary and often painful steps. In their absence, no external influence, even from the most powerful countries in the world using the most logical arguments and with the largest inducements or sanctions, would make a difference.

For Israel, progress on peace with a second Arab state, although more easily achieved on this occasion, was a considerable bonus. That peace has stood the test of time and the signing of the Oslo Accords the following year was to give some encouragement to both Israel and Syria to contemplate opening negotiations. That proved to be a much harder nut to crack and will be the subject of Chapter 22.

CHAPTER 17

More Faltering Steps towards Peace

BEFORE DISCUSSING NETANYAHU'S PREMIERSHIP of 1997–9, we should try to see it through the perspective of previous and subsequent events.

The Oslo Accords of 1995 had opened the door to a possible negotiated settlement between the Israelis and the Palestinians. Not amounting to a peace treaty, the Accords simply enabled the two sides to reach an interim agreement and to talk, sometimes directly to each other, about a potential future. Subsequent memoranda of agreement in 1997 and 1998, and the Wye River Agreement also of 1998, allowed the interim process to inch forward. But final status discussions never got off the ground. Despite much painstaking negotiation Israel remained subject to terrorist attacks and hidebound by its security needs. How could it tolerate another belligerent state on its long, exposed border? Could security ever be guaranteed for Israel's parliament and international airport within a mile of that border? Could the Palestinians be trusted after more than fifty years of enmity and was the rescinding of the wording in their National Charter watertight? The Palestinians on the other hand were stuck with a limited autonomy deal that seemed to be going nowhere. They could only see a future without a state or status of their own and facing a power that was rapidly eroding their territory.

Three later Prime Ministers of Israel made strenuous efforts to reach a peace agreement with the Palestinians. Barak, Sharon and Olmert tried various tactics and Netanyahu only dragged his heels. In all three cases they were faced with scepticism and outright revolt from their own parliamentary parties and Barak was ultimately unsuccessful in overcoming that opposition. They were not helped by Palestinian terrorist attacks on their civilian population and the failure, first of Arafat and later of Abbas, to exert any control.

Barak tried to do everything too rapidly, including aiming for peace with Assad, withdrawal from Lebanon and a deal with the Palestinians, all within two years. He tried to bite off too much and he did not prepare his government or public well enough. When his domestic problems are combined with an Arafat and an Assad, neither of whom gave any clue that they were interested in a peace deal, it is not difficult to understand why he failed.

Then Sharon, a changed man from his days as a cavalier commander and architect of the ill-fated Lebanon adventure, was so desperate to move the peace process forward that he decided on a unilateral withdrawal policy in the absence of a negotiating partner. He withdrew from Gaza and was clearly planning withdrawal from some of the West Bank when he had his stroke. The trials and tribulations he faced within Israel before he was able to make these moves provide useful examples of how difficult it is for a leader, even one intent on making peace, to be able do so.

Later still, Olmert too fought internal battles and seemed to have made some progress in negotiations with Abbas but was ultimately brought up short when he was indicted for fraud and had to resign. Whether Abbas was ready, even given a more stable Olmert, remains a moot point.

In each of these cases there is something to be learnt of what might be necessary if a peaceful resolution is to be reached. How did Netanyahu in his first term tackle the issues?

Netanyahu's First Government, 1997

On 29 May 1997 Benjamin Netanyahu was elected Prime Minister by a narrow majority in a surprising victory.

The *coup de grâce* for Peres came with the wave of Hamas suicide bombings that killed fifty-nine Israelis over a few days. The attempt by President Clinton to bolster him by calling a summit of peace makers in Egypt came to nought. Fine words of condemnation of terrorism from Middle East participants failed to cool Arab tempers. They were not assuaged either when, in retaliation for attacks by Hezbollah, the Israeli 'Grapes of Wrath' raids into Lebanon killed more than 100 civilians at Cana. Nor was the Israeli public's support for Peres improved, so it was now Netanyahu's turn.

This, his first premiership, can be loosely characterised as one of consolidation. He had not been favourably disposed towards the Oslo Accords but reluctantly accepted that he should stand by agreements reached by his predecessors. He came into office on a wave of hubris and in his first visit to America set the tone for his subsequent dealings with the administration there. He did not go down well but his reception improved as Arafat did everything he could to make him look reasonable. He also became much firmer in his negotiating stance with Syria, making it even more difficult to prise Assad away from his fixed position. It is doubtful, however, if anyone could have shifted Assad.

The Palestinian Council stated that they had revoked the parts of their National Charter that denied the existence of Israel but Netanyahu was much more sceptical. He was correct in wanting to see something stronger and it took thirteen years before the PLO finally produced a ratified and amended charter that omitted articles supporting Israel's destruction. Netanyahu had sufficient reason to be suspicious when it emerged that there were two versions of the amended charter in English but the version seen by the Israelis differed from that retained by the Palestinians. In 1988 the amended charter had included PLO recognition of Israel and its borders, and of the need to reject violence and to adhere to Resolutions 242 and 381, but it came in a paper written by Arafat's lieutenant Bassam Abu Sharif, a paper that Arafat initially denied having even seen. This dragging of heels as Netanyahu saw it did little to improve his suspicion of Arafat's intentions.

Under pressure from the USA Arafat belatedly started clamping down on Hamas and Islamic Jihad with the intention of giving Netanyahu little excuse for delaying progress on extending Palestinian developments in the West Bank. It had little effect as Netanyahu continued his programme of West Bank settlement building and other provocative actions. The continued rocket-fire from Hezbollah in the north did little to discourage him and gave sustenance to right-wing views in his cabinet.

It was inevitable that there would be a Palestinian reaction. The blue touch paper was lit when a superficially innocuous archaeological dig opened the end of the Hasmonean Tunnel within the Muslim quarter of the Old City in Jerusalem. Although this tunnel opening was nowhere near the Dome of the Rock or the mosques on top of it, it was portrayed throughout the West Bank and Arab world as undermining Muslim holy sites. Just as now, malicious rumours that Israel was about to take over the mosques on the Dome of the Rock created enormous unrest within and without Jerusalem. Riots broke out with a disastrous loss of life on both sides. In desperation Clinton called Arafat and Netanyahu to Washington for talks but there was little movement on either side.

A significant bone of contention was how Hebron might be handed over to the Palestinians. This city stood out from the others that were being transferred in the West Bank because of its strong connections with the three dominant religions. It was the site of the tomb of Abraham, the father of all three faiths, as well as tombs of the patriarchs, and it would not be easily given up. The home of 20,000 Arabs but with 400 Jews living in the centre, any arrangement for transfer rapidly became bogged down in matters of security and access. In the end most of Hebron was handed over but tortuous and tedious steps were necessary before agreement was finally reached, as spelt out in painful detail in Dennis Ross's book *The Missing Peace.*[1] Hebron and the Jewish presence there have remained thorns in the side of both Israel and the Palestinians.

Although Netanyahu was slow to implement the Oslo II Accord he did go ahead with the release of Palestinian prisoners and dramatically increased the number of permits for Palestinians to work in Israel. He also finally agreed to sign the Wye River Agreement, as we will see.

Despite American pressure both sides remained resistant to movement or compromise. It did not help that neither Arafat nor Netanyahu trusted each other, no doubt with good reason. Netanyahu would not move without signs that Arafat was clamping down on terrorism and Arafat needed evidence of movement on the handover of territory. Arafat had not been able or willing to control or condemn terrorists and whenever Netanyahu seemed about to offer something useful another severe act of terror made him retreat. Five killed and 181 wounded in the Mahane Yehuda market in Jerusalem, three women killed in a café in Tel Aviv and so on – this was not conducive to improving relations. Netanyahu's party would not have backed him in making concessions in those circumstances and it is doubtful if the public would have done so either.

It was also as true then as now that little was done by the Palestinian leadership to dissuade children from violence against Israeli civilians and soldiers. And the Israeli response was harsh. *Plus ça change.*

The Wye River Meeting, October 1998

In October 1998 the Americans brought the parties together at the Wye River Plantation in Maryland. It was a remarkable initiative for the Americans, coming as it did when President Clinton was deeply embroiled in the Monica Lewinsky affair.

Netanyahu suspected that the Americans had ganged up with the Palestinians. The US administration certainly found him difficult to deal with and relationships were not as constructive as they should have been. He has not been able to overcome his suspicions of the United States since then and this may have determined his more recent stand-offs. It is also true that Arafat believed the opposite of the Americans and, at least at first, refused to meet Dennis Ross, the US special envoy. The Americans must have been doing something right when both sides mistrusted them. Even so, after much unhappy manoeuvring over details of security and percentages of land transfers, an agreement was signed by Netanyahu and Arafat on the eighth day.

Of course, Wye River was not the end of it. Netanyahu delayed getting Cabinet approval and each side accused the other, with justification, of reneging on the agreement. Even President Clinton's remarkable and unique visit to Gaza to persuade the Palestinian bodies assembled there to confirm that they were rescinding the parts of the National Charter calling for Israel's destruction failed to ensure that the agreement was fulfilled.

The Fall of Netanyahu, 1999

Netanyahu's position became increasingly untenable. He did not win any American friends by going ahead with the contentious building of a settlement at Har Homa, overlooking Jerusalem. Mossad's botched attempt to poison Khalid Mashal, now a leader of Hamas, had been a diplomatic disaster. This episode, in October 1997, caused much dismay as King Hussein forced Israel to provide the antidote to the poison. He also demanded the freeing of the jailed Hamas leader, Sheikh Ahmed Yassin, thus embarrassing Arafat, who was then trying to control Hamas.

Netanyahu constantly portrayed himself as being in hock to his right wing both in and out of Parliament and used this to hold back on giving away too much to the Palestinians. He may have had ambitions of being seen as a historic peace maker but he hid them pretty well and in the end his overwhelming political nose led him elsewhere. By 1999 he had failed both in moving forward on agreements with the Palestinians and politically at home where he was criticised not only by a large majority of the public for not achieving enough on the security front but also by his right-wing base for giving too much away. He lost a vote of confidence in the Knesset and, in May 1999, lost the election by a large margin to his left-wing opponent, Ehud Barak.

The year of Netanyahu's fall, 1999, coincided with year five of Oslo II, when a permanent status for the Palestinians was to be achieved. Arafat was tempted to go for unilateral statehood but he was pressed by the Americans to hold back. He agreed to do so but only for twelve months, thus putting pressure on the next Prime Minister to move more quickly to negotiate a deal. He was also a keen observer of Israeli politics and was keen to avoid strengthening Netanyahu's hand in the elections. When Barak was elected he again held off in the hope that Barak would offer better prospects.

It is easy to dismiss Netanyahu as someone who would not or could not make peace. This would be a misreading of a stubborn but not unrealistic man. He was steeped in the profound Zionism of Jabotinsky and Ben Gurion and never forgot that if Israel had existed before World War II the Holocaust would not have happened. He saw Israel as a tiny land, covering no more than 8,000 square miles, in the midst of hostile Arab countries whose vast combined area was hundreds of times bigger. His pre-occupation with security was based on his experience of the many years of constant Arab threats to annihilate Israel. He knew that, while Germany continued to exist despite having lost two wars, the loss of any war by Israel would have seen its disappearance. His trust in the Palestinians was in direct proportion to his view of the defensibility of the 10-mile-wide strip of land that would remain of Israel if an independent state of Palestine was to be established in the West Bank. He neither trusted the PLO nor believed Israel was defensible with them as neighbours.

It was these ideas that drew him to the position in which he found himself cornered. The impression he gave then and still does, of someone who prefers personal power to the good of the country, may be a little unjust but it has done little to enamour him in the eyes of many Israelis. And a self-opinionated arrogance has not helped him to win many friends internationally. It is wrong, however, to think that he did not want peace. He just did not believe that the risks of making peace were low enough to eliminate the threat to Israel's existence. So he placed the bar very high, probably too high.

Many Palestinians still had hopes of a return to the whole of Palestine while most of them, as well as the rest of the Arab world, saw Jerusalem as their own inalienable capital. It would take a hugely courageous step by the leadership of both sides to make the painful concessions that would inevitably be unpopular with their publics. Were there any leaders around who could do this? Ehud Barak thought that he might.

CHAPTER 18

The Road to Camp David II

IN 1999 EHUD BARAK came into office with high hopes but was faced with a depressing series of problems. At Oslo, six years earlier, a group of reasonable Israelis and Palestinians had shown for the first time that they could see ways in which they might be able to resolve their differences. But by the time Barak was elected the Accords accepted at Camp David had been stymied. Rabin's assassination and Peres's truncated leadership followed by Netanyahu's intransigence impeded implementation. And Arafat had proved less than reliable. It was borne in on both sides that peace process discussions are always easier than implementing agreements. And increasing Palestinian acts of terror ensured that progress became impossible. In the five years leading up to 1995 and the Oslo II Accord there had been 134 Israelis killed in terror attacks while in the five years afterwards the number killed more than doubled to 305.

There was a complete breakdown of trust. The Israelis saw the violence as being encouraged and orchestrated by Arafat. What Israelis believed to be his true face was being revealed and it was clear to them that he had no intention of making peace no matter what he said. The right of return, on which he insisted, would see the end of Israel as a Jewish state and this was clearly his aim. On the other side frustration and disillusion characterised the Palestinian view. They saw the colonisation of their land by increasing settlements, turning their homeland, already reduced to 22 per cent of pre-1967 Palestine, into a number of isolated enclaves. They could not see any signs that Israel would willingly allow them a state of their own and were further humiliated by the heavy Israeli responses to the escalating violence.

Barak was recognised as a highly intelligent and logical strategist who played his cards close to his chest. He did not suffer fools gladly and won few close friends.[1] His difficulties started early with forming a government, which led him to take almost two months to produce a somewhat unstable coalition. It took a further two months before he was able to appoint someone, widely regarded as unsuitable, to lead his negotiating team. People management was not his strongest suit.

A graduate in maths in Israel and of systems analysis engineering from Princeton, Barak became the most decorated army chief Israel had ever had. His bravery was beyond dispute and his night-time exploit into Beirut, disguised as a woman, to dispatch three members of Black September thought to be responsible for the massacre in Munich of Israeli athletes at the 1972 Olympics, became part of his folklore. A talented pianist, he dismantled and re-assembled clocks as a hobby. He had strong opinions about what could and should be done to resolve the stand-offs with Israel's neighbours and put to one side many of the domestic problems besetting Israel at the time.

He rapidly set out a stall that included a peace agreement with Syria, withdrawal from Lebanon by 2000 and a new 'framework for agreement' with the Palestinians, in that order. He was acutely aware of the need to move quickly on two grounds: to be ahead in peaceful settlements before the Iranians developed their weapons of mass destruction, and to take advantage of his initial position of strength with his public if not within his government. And Arafat's stated intention to go for independent statehood lent a further stimulus for rapid action.

His three-point strategy, Syria, Lebanon and the Palestinians, soon came up against the buffers. His efforts with Assad came to no avail, as we will see (Chapter 22). Perhaps they never had a chance in view of the different interpretations of where an acceptable border might be drawn after withdrawal from the Golan. Although there was a relatively small difference between them about the areas of land that would be handed over the two parties never got near to agreement.

Barak knew that withdrawal from Lebanon would have been more straightforward if he had been able to do a deal with Assad but he decided to go ahead in any case. He successfully brought the troops out of the buffer zone in Lebanon but only at some cost. He coordinated the action with Kofi Anan and the UN, leaving the South Lebanese Army and UN forces in the gap, and managed to do it quickly and without loss of life. However, Hezbollah forces, based in and around the local villages, claimed victory and Barak's fears that this would encourage them and others to continue their resistance and promote further violence were soon realised. But Hezbollah also lost something in Israel's withdrawal despite hailing it as a victory. Although the South Lebanese Army disintegrated, Hezbollah had lost some of its reasons for attacking Israel. That was likely to be part of the reason why they argued about Israel's continued occupation of the Shebaa farms, sited on Syrian and not Lebanese land. Despite UN agreement that withdrawal from Lebanon had been complete, Hezbollah has not been deterred from using the farms as an excuse for further action. Over the years since then, Israeli bombing raids have inflicted severe damage on Beirut and Lebanese infrastructure with a terrible death toll while border clashes continued between 2000 and 2006.

Now labelled a terrorist organisation by America and the EU, Hezbollah's avowed purpose is the elimination of Israel. Although it is clearly not in a position to achieve that aim by itself, it can inflict significant damage as an important part of the Iranian and Syrian plans for Israel's demise.

The build-up of missiles and entrenched positions in Southern Lebanon has continued despite a series of negotiated cease-fires. Hezbollah has been distracted recently by joining Assad's fight for survival in Syria but it has continued to build up a formidable arsenal of sophisticated missiles in Lebanon, all pointing at Israel. They await the signal from Iran.

The 'Framework' Proposal

In 2000 Barak had earned relief and support at home and in America for coming out of Lebanon but had difficulty selling his 'framework' idea to the Palestinians. The 'framework' incorporated the concept that all the bones of contention between Israel and the Palestinians should be settled in one package rather than in a piecemeal fashion. He felt that a step-by-step approach left too many opportunities for disagreement and failure. His motives were impeccable but his personal and management skills left something to be desired. He must share some of the responsibility for the subsequent failure of the negotiations.

On the Palestinian side, Arafat failed to control the violence and may even have provoked it as a way of pressurising the Israelis. Arafat's promotion of an educational system that bred hatred and glorification of violence and his failure to curb terrorism undermined Barak's negotiating position in his Cabinet and the Knesset. Arafat did little or nothing to prepare his people for the compromises that would be necessary and pressed on with demonising Israel and the Jews in his media. He maintained his maximalist demands on rights of return and on sovereignty of the Temple Mount and his position was not strengthened when he made the extraordinary claim that the Jewish Holy Temple had stood in Nablus and not in Jerusalem. Nor was he helped later, at Camp David, by the bickering between his lieutenants Mahmoud Abbas and Abu Ali, who presented opposing views.

On the other hand, Barak had failed to give any encouragement to Arafat that he was serious. In focusing first on Syria, he did little to ease Arafat's concerns that he was being ignored and after withdrawal from Lebanon he halted progress on the Wye River interim agreements. Further withdrawals from the West Bank and release of prisoners were put on hold pending the 'big bang' of the final and, as Barak saw it, the total resolution of all their differences. He held Arafat at a distance, giving little chance that the two leaders would form the sort of bond that had characterised the relationships of previous Israeli leaders with

Sadat and Hussein. He turned down Arafat's request to hand over three villages near Jerusalem to his jurisdiction in his rush to get to a summit where all their differences might be on the table.

Barak viewed this plan as having the most potential for progress with the PLO. He had met Mubarak of Egypt and Abdullah of Jordan and gained a modest measure of support, and Clinton was clearly interested in ideas that might give him a win in the Middle East during his last year as President. In not giving sufficient encouragement to Arafat before the invitation to Camp David, Barak created problems for himself. And all this made it more difficult for Arafat to persuade his own restive population that he was achieving anything that they would find encouraging. Hezbollah was seen as having successfully driven out the Israelis by force and Arafat appeared weak in contrast. This made him even more reluctant to control the violence. He had little to show his people with so few concessions on prisoner release, tax revenue transfers and hand over of the villages for which he had asked. Desperate to see some something positive he could sell to his public, he was rebuffed for the time being on all he sought, including the symbolic transfer of Abu Dis, a village overlooking Jerusalem. Barak, on the other hand, was reluctant to spend any more capital on small offers that would likely provoke opposition at home.

Barak's Fragile Position

Barak was very conscious of a need to keep the Israeli public on board, making him extremely anxious to keep his ideas and tactics to himself until they were likely to be successful. He knew how fragile his support could be if he appeared to be giving too much away too soon.

As an example of how far a leader may go out on a line Barak must be one of the bravest although not the shrewdest. There was much discontent amongst the Israeli public about what he seemed to be giving up at a time when the Palestinians were inflicting acts of terror on civilian targets. The fact that no attention was being given to domestic problems did not help and gave even more fire to the Likud and opposition parties' rhetoric. Barak found himself having to give way on funding for religious education to the right-wing Shas party to keep them in his coalition and as a result the left-wing party Meretz resigned. By the time he left to go to Camp David in July 2000 he had lost control of his government, having only 42 out of the 120 seats in the Knesset, and barely survived a vote of no confidence. There were protests in Rabin Square, his approval rating had fallen to 25 per cent and his Foreign Minister refused to go with him to the US. Only someone exceptionally courageous and supremely self-confident could manage such an unpromising start to negotiations.

Arafat had uncertainties about his own support but he paid little attention to Barak's fragile position in the negotiations that were to follow. Barak, finding himself in the position of having failed with Syria, felt the need to move rapidly to an ambitious settlement on statehood for the Palestinians. He was pressing Clinton, who he knew was well into his final year as President, to call a summit meeting before it was too late. Arafat, on the other hand, was slow to move. He had lost trust in Barak and was angry that so little progress had been made on the Oslo II interim agreements. He was only reluctantly willing to hang out for a better deal on the final status negotiations. For more or less the same reasons Barak felt, probably correctly, that small steps would undermine his negotiating position. Needless to say trust between them was very low and it was in this dispiriting position that Clinton agreed to bring the parties together.

Camp David II

Barak was in a hurry. He knew how fragile his support was at home and if he was going to achieve anything involving sacrifices and compromise it would have to come as a complete and watertight package to reassure his public. Arafat's public was equally difficult, restive and prone to violence. Little wonder that he was reluctant and angry as he arrived at Camp David. He was also no stranger to using violence as a means of exerting pressure.

It was at Camp David, however, that the most serious attempt by an Israeli Prime Minister to resolve all their differences with the Palestinians was made. The fact that it ultimately failed is due to many factors but it is difficult to escape the conclusion that Arafat was not ready. Certainly Clinton laid the blame at his door and Prince Bandar bin Sultan, Saudi Arabian ambassador to the US, had told Dennis Ross that if Arafat did not accept what was on offer 'it won't be a tragedy, it will be a crime'.[2] On the other hand, Arafat was fearful for his life; he had survived previous assassination attempts, and asked Clinton if he wanted to go to his funeral. The rapturous response when he arrived home, having not given way to the Americans and Israelis, shows his reluctance to be well founded. He clearly had not prepared his people for any compromise for peace.

The first few days of the fourteen-day summit were marred by anger and frustration. Barak studiously avoided direct contact with Arafat, even though he later entertained him at home in Tel Aviv for head-to-head talks. Clinton lost his temper in a tirade against Arafat in a private meeting and had angry words for Barak on another occasion. He was now in the last months of his presidency and could see time slipping away. He knew that his probable successor, either Al Gore or George W. Bush, was unlikely to place this Middle East conflict high on their agenda when they arrived in office in January 2001. Nor were they ever likely to invest as much personal energy as he did in trying to push Arafat and Barak into a deal.

According to Stanley Greenberg, an American pollster, Barak's tactics were to use the first few days of the summit to rack up the pressure on Arafat by not placing too many offers on the table.[3] There was much poring over maps and detailed discussions by the negotiating teams about borders, land swaps, refugees and security. The more sensitive issue of Jerusalem was not discussed until about day eight, when Barak had heard more about public opinion in Israel. Greenberg, who had helped mastermind Barak's (and Clinton's) election campaign, was busily feeding Barak with daily reports of opinion polls and focus groups he led on every aspect of the negotiations. Barak asked him to sound out the public on Jerusalem and Greenberg was amazed to discover that, whatever Likud parliamentarians were saying, the public at large took a more pragmatic approach.[4] The majority accepted that Arab East Jerusalem and the Muslim and Christian quarters of the Old City could be handed over to the sovereignty of the Palestinians together with the Muslim places of worship on the Temple Mount, in exchange for a secure peace. That was the basis of the offer that Barak felt able to make.

Some in Israel have said that it was a tactical mistake to make this offer then and Jerusalem should have been held back as a bargaining chip for when all the other issues had been settled. The belief that Arafat would always hold out for more was borne out when he turned it down probably in an effort to gain the whole of Jerusalem. It was then that he expressed the spurious view that the Jewish Temple had been in Nablus and never in Jerusalem.

The Americans were in despair and Barak was morose as negotiations ground to a halt. The summit had failed and an innocuous statement was released in which Clinton praised Barak but, by omission, blamed Arafat. That did little to bolster the Palestinian cause and was probably a diplomatic error.

The Clinton Parameters

Camp David was not the end of the efforts to reach agreement. Despite the fact that Barak had now lost a vote of no confidence in his Knesset, he decided to go to elections for the premiership. Although well behind

Ariel Sharon in the public opinion polls, he encouraged his negotiators to meet again. Clinton too would not give up and, in his last few weeks, made one final attempt. He invited Barak and Arafat to Washington and presented them with a paper outlining the parameters of an agreement that he had gleaned from the summit should be acceptable to both parties.[5] It included: sovereignty of over 90 per cent of the West Bank for the Palestinians, with land swaps to allow Israel to retain some of its settlement blocks near Jerusalem; addressing the security challenges for Israel with early warning stations; a presence along the river Jordan followed by a phased withdrawal and a demilitarised Palestine; Jerusalem to be divided into Arab and Jewish sections; Palestinian sovereignty over the Haram (the top of the Temple Mount); and Israeli sovereignty over the Western Wall and adjacent plaza. Several possible ways in which this might be achieved were offered. For refugees, five possible homes were proposed: the new state of Palestine, areas of Israel that formed the land swaps to be handed over, rehabilitation in their current host country, re-settlement in a third country and admission to Israel for some (numbers left to be defined).

The paper was presented to both parties on 23 December, three weeks before Clinton was due to demit office, and he gave Arafat and Barak five days to respond with no opportunity to re-open negotiations. Barak took it to his government, where, considering his broken position, it was remarkable that he was able to gain their reluctant approval. Not so Arafat. He vacillated beyond the five days and finally turned it down.

The last chance for an agreement arose in a meeting arranged at Taba in the Sinai to look again at the 'Clinton Parameters'. Even though Yossi Beilin at that meeting exceeded Barak's brief and offered Arafat more than had been agreed, he still could not get Arafat's agreement. In any event it was far too late and the mood music was depressing. Barak and Clinton were on the way out and little was going to be achievable at this stage.

It might be asked what was going through Arafat's mind to make him unable to accept the best chance he had of gaining a state of his own. Several possibilities emerge. His background of hostility to the very idea of an Israel in what he regarded as his land must have conditioned him to require more than was on offer. The continuing erosion of his land by progressive settlement building and the restrictions placed on movement of his people were humiliating and frustrating. He could not avoid remembering that the Palestinians had already given up 78 per cent of the land they had considered theirs and were now being offered less than all of the remaining 22 per cent. His maximal position, from which he found it impossible to retreat, included the whole of Jerusalem, much greater freedoms for his Palestine and the return of refugees to the whole of Israel. His own public were completely unprepared to allow him to accept anything less and on Jerusalem, the rest of the Arab world was watching anxiously. The Palestinians were growing dissatisfied with their leadership, a situation that was simply exacerbated by the endemic corruption, mismanagement and incompetence amongst Arafat's inner circle. This did nothing to improve their deteriorating economic situation either. His tenuous support from Syria would have been eroded still further by any agreement with Israel and, although he would have had some back-up from Jordan and Egypt, he had a not ill-founded fear for his life. And the fact that Sharon had marched across the Temple Mount with a group of Likud politicians and security guards not long after the Camp David summit fulfilled its purpose in provoking a reaction in the Arab world and amongst the Palestinians. Arafat did little to control the intifada that followed and that consumed many Israeli dead and many more Palestinians before it slowly subsided after some years. Only a strong Palestinian leader much more committed to peace than him would have been willing to reach agreement with Israel. By then the Barak and Clinton initiatives were no longer visible. Sharon had been elected Prime Minister and Bush President.

Lessons Not Yet Learnt

I have laboured over describing this unhappy experience because it exemplifies what might be necessary if we are ever to see a stable solution to this conflict. Firstly, it will require brave leaders who are willing to go out on a limb and take unpopular decisions. They must have a vision and they must be able to persuade their own government and public of the value of their vision. And it will take two of them, one on each side, at the same time. Only the strong will achieve anything in this precarious world.

Secondly, these leaders will need to tread the difficult path between preparing the public and presenting the case for sacrifices for the overall good while at the same time not publicising the detailed debates and partial solutions that are being considered until they are strong enough to withstand close scrutiny. Better to negotiate in secret away from the prying eyes of the media until a position is reached that has a realistic prospect of being accepted.

Thirdly, before going to summits that inevitably raise hopes and expectations it is vital to have negotiated the basic outlines of what is likely to be acceptable to both parties beforehand. Too many surprises at the last moment are difficult to take on board and they inevitably have to be taken away for further discussion and thought. Barak was in a hurry and Arafat was pressing him but he did little to put himself or his people into a receptive position even had Arafat been willing to compromise.

The influence of the actions of terrorists is considerable. Unfortunately they will always try to frustrate efforts to make peace. The inevitability of such actions should prepare leaders to press on with even stronger and more rapid efforts to resolve differences. Unhappily that is often easier said in isolation than in public when the people are incensed.

At Camp David, Barak was brave enough but had poorly prepared his public and his government. He had given little prior encouragement to Arafat, who had done even less to prepare the Palestinians. In his speech to the Knesset on his resignation, Barak spoke out on the need for Israel to have a smaller state behind much more secure borders that would follow Palestinian statehood. It is unfortunate that he had not spoken so clearly earlier. Before the summit Barak had not agreed to much direct contact with Arafat, who felt increasingly alienated and ignored. Too much was left to negotiation at the summit. And there were leaks to the press in Israel that were often inaccurate but sufficiently worrying to create obstacles to Barak's ability to make concessions.

This was a missed opportunity that did not come easily again. It was now Sharon's turn to try his arm.

CHAPTER 19

Ariel Sharon Elected, 2001

IN MARCH 2001 ARIEL Sharon was elected as Prime Minister by a large majority in the midst of a raging intifada. Head of the Likud party, he was seen as a tough man who could sort out the Palestinians and put a stop to the violence. Here was a man with a chequered history. He first came to prominence as a national hero of the 1973 war in the Sinai, where the myth was perpetuated that he had single-handedly beaten the Egyptian Army and crossed the Suez Canal in spite of commands from his superior officers to stop. He did little to correct the myth. 'Arrogant, swashbuckling, manipulative, loved or hated, always controversial, master of self-promotion, contemptuous of his superiors',[1] he was the man Israel wanted for the job after Barak's failed peace initiatives, despite his ill-fated Lebanon adventure, the Sabra and Shatila camp disaster that caused his dismissal as Defence Minister, and his recent provocative walk on the Temple Mount. None of that interfered with his election.

But if Sharon's relationships with the public were good, they were poor within his own party. His colleagues thought of him as untrustworthy and unreliable and, at the age of seventy-five, he was considered a stopgap candidate before the full general election due eighteen months later. He, of course, did not see it that way and stood again in the general election.

For the first eighteen months he headed a coalition government with Labour, a situation that was not nearly so much anathema to him as it would have been to Begin or Shamir. He had already flirted with Labour over ideas for peace negotiations and although he had abhorred the Oslo Accords he spoke out in his first speech to the Knesset about his plans for Gaza and the West Bank. He talked even then of withdrawal, with or without Palestinian agreement, and about the need for painful concessions. The idea of unilateral withdrawal was already in the mind of Ehud Olmert, his deputy leader, and it may have been planted there by Dan Schueftan, an advisor on national security, whose book *Disengagement: Israel and the Palestinian Entity* had considerable influence when it was published in Hebrew in 1999.[2]

Sharon had been the leading architect of the settlement programme in previous governments, and here he was now talking of removing them. A remarkable transformation if he meant it. That he did was soon to be revealed. This was not exactly manna before his Likud colleagues but as they thought of him as only a temporary leader they were not too worried. It was only when he was firmly established on his re-election that they began to take him seriously and by then he was in a position of considerable strength although not in his own party.

His immediate problem was the intifada. Arafat was doing little to quench the flames as Palestinian frustration blew up. Barak's handling of the intifada had been uncompromising and the loss of Palestinian life screened on television in Europe and America brought much appalled criticism. Many in Israel feared the worst. Sharon, the ruthless warrior and uncontrolled Defence Minister, was going to cause even more havoc. He surprised everyone, however, by his use of the phrase 'restraint is strength' and he slowly but surely eased the response to the increasing number of suicide attacks.

A Special Fact Finding Commission was set up in October 2000 to investigate the causes and impact of the intifada and Senator George Mitchell was asked to lead it. An experienced negotiator who had been well regarded for his efforts in Northern Ireland, he produced a report that made a series of proposals to end the violence and despite a devastating suicide attack on the Dolphinarium seaside club in Tel Aviv in which twenty-one teenagers were killed and many more injured Sharon accepted it and curtailed the army's response. He was far from soft on the Palestinians but encouraged his son Omri to meet Arafat to discuss possible peace moves. His change of character into a leader respected, albeit reluctantly, on the world stage surprised everyone and it was the strength he gained from the public by his actions that allowed him later to withdraw unilaterally from Gaza. Too conciliatory a leader probably could not have taken the Israeli public with them in a decision that has had such profound repercussions. But he showed that 'restraint is strength' fitted well with a public worried and anxious about unpredictable terrorism.

In his ability to appeal to the public he stood in contrast to Barak, who was aloof and whose interpersonal relationships were poor. International opinion of Israel had been almost uniformly condemnatory and Arafat had played it up as much as he could but now Sharon was beginning to gain brownie points.

In summer 2001, George Tenet, head of the CIA, presented a paper proposing a cease-fire that Sharon and, eventually, Arafat accepted. But neither Hamas nor Islamic Jihad was party to the agreement, more Israelis were killed and the agreement was lost.

This was the moment when the 9/11 attack on the Twin Towers in New York diverted the world's attention. During the 1991 Gulf War, Palestinians in the West Bank had danced on their roofs as Scud missiles from Iraq rained down on Tel Aviv, and now Arafat feared again being painted with the same brush as he had been then. This time he hurriedly clamped down on the celebrations that had begun in the West Bank and sent condolences to President Bush. But terrorist attacks against Israel continued and when an Israeli minister was assassinated in Jerusalem by the PFLP, American antipathy to the PLO increased. Then when the *Karine A*, a ship carrying illegal arms to Gaza, was intercepted by Israel, Bush was incensed, especially when Arafat was shown to have lied about his direct involvement.

Meanwhile 2001 and 2002 saw a spiralling of the intifada with numerous attacks on civilian targets in Israel. Suicide bombers were busily creating havoc and faith in Sharon was shaken. Multiple deaths in buses, hotels and restaurants were weekly tragedies and the population became fearful and depressed. Arafat was now under house arrest as the Israeli Army encircled his compound in Ramallah yet the terrorism continued.

Finally in March 2002 the IDF put its 'Operation Defensive Shield' into action, to devastating effect. Huge damage to the Palestinians and their property and the undisciplined behaviour of some in the IDF caused enormous distress. But accusations of a massacre of civilians by the IDF at Jenin were soon shown to be a fabrication, although not soon enough to inhibit the continuing condemnation of Israel. By the end of the mission the tally of Palestinians killed in the West Bank was 260, mostly armed militants. Ninety-four Israelis were killed of whom thirty-four were soldiers. The fact that Sharon had exerted strong control meant that the death rates and damage, although severe, were less than might have been expected from the size of the huge army he deployed. But it is the unhappy case that between 2000 and 2004, 904 Israelis and 3,000 Palestinians were killed.

Genesis of the Security Fence

Defensive walls in the Middle East are not entirely novel. During the mandate times, in 1936, the British had constructed a wall along the border between Palestine and Syria and Lebanon. 'Tegart's Wall', named after the architect of the wall and its forts, Colonel Charles Tegart, was built to keep out raiding hordes from the north.[3] Fences and barriers had been built in Jerusalem between 1948 and 1967 and now the idea of a barrier was being raised again.

Operation Defensive Shield had been successful in moderating the intifada but in Israel it was recognised that it had done so at a huge cost and that continuing aggressive Israeli actions in the West Bank were blunt instruments. The idea of a defensive wall had been mooted for some time, popularity for the suggestion was rising, and in June 2002 the Israeli Cabinet approved a proposal to go ahead.

There was opposition from both the Palestinians and the Israeli settlers. The former were unhappy because the proposed siting would not only cut a slice off the future state they envisaged but also divide villagers' farmland and olive groves, while the latter saw themselves being cut off. In Israel Likud saw the fence as defining a border between Israel and the Judea and Samaria that they regarded as part of a greater Israel. The barrier, most of which is a fence, was successful in at least one sense in that it markedly reduced the number of terrorist attacks from the West Bank. It has, however, been used as the symbol of the isolation of Palestinians in the West Bank, especially the 5 per cent that is truly a high concrete wall in and around Jerusalem.

Sharon bludgeoned his way through the Cabinet against his own Likud party and against the constant sniping of Netanyahu. The significance of the fence and its position was far from lost on Sharon, who regarded it as much more than simply a barrier to deter terrorist attacks. He saw it as part of his wider strategy of withdrawal from the West Bank. He repeatedly spoke of the absolute necessity of coming out of the West Bank and Gaza as a prerequisite for a secure and democratic Jewish state. He could see very clearly that incorporating the Arab population of the West Bank would soon lead to an Arab majority and Israel would lose its essential Jewish nature. He talked of the two alternatives – the whole of an *Eretz Yisroel* incorporating the whole of the West Bank but no Jewish state or a Jewish state but not the whole of *Eretz Yisroel*; and he chose a Jewish state. He was clear in his desire to break from the cherished illusion of occupation for ever but with this sort of talk he set himself on a collision course with his Likud party.

He was bolstered by a supportive letter from President Bush, who had by then become completely disillusioned by Arafat. The letter set out a far-reaching American position on Palestinian refugees. Bush accepted their return to a new Palestinian state but not to Israel, and he also saw the large settlement blocks remaining in Israel within re-adjusted 1967 borders. These were part of his 'road map' for peace and have remained American policy until UN Security Resolution 2334 in December 2016 that now casts doubt on the legality of any settlement beyond the 'Green Line'.

CHAPTER 20

The Road Map and Unilateral Withdrawal

BETWEEN 2003 AND 2005 President Bush was taken up with plans to oust Saddam Hussein in Iraq. His attention was diverted from the Israeli–Palestinian dispute but international voices were being raised in Europe as well as in the Arab world that this issue had to be tackled. Whatever his motives were, whether to gain support for Tony Blair's involvement in the Iraq adventure or Arab approval, he produced what became known as the 'road map'. The Middle East Quartet (the USA, the UN, Russia and the EU), formed in 2002, was solidly behind the proposal, which was strongly promoted by King Abdullah of Jordan.

It incorporated all the previous efforts to describe what a peaceful resolution would look like, including the Oslo Accords, the Geneva Accords and the Clinton Parameters: an end to the violence by the Palestinians, a withdrawal from the settlements (with land swaps), secure borders, return of refugees to a new Palestinian state, and acceptance of Resolutions 242 and 381, while the thorny question of Jerusalem was to be left over for further debate. The difference between the 'road map' and earlier proposals was the requirement now for simultaneous action by both sides and not a series of actions each based on achievement of a condition set by one side or other. The whole 'road map' was to be phased, leading to completion by 2005. The support Bush gave in his letter to Sharon on refugees and settlement blocks provided

Sharon with sufficient ammunition to have the 'road map' accepted by his Cabinet, after much horse-trading and objections from Netanyahu.

By then, in 2003, Sharon had been re-elected and, at a meeting convened by Bush in Aqaba, Arafat's Prime Minister, Mahmoud Abbas (Abu Mazen), and Sharon each committed to the 'road map' despite unhappiness in both their camps. Against the odds Abbas managed to get Hamas to agree to a *hudna*, a temporary truce, and July 2003 was the quietest month for two years. The optimism soon ended when a huge suicide bomb exploded on a bus in Jerusalem, killing sixteen adults and seven children. Arafat's refusal to act against the militants prompted Abbas to resign and the 'road map' was in tatters. The Israelis had started dismantling illegal outposts in the West Bank but this was seen as simply a gesture when several of these small outcrops were quickly re-built as the troops moved out. Relations between the Israelis and Palestinians, already bad, worsened further as Arafat tried to spread the message that it was Israel that had pushed America into an Iraq war that was now going badly wrong.

Withdrawal from Gaza

There is a commonly asserted view that if only Israel would remove the settlements there would be a good chance of peace with the Palestinians. That may have contributed to the opinion of Ariel Sharon in 2003 although the impracticality of staying in Gaza weighed heavily with him. He constantly reiterated his message that a democratic Israel could not continue to occupy the West Bank and Gaza, incorporate a growing population of Arabs and yet remain a Jewish state. (He used the word 'occupation' several times, much to the chagrin of his right wing.) He convinced himself that his logic was so impeccable that he should come out of the occupied territories even if he could not gain the agreement of the Palestinians. He did not foresee the disastrous aggression of Hamas and the wars that were to follow. To the despair of many, the logic of this argument has been overturned by the behaviour of those, especially Hamas, who just do not want a peaceful outcome and the consequences of unilateral withdrawal have put back prospects for peace even further. There is no encouragement there for withdrawal now from the West Bank.

But undeterred by opposition in his own party Sharon pressed forward with his plan to remove the settlements in Gaza and four others in the northern West Bank. He brooked no opposition and, in June 2004, sacked two ministers from his Cabinet in order to get a majority support. His idea was to withdraw behind the security barrier, settlement by settlement, and to use the experience gained from his role in removing settlements from the Sinai in 1980.

August 2005 saw the evacuation of twenty-one settlements in Gaza completed in eight days. Despite much protest from across the settler movement, the 9,000 Gaza settlers were removed, mostly peacefully, by 40,000 well-trained police and soldiers. No one was physically hurt. The West Bank settlements were evacuated later, Sharon using 10,000 troops to move a few hundred settlers. In both cases the huge number of police and soldiers needed and the problems that followed in re-housing the settlers should not be underestimated. It should give pause for thought to those believing that the removal of the several hundred thousand settlers now in the West Bank would be easily accomplished.

Sharon Forms a New Party as Hamas Gains Control

The end of this episode saw a number of predictable and not so predictable events. Hamas moved rapidly to gain control of Gaza and destroyed the infrastructure, including a large number of greenhouses left by the Israelis. In parliamentary elections Hamas ousted Fatah and started a process of violently 'cleansing' the opposition party. Terrorist attacks from Gaza continued but now they operated solely against targets within Israel.

Sharon, completely at loggerheads with Likud, which was opposed to his policies, decided to form a new party – Kadima – and took Ehud Olmert, Tzipi Livni and several other unhappy members with him as well as Shimon Peres from a disaffected Labour Party. By December 2005 opinion polls showed Kadima would win more than Likud and prospects for more moves in the West Bank were being floated. By then Arafat had died, in November 2004, of a mysterious illness in a hospital in Paris and Mahmood Abbas was now President.

Then in January 2006 Ariel Sharon suffered a haemorrhagic stroke. He remained in a persistent vegetative state until he died eight years later in 2014. He was a man with a notorious appetite and, at 5 feet 7 inches (170cm) tall but weighing 115 kilograms, he was grossly overweight. He was always going to be at risk but characteristically paid scant attention to expert medical advice.

Sharon's bravery in facing up to his own party and to a large section of the public, although never the majority, was remarkable. His logic for unilateral withdrawal was, at the time, impeccable. But now it is clear that it was a mistake to do so without the agreement and cooperation of the Palestinians. He might have done more too to exert control over the aftermath. The consequences of leaving an enclave within Gaza of virulent enemies, violently opposed to Israel's existence, have been played out in a devastating way for both Israel and Gaza's citizens. Furthermore they have made it even more difficult to persuade Israelis that retraction from the West Bank is a desirable objective.

One can speculate about whether Sharon would have been able to go on to remove more settlements from the West Bank. He had withdrawn four, as part of a resolution of the conflict, but given the enormity of the difficulties he would have faced in embarking unilaterally on this much more ambitious target, it is unlikely he would have been able to make much progress.

With Olmert and Abbas as the new leaders, the question now arose as to whether this was an opportunity for more effort.

CHAPTER 21

Olmert Takes Over, 2006

EVEN BY ISRAELI STANDARDS Ehud Olmert's first year was unhappily eventful. A complex character, he had been Deputy Prime Minister to Sharon and had moved with him to join the new Kadima party. Before that he had spent ten years as mayor of Jerusalem. But now he did a volte-face on his view of the future of Israel. He had been a staunch supporter of a single Greater Israel incorporating Judea and Samaria. Now he believed that this was no longer a viable option and separation into two distinct states was the only way in which Israel would be able to remain both Jewish and democratic. He was fully supportive of the unilateral withdrawal concept enacted by Sharon and indeed may have persuaded him of the idea. But now he was faced with a number of distractions.

In July 2006, even though Israel was facing attacks from Hezbollah in the north and Hamas in the south, Olmert was able to begin serious negotiations with Mahmoud Abbas. But first he turned his attention to Syria, where he hoped to wean Bashar al-Assad away from supporting Hezbollah and from Iran. A vain hope, as it turned out, but a worthwhile effort as Hezbollah launched numerous rocket attacks into Israel, kidnapped some Israeli soldiers near its border with Lebanon and killed others. Meanwhile Hamas in Gaza was busily building tunnels into Israel and had kidnapped Corporal Gilad Shalit. Sporadic attacks on Hezbollah from the air by Israel failed to deter them and Olmert launched the ill-fated 2006 Lebanon ground war. It caused devastation in Lebanon, not just to Hezbollah, which lost most of its missiles and more than 600 fighters, but also to the civilian population, which suffered over a thousand dead and much loss of property. At the same time it was very unpopular in Israel, where the loss of 120 soldiers and forty-two civilians was deeply felt and the failure to remove Hezbollah completely increased Israeli disaffection. International condemnation was severe as the destruction was played out on television around the world.

A cease-fire was brokered by the UN four weeks later and although Hezbollah had been damaged, they had survived the attack and were able to trumpet survival as a defeat for their enemy. Symbolic victories go down well in the Arab world. Within a year of taking up office Olmert's popularity sank to very low levels. Enormous dissatisfaction in Israel with the results of the Second Lebanon War prompted an internal inquiry (the Winograd Report)[1] that found serious errors. The lack of preparedness by the army led to the dismissal of the Chief of Staff while gross errors of judgement by Defence Minister Amir Peretz caused him to retire. Although Olmert was severely criticised he managed to survive.

Even more depressing to Israel was the fact that it had not managed to rescue the abducted soldiers nor had it fully knocked out Hezbollah's military capability. Hezbollah was soon able to call on Iran to rapidly rebuild its missile base with yet more sophisticated weapons and today it has a formidable array of 'defensive' missiles pointing at Israel. Olmert then turned his attention again to Syria, but, as we will see (Chapter 22), this was to no avail.

Serious Talks between Abbas and Olmert

Israel reached a cease-fire with Hezbollah in August 2006, after which serious efforts were made to reach final status agreements between Abbas and Olmert, despite the distractions in Syria. They were far reaching and constructive and their eventual failure deserves careful assessment.

It was clear that Olmert much preferred to go straight to a final status agreement rather than press on with interminable interim arrangements. And Abbas seemed ready to engage. They both wanted to face head on the major sticking points of right of return of refugees and the status of Jerusalem. Despite enormous effort these were the sources of failure.

Olmert first met Abbas in December 2006 and they continued to meet no less than thirty-six times during the next two years. President Bush, although reticent at first to become involved, was persuaded by Olmert to lend his support. He did so by setting up a high-profile meeting at Annapolis, Maryland, to which he invited not only Abbas and Olmert but also representatives of the Quartet and a number of Arab countries. As a result bilateral talks were immediately set in motion. Two parallel tracks were started. The most significant was the series of bi-weekly direct meetings between Abbas and Olmert themselves. The meetings of the negotiating teams, headed by Tzipi Livni for Israel and Abu Alaa for the Palestinians, were less successful. Olmert was later critical of Livni for being too resistant to compromise even though Palestinian brinkmanship played its part in the subsequent failure to reach agreement. The tone of the Livni–Abu Alaa meetings can be gleaned from the records of parts of their discussions published by Al-Jazeera in 'The Palestine Papers'.[2] These papers have been interpreted as showing the PLO giving too much away under Israeli and American pressure. It is, however, worth noting that verbatim discussions held during the circumstances of a negotiation will include a full range of options and ideas and may not give the full picture of agreements or disagreements.

Accounts of the Olmert–Abbas meetings revealed later by both of them present a somewhat different picture. On the Israeli side Olmert went further than any previous leader in his propositions and Abbas agreed with that assessment in later interviews.[3]

The bones of what was placed on the table are as follows: a two-state solution was accepted as a given. The focus was then on the position of the borders. Abbas offered to swap 1.9 per cent of the West Bank while Olmert suggested a 5.9 per cent swap. Abbas reasoned that his offer would give Israel the ability to retain 60 per cent of the 300,000 settlers leaving about 120,000 to be moved. There was much poring over maps and argument about which settlement towns might be retained but it was the town of Ariel that proved the most contentious. Finally Olmert presented Abbas with a map of what he envisaged as being acceptable borders and land swaps. Abbas was not allowed to take this sensitive map away with him unless he immediately signed up to it, something he was not about to do. But he did try to memorise it and re-drew it from memory on a piece of paper on his return home.

The debate on Jerusalem was moved forward with proposals that Arab East Jerusalem together with the Arab and Christian Quarters of the Old City should become Palestinian while Jewish West Jerusalem and the Jewish Quarter of the Old City would remain Israeli. The holy sites, then termed the 'Holy Basin' according to Olmert, should come under some sort of custodial committee made up of Israel, Palestine, Saudi Arabia, Jordan and the USA. These were remarkable proposals from a man who had been the mayor of the whole of Jerusalem for many years but when he sought to include the City of David and the Silvan valley within the 'Holy Basin' Abbas strongly objected.

The principle of right of return of refugees was accepted by Olmert but the quantum became the main issue. He accepted the idea that 10,000 refugees could be allowed back into Israel proper with compensation for others who could return, if they wished, to the proposed Palestine. He also sought compensation for the Jews who had been expelled from Arab lands in 1948. Abbas saw 10,000 as a trivial number compared with the burgeoning numbers of refugees that had grown from the original, less than a million, to five million by then.

So Near but So Far

On the face of it Abbas and Olmert were not far off an agreement. Abbas admitted as much later. On borders and land swaps it does not seem beyond the bounds of possibility that they could have reached a compromise somewhere between Abbas's 1.9 per cent and Olmert's 5.9 per cent. On Jerusalem a division was virtually agreed, at least by the two leaders, but was stymied by the inclusion of the City of David in the 'Holy Basin', and on refugees there was some room for manoeuvre that might have been spelt out in further work.

But there were powerful arguments against finally doing the deal. On borders, Abbas would have found it difficult to persuade his opponents of the deal, of which there were many on his side, who believed that having lost 78 per cent of their land after 1948, giving any more away was unacceptable. Olmert on the other hand knew that the pre-1967 'borders' were simply armistice lines drawn after the cease-fire of 1948. In his mind they were always going to be negotiable to the extent allowed for in the wording of Resolution 242. On Jerusalem, Abbas had to face not only his Palestinian population but the rest of the Arab world, where it was adamantly held then that Jerusalem was the undivided city of Islam. Dividing it and sharing it with others was deemed by many to be unacceptable. A similar view, reached from completely the opposite direction, was held by many on the Israeli side where the idea of a divided Jerusalem, the capital of Israel, was anathema. Yet here was Olmert offering a division while Abbas was too fearful or too weak to take this leap. And on refugees the pressure on Abbas to bring 'home' five million refugees was enormous while Olmert knew that less than a fifth of that number had fled from Israel in 1948 and most had been born subsequently. More importantly he could never accept anywhere near the millions Abbas sought while retaining the essential Jewishness of the state of Israel. He was therefore keen on the proposals for refugees laid out in the Clinton Parameters, in which it was suggested that they should be re-housed in a variety of ways. Abbas could not find it in him to accept this nor was he strong enough to present it to his people. A missed opportunity with tragic consequences.

These are the difficulties that have continued to plague negotiations ever since. They will have to be faced again if any progress is to be made but there is little doubt now that the Olmert–Abbas discussions were as near to reaching a successful conclusion as they could be at the time. It could be thought that Abbas was fearful of the attitude of the other Arab states to any concessions he might make to Israel. As we will see, his persistent resistance to direct negotiations with Israel cannot continue to be blamed on the attitudes of the Sunni Arab states that are now much keener on making peace with Israel themselves and see the continuing Israeli–Palestinian conflict as an obstacle to that end.

There were two other matters that probably contributed to failure. Firstly Olmert had been indicted for a number of criminal charges including fraud and bribery and was under heavy pressure to resign. Under these circumstances Abbas may well have felt that reaching an agreement with a lame-duck leader was risky. It is unfortunate then that he did not grasp even a fleeting opportunity. Olmert did resign and although many of the charges against him were later dropped he was found guilty of the remainder and, since January 2016, has been serving a jail sentence.

The other problem was the view, increasingly voiced, that Abbas was too weak a leader to be able to take difficult steps. His inability to control Hamas after it threw the Palestinian Authority out of Gaza in 2007 did little for his capacity to negotiate. His popularity was in decline and has sunk even further since then. His autocratic management style, the rumours of corruption, and his failure to achieve any relief for his population coupled with a lack of any elections for many years did not improve the common view. His Prime Minister, Salam Fayyad, appointed in 2007, was widely regarded as a pragmatist with whom Israel could have done business. He had embarked on a programme to build the infrastructure of a future Palestinian state, to improve the economy and security and to clean up some of the corruption. It is mere speculation about how far he might have been able to go with Olmert if he had been leader. Perhaps he was too flexible to survive and indeed Abbas removed him in 2013.

This Olmert–Abbas era was the last occasion when both leaders took a significant step towards a final status resolution. Yet another missed opportunity for the Palestinians to have their own state and Israel to have a peaceful neighbour.

Olmert's resignation brought Netanyahu back to the premiership and in America, Barack Obama was elected President. They had to cope with each other as well as with the turmoil that was enveloping the wider Middle East. These were times of radical change, mostly for the worse.

CHAPTER 22

The Syrian Track

WE CAN NOW EXAMINE the multiple efforts, over many years, to reach an agreement with Syria's leaders.

With its increasing disintegration the prospects for peace with Syria have by now, in 2017, become unthinkable. Until some semblance of stable government has resumed, in whatever borders emerge, it will be impossible for Israel to find anyone with whom to negotiate. The current disarray has left a range of rebel troops, including Al Qaeda and IS, on or near Israel's northern border, posing a severe security threat, and confirms the views of many in Israel that it was fortunate that the Golan Heights, occupied by Israel in the 1967 war, were not handed back to Syria in the 1990s. The recent flight of UN troops across the border into Israel has also emphasised, as if emphasis was needed, that reliance on international peace-keeping forces for Israel's safety is not a viable option. But relations have been fractious since mandate times and it was only in the 1990s, during the Rabin and Peres premierships, that any prospect of a peace agreement began to be seriously mooted.

Despite the current hopelessness of Israeli–Syrian relations, it is worth re-examining the history of that interface since it impinges on past and current negotiations with the Palestinians. Syria's role both in exerting control over Arafat's PLO and in support of Hamas and Hezbollah has clearly been significant. And Syria has always played a vital part in the peace process, largely in efforts to undermine it.

Paradoxically, when a peace treaty with Syria did briefly appear on the horizon, Damascus was festooned with banners extolling peace.

The borders of Syria and Palestine set out in the 1923 League of Nations mandate became the subject of repeated incursions by both sides, especially after 1948 with the establishment of Israel. The original arrangement left Syria unhappy and would have continued to be a source of irritation. It was only with the occupation of the Golan Heights that Israel found itself with a bargaining chip that it could use to try to settle the border issue.

But to imagine that the Golan occupation created Syria's implacable enmity would be a misreading of history. Long before 1967 Syria had worked to undermine Israel's position with repeated skirmishes along its border and uncompromising speeches by Hafez al-Assad to his people. He led the charge at the Arab summit in 1967 in denouncing Israel and made vicious attacks on Anwar Sadat when Egypt made peace with Israel in 1978. There is little evidence of a willingness to make peace before Rabin's initiatives of 1993.

For Israel a peace with Syria was seen as vitally important. Compared with the Palestinians, Syria was a sovereign state with a strong army and a leader with whom they could deal, at least in theory. A peace there would allow a safer withdrawal from Lebanon, Hezbollah and Hamas would lose support and become less of a threat and, equally importantly, a buffer between Israel and a belligerent Iran with its nuclear ambitions would be invaluable. Perhaps Assad was always aware of that and continued to hold out for the best deal he could get.

Assad regarded his Syria as the natural guardian of the Palestinian cause. He could not escape the fixed idea that Palestine was simply a region of southern Syria and his grand plan was to exert his hegemony over Palestine, Lebanon and Jordan. He held the PLO close, tried to control their aspirations for an independent state and used their cause only while it was convenient for him in his battle to oust Israel.

The Golan Heights were just a further source of enmity. While Syria had little strategic need for them apart from some hyped-up security requirements, national pride and lost dignity demanded their return. In 1981 Israel went beyond 'occupation' to annex the Golan Heights since by then they seemed much more significant. The Israelis remembered Syrian rocket attacks launched on their northern towns from there and would not willingly hand them back without a full peace and adequate security arrangements. Israel's current Prime Minister, Benjamin Netanyahu, is now using similar arguments but at the time, Yossi Beilin was far from convinced of the need to hold on to the Golan for security reasons alone. He pointed to the more significant threat posed by the numerous Scud missiles aimed at Israel from the plain behind the Heights. But it would have been extremely difficult to persuade the Israeli public of that logic then as now.

Assad stuck out for complete withdrawal from the Golan before giving any detail or commitment to a firm peace arrangement. Yitzhak Rabin on the other hand was unwilling to give up any land without that commitment. The idea of returning the tangible asset of land for an intangible asset of an uncertain peace that was always vulnerable to reversal was a step too far for him. Much later, Ehud Olmert was more interested in a severance of Syria's ties to Iran and Hezbollah than a full peace treaty yet he was equally unsuccessful. Assad continued until the end of the century to resist US inducements, including those of Henry Kissinger, to negotiate with Israel, although he softened his stance just a little when the Americans redoubled their efforts and Warren Christopher shuttled backwards and forwards between Damascus and Jerusalem in 1992, Assad having restored relations with Egypt in 1989. He preferred instead to rely on Russian support and only changed tack with the weakening of Russian influence and a drop in its supply of arms, and with restrictions on trade imposed by the US and Britain when they placed Syria on their terrorism list.

It was the unlikely pair of Assad and Yitzhak Shamir that eventually agreed to join the Madrid conference pressed upon them by the Americans. The agreement of these two figures with their intractable natures, although remarkable, was hedged about with all sorts of pre-conditions.

The meetings were never a success. They were held in icy cold moods with no shaking of hands and absolutely no social contacts between the negotiators. Each side stated their case without any signs of compromise. But the fact that they were talking to each other, or at least at each other, for the first time could be regarded as progress.

With the election of Rabin in 1992 a serious effort was made to move the debate on. He was anxious to see movement on both the Palestinian and Syrian fronts while the Americans strongly held that a peace with Syria was a much more important immediate aim. Assad proved sluggish in his responses. A return of the Golan, although not straightforward, and strongly resisted by the Israeli public since it was now populated by Israeli agricultural villages, would not have been hidebound with the biblical implications of the West Bank for Israel. It was always going to be easier to let the Golan go. But as Assad blew hot and cold and dragged his heels Rabin decided to concentrate on the negotiations with the Palestinians.

Time was running out and as so often, events intervened. Rabin was assassinated in 1995 and Shimon Peres, made Prime Minister immediately after Rabin's death, made a further effort to focus on a peace deal with Syria in the short time available to him. The bilateral talks in Washington had driven into the sand and Peres pressed Christopher and his President to try to bring the parties together again. The Americans did not need much convincing since they too were keen to see some progress in Clinton's re-election year and further meetings were organised at the Wye Valley Plantation.

The Israeli delegation tried hard to push the Syrians to move quickly to a decision, pointing to the domestic pressures facing Peres. They were anxious to show that he was investing his personal standing and future political survival in the process and could easily lose his premiership in the few months remaining to him. The Syrians had difficulty understanding this manifestation of democracy and the need to convince a fractious public of the wisdom of this initiative. But Assad was not without his own domestic issues. His Ba'ath Party was not uniformly supportive of his efforts to make peace and needed some sign of success after four years of discussion. His minority Alawite sect had not earned much public affection either but despite, or because of, these domestic weaknesses he continued to vacillate.

Assad lacked Sadat's vision and the ability to make the unpopular decisions of an inspired leader. He was cautious, rigid and calculating, leaving him unable to take risks or make any compromises. He controlled the Wye River talks at a distance and while some small advances were made in understanding the issues no substantive progress was made. The meetings eventually ground to a halt and for Peres, the last straw was Assad's failure to condemn the acts of terror by Hamas that were beginning to escalate.

Meanwhile Iran was doing all it could to prevent Syria signing any peace deal with Israel. Once it was clear that all progress had ceased, Syria, at Iran's urging, prompted Hezbollah to resume its missile attacks on Israel. At the same time it encouraged the Hamas leadership, based in Damascus, to continue their terrorist activities. Assad never, at any time, agreed to meet face to face with any of the series of Israeli Prime Ministers, including Rabin, Peres and Barak, who tried to engage him in negotiation. The closest contact Assad permitted with the Israelis was through the Americans, including Warren Christopher, Dennis Ross and, on occasion, with Bill Clinton himself.

In May 1996 Benyamin Netanyahu swept to victory in the wake of a series of terrorist attacks and on the platform of the security he promised to provide. Public reaction against any peace with either the Palestinians or the Syrians was running high and Netanyahu took advantage of that to denigrate the policies of his left-wing rivals. No further progress was on the horizon. Not everyone in the Arab world was disappointed. While Arafat and the PLO became anxious and Assad seemed taken aback, the Iranians were delighted and the Egyptians, Jordanians and Iraqis were pleased that a check had been placed on what they saw as Israel's plans for Middle East hegemony.

It was then Ehud Barak's turn when he succeeded Netanyahu, in a wave of enthusiasm in 1999, and he put enormous effort into trying to reach an agreement with Assad. He saw Syria as both a threat with its large army and as an opportunity. As head of a nation state, Assad was someone with whom he could negotiate, and a successful peace deal would give him a big win at home. It would provide the buffer he desperately wanted between Israel and the increasingly dangerous Iran and allow him to withdraw from Lebanon with Syrian support. All of that was to no avail as Assad became increasingly resistant to a peace deal. Furthermore, when Assad finally and reluctantly deigned to meet Clinton in Geneva, he resisted all efforts by the American to persuade him to sit down and listen to what was on the table. For Clinton this slap in the face made him realise that further efforts were futile. Dennis Ross describes Assad at this stage as physically weak and he may also have had early signs of dementia.[1] Assad probably recognised that he was dying and was distracted by the need to leave his son, whose succession he was planning, without too many headaches within his fractious Ba'ath Party at home.

By the year 2000 the world had moved on. Syria had cemented relations with Iran, exerted its dominance over Lebanon and increased its support for Hezbollah in its efforts to attack Israel. That was the year that Israel managed to withdraw from Lebanon. The hosting of the Hamas leadership in Damascus hardly helped persuade Israel that Bashar al-Assad was any more interested in peace than his father, whom he had succeeded. By then it was clear that any attempt to raise prospects for a negotiated settlement faced almost impossible barriers. It would have required more than strong inducements by the Americans to wean Syria off its embrace of Iran and its liaison with Hezbollah. Furthermore the renaissance of Russian influence and support was rendering American involvement a less attractive proposition. And in Israel, the thought of giving up a Golan that many felt had become even more strategically important was anathema as its northern neighbours continued rattling their sabres. Even though the Sea of Galilee as a source of Israel's water supply was of diminishing importance as desalination and recycling took over, by this time Bashar Assad was no longer interested in giving away access to the lake that had been Syria's before 1948, or indeed anything else for peace.

It was against this unpromising background that Olmert tried to re-open negotiations with Assad. By then, Assad had lost the confidence of President Bush during the Iraq War and sanctions imposed on him were beginning to bite. He had tried to placate the United States by withdrawing his troops from Lebanon in response to UN Resolution 1559. But while earlier overtures with Sharon had been rebuffed, now Olmert chanced his hand.

A secret channel was opened in Turkey with the support of President Erdoğan. Meeting in Ankara, Turkish diplomats ran between representatives of the two countries as they sat in separate rooms. By September 2007 the talks were no longer secret and both sides were talking up the potential benefits of an agreement. Olmert's aim was to disassociate Syria from Hezbollah and from Iran rather than necessarily a full-blown peace, while Syria simply wanted the return of the Golan.

A Nuclear Hiccup

A remarkable event then took place. On 6 September 2007, in 'Operation Orchard', the Israeli air force destroyed the Deir ez-Zor nuclear reactor being constructed at Kibar in northern Syria. Supplied by the North Koreans in secret, Assad had even kept his nuclear ambition from his army, and was constrained in publicising the attack. He certainly did not want it to be known that he was collaborating with North Korea, a member of President Bush's 'axis of evil'. He tacitly conspired with the Israelis to keep the existence of the reactor, and its destruction, out of the public eye.

Surprisingly this dramatic event caused only a hiccup in the negotiations. What stopped them dead was not this but three other developments in 2008. Olmert was being indicted for criminal offences and

Assad became reluctant to complete an agreement with a lame-duck leader. He was also increasingly unhappy with the way the discussions were heading on how much of the Golan was to be handed over. But the final straw was the unleashing of 'Operation Cast Lead' on Gaza by the Israelis. Erdoğan was incensed. A long-time supporter of Hamas, he immediately drew the meetings in Ankara to a close. Talks with Syria have never been possible subsequently nor, as we saw earlier, are they likely to be resumed any time soon.

Over the years a number of attempts to lower the resistance to negotiations have failed. One such, the far-sighted but fanciful proposal put forward by the United States Institute of Peace's Center for Mediation and Conflict Resolution for a joint Jordan Valley–Golan Heights environmental reserve, a sort of haven of peace between the two countries, fell on stony ground.[2]

In retrospect there was never a time during the periods 1992–6 and 1999–2001, while representatives were meeting, that there was more than a distant glimmer of hope for peace. There were enormous benefits to be gained by both sides but neither found it possible to give up on their demands. Patrick Seal, Assad's biographer, laid at least as much blame for the failure on Israel's shoulders as on Syria's,[3] but Warren Christopher's account leaves little doubt that it was the recalcitrance of the Assads, father and son, that was the major cause of the breakdown.[4]

When Syria became subject to rebel revolts and invasion by IS, all thoughts of peace with Israel were off the table anyway. Threats of invasion by the US and the later military involvement of Russia have complicated matters still further and Syria's future is now impossible to predict. What position will President Assad occupy? Will he be in situ or exile? What proportion of the country will remain as Syria and what under rebel administration? Who will govern what and where? What role will Russia play? And Iran? These are the imponderables that Israeli think tanks must now be considering. They will have the unenviable task of working through the options for a future relationship with what remains of a divided Syria. Are there any opportunities at all for some sort of accommodation with what will exist when all the dust settles in some undetermined future? It seems extremely unlikely that Bashar al-Assad himself will change his position on Israel unless he sees the remote opportunity of using it to strengthen his position in his remaining Syria against the various opposition groups. It is equally improbable that any of the various warring factions might be interested in dropping their enmity to Israel. If they ever lift their heads up from fighting each other, they are more than likely to turn their morbid attention to their common enemy. That is certain for Hezbollah, Al Qaeda and IS but their divisions are so deep that for now at least the likelihood of any collaborative effort is remote. Israel will then be looking at ways in which it can increase its defence rather than returning the Golan or indeed making any other concessions. Netanyahu's recently reported statements that Israel will never give up the Golan Heights may be undiplomatic and even unwise. But in the absence of any comment by the UN about the erosion of Syria by the Kurds, IS and rebel groups, its efforts to censure Israel for occupation of the Golan smacks of moral relativism by the General Council.

For Israel, peace with Syria is unlikely to re-appear on the agenda for the foreseeable future.

CHAPTER 23

Abbas, Netanyahu, Obama and a Roller-Coaster Ride

AS OLMERT RESIGNED TZIPI Livni took over as leader and although her party, Kadima, gained the most seats in the election of 2008 she was unable to form a coalition. Netanyahu was then able to slip in in March 2009 and form a right-wing majority coalition government.

He arrived in the wake of a hail of rockets from Hezbollah and Hamas but despite this his pre-election addresses had focused more on the Iranian nuclear threat than the Palestinian question. He had a quite different agenda from Olmert for dealing with the Palestinians, whom he regarded as never being capable of reaching an agreement, and pressed forward instead with the idea of boosting the Palestinian economy. Important though that must be, it has failed for a number of reasons, not least because of Abbas's resistance, a lack of the robust Palestinian administrative infrastructure that a state requires and rampant corruption in Fatah.

Netanyahu was then faced with a newly elected American President who also had completely different ideas from his predecessor. They were soon set on a collision course.

It is worth our while examining the changing pressures that were then brought to bear that made it difficult if not impossible for the Palestinians and Israelis to reach an agreement. First, the American role.

Obama Tries His Hand

It is the norm for American Presidents to start out with the idea that their immediate predecessor has played mistaken games in foreign affairs, especially in the Middle East.[1] President Obama was clearly in that camp and distanced himself from Bush's policies.

In 2008, a critical review of previous American presidential policies and tactics had been published together with a series of recommendations for future Presidents.[2] The presumption in this report, by a study group at the United States Institute of Peace, was that given the correct tactics, carefully thought through and delivered, America could sort out the Israeli–Palestinian conflict once and for all. Obama's Middle East agenda seems to have been based on some of these ideas. Little was made of the fact that Oslo, and the peace treaties with Egypt and Jordan, had each been initiated by the parties themselves and only once they had started was American involvement so vital. As he stepped into the complex arena of Middle East interrelationships Obama began by focusing on improving relationships with the Arab states after Iraq and, in order to gain key allies, introducing some separation from Israel and exerting pressure on Israelis and Palestinians to come to an agreed solution to their differences. Unfortunately these tactics have proved to be not a little inept and the impact of his involvement on Israel/Palestine is yet to be played out.

Obama, in believing that he should exert strong pressure on the Israelis while distancing himself from them, was following in the footsteps of Eisenhower, Nixon, Carter and Bush Senior before him. A combination of actions he felt would enable him to press for a rapid resolution of the conflict with the Palestinians. Obama may have fondly imagined it would also improve relations between the US and the Arab states. Unfortunately he may not have recognised that, when some of his similarly minded predecessors had tried the same line, far from improving relations, the situation had worsened. On the other hand, Presidents who had taken a more supportive position with Israel, including Truman, Kennedy and Clinton, had not damaged US–Arab relationships. The truth is that while resolving the Israeli–Palestinian stand-off was important for other Arab leaders, they gave much greater priority to their own internal problems and external threats. These were now becoming severe.

Obama set out with a laudable aim of trying to repair relations in the Middle East that he felt had been damaged during the Bush years. He promised to withdraw American troops from Iraq and held his hand out to Syria, Iran, Turkey and Egypt. In a speech he made in Cairo in June 2009 he spoke of a changed American attitude towards Islam and the Iranian nuclear programme. But his desire to see more democracy did not go down well with Mubarak in Egypt or the other Arab autocrats. He also included mention of his new, stronger line on Israel in an effort to convince the Arabs of his seriousness. He had already stated his ambitious aim of a rapid resolution of the Israeli–Palestinian conflict and spoke of an early freeze on settlement building in the West Bank and a return to the 1967 borders. Netanyahu was dismayed with Obama for giving away all his bargaining positions without an obvious quid pro quo. Of course Obama deserves some credit for trying but his belief that if he could sort out this conflict, US relations with the rest of the Arab world would be all sweetness and light, was misplaced.

When Iran's Mahmoud Ahmadinejad twisted Assad's arm, the Syrian leader rebuffed Obama's overtures, and Egypt was shortly to go through the 'Arab Spring', in which Mubarak was deposed and the Muslim Brotherhood under Mohamed Morsi was elected. As a strong protagonist of democracy, Obama was supportive of these Egyptian changes but the autocratic regimes in Saudi Arabia and the Gulf states, hitherto allies of the West, were appalled at what the 'Spring' might bring to their own shaky regimes. The American support for the Muslim Brotherhood in Egypt sent shivers down their spines. The Saudis, who thought that he had forced Mubarak out, began to question Obama's judgement. He had indeed tried to convince Mubarak to stand down voluntarily. The Saudis' view was not improved when the Brotherhood regime in Egypt was later overturned in a military coup and Obama withdrew his support for the new government of Abdel Fatah el-Sisi. Nor were they pleased with his initial overtures to their feared enemy, Iran. He was made to appear weak in their eyes when he changed his tune on Iran from one of 'prevention' of its nuclear ambitions to one of 'curtailment'.

Obama's attitude to Assad's atrocities in Syria weakened his position still further. Obama spoke of his 'red line' that would be crossed if Assad used chemical weapons against the rebels. When Assad did just that in 2013 and killed 1,400 rebels, including 400 children, Obama agonised and vacillated.[3] No one could accuse Obama of being gung-ho, he was more gung-no. Assad only gave up his stores of chemical weapons (although probably not all of them) when Russia intervened. Obama's reputation had already been sullied in the Middle East when, after initial reluctance to intervene in the disastrous Libyan civil war in 2011, he was accused of failing to prevent the post-war chaos that allowed Libya to become a haven for large numbers of jihadist groups. Obama justified his belated and limited action in Libya and Syria since he had managed to avoid American involvement in yet more wars in the Middle East, wars that the American public would have been unlikely to support. But the net result was that Saudi Arabia, Egypt and the Gulf states, as well as Israel, began to regard Obama as unreliable as well as weak.

Turkey, an important NATO ally, was not particularly pleased either that Obama was making overtures to Iran and Syria and offering support for the Kurds. Obama misread the internecine rivalries and enmity between these various regimes and the antipathy amongst many of them to the West and America.

Another nail in the coffin of the US–Israel relationship was hammered in when, without warning the Israelis, Obama gave a speech in 2011 in which he made a push to settle the Israeli–Palestinian conflict by pressing for a withdrawal to the pre-1967 borders and return of refugees. He calculated that the turmoil in the rest of the Middle East gave him an opportunity to sort out this particular issue when, in fact, it was quite the wrong moment. The rest of the Arab world were taken up with their own problems and had little time for Palestinian difficulties. This miscalculation was compounded when Netanyahu publicly rebuked Obama in a joint interview in the White House. Personal relations between the two were never more than distant.

In trying to solve the Israel–Palestine conflict once and for all Obama succeeded only in alienating Netanyahu. Whatever one thinks of Netanyahu, and there is much to criticise, it is unlikely to be productive or diplomatic for one head of state to alienate another with whom it is important to do business. And that went both ways.

Obama was correct in wanting to improve America's relationships with the Arab world but he and they were soon overtaken by profound changes that were completely unpredicted. It is now that we can try to assess the activities of the PLO, Hamas and the Israeli government as the world immediately around them began its dramatic shifts.

Netanyahu's Conditions

Netanyahu did not believe that the Palestinians under Mahmoud Abbas were ready or willing to reach an agreement with Israel. He pointed to the repeated failures of all his predecessors to make progress with the PLO and Hamas. Abbas's refusal to recognise that Israel was a national Jewish state was completely unacceptable to Netanyahu and the belligerent stance of the Hamas leadership with their constant message of death and destruction for Israel was unlikely to soften his attitude.

In a speech he gave at Bar-Ilan University in June 2009 he had presented his vision of two states, one Jewish and one Palestinian, living in peace side by side.[4] He then set out his ideas of what could lead to an end of the conflict, including the need for security, defensible borders and an undivided Jerusalem as Israel's capital. Not much new there then, and little chance that all these conditions might be acceptable to the Palestinians. It was small comfort to Abbas that Netanyahu spoke of two states or that he did not say that these were final, irrevocable pre-conditions.

For the two years between 2009 and 2011 there had been a stalemate in Palestinian–Israeli negotiations in spite of, or because of, Obama's interventions. In May 2011 Netanyahu expanded on his vision for a resolution that included:

- Palestinian recognition of Israel as a Jewish state;
- acceptance of an end to the conflict;
- Palestinian refugees to be settled largely, but not entirely, outside Israel's borders;
- large settlement blocks to remain within Israel with land swaps for the remainder;
- demilitarisation of the Palestinians and an Israeli presence along the river Jordan;
- Jerusalem to remain the undivided capital of Israel.

Most of these were never going to be interesting enough to a reluctant and untrusting Abbas to tempt him anywhere near the negotiating table. It is conceivable that Netanyahu knew this and was playing to his own right-wing coalition partners. He was later to modify and soften his public utterances, as we will see, but that has been no more successful in luring Abbas to the table.

Under pressure from the US, Netanyahu agreed to a settlement 'freeze' that lasted ten months in 2010. The 'freeze' was restricted to new builds and did not include building already under way or building in Jerusalem. The fault for not taking advantage of the 'freeze' lay mostly with Abbas, who clearly was suspicious of Netanyahu and was holding out for more offers. As a demonstration that the settlements might not be the only, or even the most important, sticking point, Abbas moved on to the matter of return of the refugees and the position of the 1967 borders before offering to re-start negotiations. Having failed to take up

Olmert's earlier blandishments it was never likely that he would now accept any of the more hard-line Netanyahu offerings. It was only in the last month of the 2010 'freeze' that Abbas was persuaded to meet with US Secretary of State Hillary Clinton in Annapolis. By then little was going to be achieved and while Abbas pressed for an extension to the 'freeze' Netanyahu could see little point in trying to convince his right wing to continue in the face of a lack of any progress.

Abbas under Pressure

Meanwhile Abbas was becoming increasingly unpopular at home; he continued to be perceived as weak and achieving little for his people. He felt under pressure to do something positive and sought help from other Arab leaders, but by then they were distracted by their own internal problems.

By 2011, Salam Fayyad, Abbas's Prime Minister, had produced his two-year plan to build the state institutions that the Palestinians desperately needed but, in the absence of progress with Netanyahu, Abbas simply fired him. Abbas decided to take a bold step and seek unilateral recognition at the United Nations for a Palestinian nation state. Needless to say, this was strongly resisted by Israel. Obama and the USA were less than enthusiastic too and did all they could to dissuade him. While it would have been relatively easy for Abbas to gain the necessary two-thirds majority in the General Assembly, Obama dearly wanted to avoid the embarrassment of using the veto in the Security Council, where approval was also required. Such a course of action would have alienated the Arab world. He exerted enough pressure to deter Abbas, at least for the moment but only at the expense of increasing the difficulties faced by Abbas at home.

In an effort to break the impasse Obama had sent Senator George Mitchell to the Middle East in 2010. He tried to employ the patient step-by-step approach he had used successfully in Northern Ireland but this was soon recognised as inappropriate in the cauldron of the Middle East and came to nothing. Netanyahu was not budged from his firm line and Abbas was left to wallow in his increasing unpopularity in the West Bank.

The Brief Hamas–Palestinian Authority 'Unity Government'

Negotiations with the Palestinians have been bedevilled by the extreme animosity between the separate factions, Fatah and Hamas. An uncompromising split between them had opened up when the latter forcibly took over Gaza. The brutal suppression of the Fatah opposition in Gaza by Hamas was unsurprising in light of their polar views on relations with Israel. The fundamentalist Muslim Brotherhood ideology of Hamas runs counter to the more secular views of Fatah and while Fatah, under Arafat, had removed those parts of the PLO Charter that were aimed at the destruction of Israel, it was a charter that Hamas had never signed up to. Their own charter remains vehemently opposed to the existence of Israel. The fatwa issued in 1990 by Muslim scholars in Egypt against anyone buying or selling Islamic land lent justification to Hamas's position.[5] Accordingly Israel is viewed as sitting in the *waqf* category of land, an Islamic endowment that belongs to God and cannot be sold even to another Muslim.

As a strict adherent to this doctrine that Muslim lands can never be negotiated away, Hamas was always an unlikely partner for peace. Little wonder that it and Fatah had difficulty finding common ground and the Palestinians could not present a common face in any negotiations with Israel. And for Israel, a deal with the Palestinian Authority (PA) would still leave a significant proportion of the Palestinians outside any agreement.

But in 2011 these rival factions signed an agreement in Cairo to form a consensus government. It took another three years of jockeying for positions before the so-called 'Unity Government' was instituted. It never lived up to the 'unity' label although there was some understandable enthusiasm for the concept internationally. It was only to be expected that Israel would object strongly to the idea of dealing with a government containing Hamas, an organisation committed to its destruction. The US was also more than ambivalent about recognising a party labelled as terrorist.

But neither Israel nor the US had much to fear as Mahmoud Abbas struggled with the conundrum of how to incorporate, in a joint government, members of Hamas who were intent on destroying its purpose yet who would be acceptable internationally. An interim government under Rami Hamdallah, Fayyad's successor as Abbas's Prime Minister, was formed in June 2014 with what were called 'technocrats' rather than politically aligned members although all were Abbas's men and none belonged to Hamas. PA security forces continued to arrest Hamas supporters and Hamas hounded Fatah members, arresting amongst others a senior Fatah official in Gaza. The 'Unity Government' could not last and one year later it collapsed after protests from Hamas. Since then a somewhat optimistically termed 'consensus government' has limped along under Abbas with little or no Hamas involvement.

There was a considerable rationale behind the need to bring the major divisions amongst the Palestinians together to form a united position from which to negotiate. But it was not simply the irreconcilable differences between them that interfered with progress. There was much else going on, not least the profound changes elsewhere in the Middle East.

The Arab Spring

Much has been written about the so-called 'Arab Spring' and here I will concentrate on its impact on Israeli–Palestinian relations. Starting in an isolated incident in Tunisia in 2010 it rapidly spread to Egypt, where it had its most significant impact. There, the largely young, idealistic population gathering peacefully in Cairo's Tahrir Square were used by the Muslim Brotherhood to take advantage of the uproar. President Mubarak was deposed and put in jail as a traitor while Mohamed Morsi took on the presidency.

Fearful though the monarchs in Saudi Arabia, Jordan and Morocco were, they managed to survive with a range of concessions. Assad clung on in Syria by other means. He slaughtered large numbers of dissidents. And in Bahrain the rulers did not suffer the opposition gladly either.

In Egypt Morsi soon overplayed his hand by granting himself unlimited powers, clamping down hard on journalists and putting down peaceful protests with severe brutality. Protests grew even louder and it was their strength that caused his dismissal in a military coup just twelve months after he took office. He was succeeded by a military council headed by Abdel Fatah el-Sisi, who, a short time later, assumed the office of President. He in turn has been harsh in his treatment of the opposition, largely in the Muslim Brotherhood.

Spring turned to winter and by 2013 popular democracy was visible in very few places. Tunisia, where the local Muslim Brotherhood has seemed willing to make some compromises, may be the one exception.

CHAPTER 24

In the Eye of the Storm

ABBAS AND NETANYAHU WARILY watched the drama unfolding around them and tried to calculate its impact on their own negotiating positions. But worse was to follow.

The American-led war in Iraq in 2003 was regarded by some as a success but the aftermath was soon seen to be disastrous. Little thought or preparation had been made by the allies about how to deal with the vacuum that ensued, and during 2006–7 it was filled by the sectarian conflict between Shia and Sunni Muslims. This conflict became a fertile ground for the development of several groups of extreme Islamists at loggerheads with each other. One of them evolved in 2014 into Islamic State, otherwise known as ISIL (Islamic State of Iraq and the Levant) or ISIS (Islamic State of Iraq and Syria) or Daesh (an Arabic acronym), and that year saw this fundamentalist group, wedded to a Salafi doctrine of Sunni Islam, gaining ground in an Iraq that was virtually ungovernable. Its sickening acts of public executions seen on television across the world caused horror and revulsion. Its actions soon distracted international attention, at least for a short while, from the Israeli clash with Gaza in 'Operation Protective Edge' in 2014.

Of equal significance, and with a potentially greater long-term impact in the Middle East, has been the infiltration by large numbers of Iranian-supported Shia militant groups into Syria and Iraq. It is now estimated that there are several thousand such militants in over sixty groups spread across Iraq. As and when IS is defeated it seems likely that Iran will have achieved something it was never able to do in all its wars with Iraq, namely annexation of a major part of it.

It is these events, both realised and potential, that were exercising the imaginations of Abbas and Netanyahu between 2012 and 2015. Which way should they jump? As always, there were at least two schools of thought. The first was for one or other of the two parties to move quickly to try to resolve their differences while the world around them was in such disarray. It would have taken an extremely brave and possibly foolhardy leader to adopt that line. The other was the more cautious approach. The impossibility of predicting the outcome of the Arab Spring must have weighed heavily. What, for example, would be the position of Jordan if King Abdullah was deposed? Would the Muslim Brotherhood have taken over as they did in Egypt? Or, more likely, another extreme group? Or just possibly, a more secular regime? In any case Israel would become even more wedded to strengthening its security arrangements in the West Bank and Abbas would be calculating whether his own regime was in jeopardy. In short, what would a different Jordan have meant for Israel's security and Palestinian independence?

Then there were the worries posed by the Muslim Brotherhood takeover in Egypt. Its alignment with Hamas in Gaza made Israel even less willing to make concessions to the Palestinians, particularly if Hamas gained ground in the West Bank. Egyptian support for jihadists in the Sinai was of no comfort either. All that was to change with the fall of Morsi and the suppression of the Muslim Brotherhood when Sisi took over but these are the factors that must have made Abbas and Netanyahu nervous of taking any steps towards reconciliation.

The totally unstable situation in Iraq and Syria, with their toxic mix of rebel groups, Islamic jihad and Iranian interference, was watched with growing apprehension in Israel and the West Bank but, as we will see in the next chapter, a silver lining to these clouds was just appearing.

Fighting In Gaza

The prospects for meaningful negotiations between Abbas and Netanyahu were not made easier by the continuing provocation by Hamas in Gaza and were further worsened when Israel responded severely in the 2014 invasion. 'Operation Protective Edge', launched on 8 July 2014, was the third major incursion by the IDF into Gaza. Previous engagements, 'Operation Cast Lead' in 2008–9, during Ehud Olmert's premiership, and 'Operation Pillar of Defence' in 2012, had seriously undermined efforts to maintain discussions with Abbas. But the 2014 war was even more destructive in more ways than one.

There are at least two narratives about the causes of these conflicts. The Palestinian narrative is based on the blockade by Israel (interpreted by many as occupation), the strict limitation on their movement in and out of Gaza and the frequent killings of Hamas personnel. Israel's view is coloured by a Hamas charter that is uncompromising in its aim to destroy Israel, by the huge number of rocket attacks on Israel and by the construction of tunnels with the sole aim of striking at soldiers and civilians alike deep within Israel.

Ever since Sharon's unilateral withdrawal from Gaza in 2005, Hamas had been busily firing rockets into Israel. Then, in 2006, in a raid through their tunnels under the border into Israel they killed three Israeli soldiers and kidnapped Corporal Gilad Shalit. He became a *cause célèbre* until his release after five years in exchange for 1,027 Palestinian prisoners.

It was the constant rain of rockets from Gaza, several thousand over some years, together with the specific exacerbations of Hamas actions, that finally prompted the three armed responses. The toll of Palestinian deaths and casualties has been contrasted with the relatively smaller number of Israeli dead and injured and accusations of lack of proportionality have been levelled at Israel as a consequence. The Goldstone Report to the UN after the 2012 war and the report by

Amnesty International after 2014 were uncompromising in their accusations of Israel's 'war crimes'. Although Goldstone later retracted his support for the report bearing his name, the mud has stuck.

The validity of both reports is questionable on a number of grounds. Neither took account of the tactics of a Hamas that had been firing numerous rockets into Israel for some time, had been smuggling arms into Gaza, largely through tunnels from Egypt, had attacked and killed Israelis via their tunnels and instead of protecting their civilian population had deliberately placed them in the front line against Israel's attacks. And suggestions of a lack of proportionality take no account of the efforts that Israel took to protect its citizens with shelters in every home and the deployment of anti-missile technology such as the Iron Dome. In contrast Hamas used schools and hospitals from which to launch rockets, and ordered civilians not to flee when Israel warned them of an attack through telephone calls, leaflets and small arms 'knocks on the roof'. Little wonder that there were many more Palestinians killed than Israelis.

Of course, the parlous position of the citizens of Gaza is devastating and restrictions on their entry and exit, made worse by the closure of the Rafah Crossing into Egypt, has had a profound effect on their morale. But around 2,000 civilians from Gaza come through the Erez Crossing into Israel every day for business or family visits and for medical care. A visit to Israeli hospitals reveals many children, with their parents, from Gaza being cared for in cardiac surgery and cancer care wards. Although life expectancy and infant mortality rates are no worse than those of Jordan, Egypt and Saudi Arabia the health of children in Gaza is worrying and restrictions on their water supply and sewage disposal must play a part.

Can Israel bear all the blame for this? The fact that Hamas clamped down hard on UNESCO when it tried to install a desalination plant with equipment and expertise derived from Israel suggests that Hamas is not entirely blameless. The failure of the PA to send across medical supplies that Israel has provided and the block imposed by Hamas on the transfer of a huge consignment of bottled water that Salam Fayyad had authorised are hardly likely to help Gaza's children. And diversion of cement and building materials, meant for rebuilding homes, to the construction of tunnels into Israel only damages their citizens further.

Hamas has not been aided either by Sisi in Egypt, who has clamped down on its ally, the Muslim Brotherhood, and has been waging a war on Al Qaeda and other jihadist groups in the Sinai. As a result Hamas has found its tunnels into Egypt blocked and smuggling severely curtailed. It now faces even more difficulties yet its anti-Israel rhetoric has not softened.

Israel meanwhile continues to maintain the blockade on goods that may be used for military purposes while allowing food and humanitarian aid across. Its recent agreement with Turkey to allow it to send aid to Gaza via Ashkelon and to assist with the development of a desalination plant and electrical generator are positive steps. A similar agreement in 2010 would have avoided the *Mavi Marmara* disaster when the Turks tried to break the blockade by sea.

The lack of any coherence between Hamas and the PA and the outright rejection by the former of any negotiation with Israel cast even longer shadows on the prospects for an agreement with the Palestinians. Even if there is ever a settlement of Israel's differences with the PA there will remain an isolated belligerent Hamas opposed to both parties. That prospect has yet to be faced but it must have played on the minds of Olmert and, later, Netanyahu, as well as Abbas.

CHAPTER 25

Public Pressures and Government Constraints

THE COLLAPSE OF THE Camp David negotiations in 2000 followed by the second intifada heralded a marked deterioration in the 'peace process'. Negotiations had begun with high hopes with the Oslo I Accord of 1993, but efforts to re-start them, at Annapolis in 2007–8 and by John Kerry, Obama's Secretary of State, in 2013–14, ultimately failed. Now neither the Israeli nor Palestinian leadership gives the impression that they want to resolve their differences. Netanyahu often seems to follow the dictum of Yitzhak Shamir, who spoke of 'managing' the conflict rather than resolving it. The source of Abbas's reluctance to negotiate is complex but he has been even more unwilling in recent years. Equally, there seems little doubt that a majority of the population on both sides want peace although for a minority the price demanded by the other side has been too high.

That compromises will be necessary is accepted by most Israelis and Palestinians. That has not prevented their leaders putting seemingly impossible barriers in the way. If a resolution was easy it would have been agreed long ago. Misunderstandings, misconceptions and lack of trust have compounded the basic problem of incompatible aims.

The fact that few Palestinians have met an Israeli who is not a soldier in full battle gear and that most Israelis see Palestinians as knife-wielding terrorists does little to improve understanding and tolerance. According to polls in December 2015, 82 per cent of Palestinians thought that Israel's goal is to extend its borders from the sea to the river Jordan and 25 per cent think that they aim to deny the political rights of the Palestinians.[1] Of the Israelis 43 per cent believe that the Palestinians aspire to conquer Israel and destroy most of the Jewish population. Two peoples, each with a legitimate claim to the same piece of land, has not been the best place from which to start and the constraints posed by domestic pressures within Israel and the Palestinian Territories weigh on their leaders.

Pressures In Israeli Society

Israel's society is rich in diversity but has a common thread in that everyone has an opinion about how to run the country better than the government. The generally accepted divisions of society into right and left are only loosely relevant in Israel where they mainly apply to views on Israel's relationship with the Palestinians. The right is usually taken to include the settler movement, of whom many, but by no means all, are also orthodox, while the orthodox religious Jewish groups include the ultra-orthodox and Haredi communities. Some Haredim are not Zionistic and will not accept Israel's existence until the Messiah arrives. The left, on the other hand, are largely secular and tend to be of western European, Ashkenazi origins. These are very broad generalisations and include many exceptions and further divisions. Those of eastern Mediterranean, Sephardic origins tend to be on the right and are often observant Jews but the more recent Russian immigrants, although also on the right, are more likely to be secular. They are divided still further by geography. The secular left are found mainly in Tel Aviv and Haifa while the right congregate in Jerusalem and each regards the other as living in an unreal bubble.

There is, of course, the usual domestic divide between the 'haves' and the 'have-nots', between the rich and the poor. Three years ago a protest movement gathered momentum against the inequalities in

Israeli society. Large numbers of young protesters 'sat in', demanding more equitable wages and lower prices for basic foods and housing. This soon fizzled out as winter arrived.

The demography of Israel is intriguing. Of the roughly 8 million Israeli citizens, about a million arrived from Russia in 1991 after the collapse of the USSR, a few thousand from Ethiopia who came in two waves in 1984 and 1991, and now an increasing number are reaching Israel from France. There are over 400,000 settlers in the West Bank, although most of these live around Jerusalem. Within Israel there are about 1.2 million Israeli Arabs, mostly Sunni Muslims but including some 10 per cent who are Christian. There are about 180,000 Bedouin in the Negev and Galilee while the Druze comprise some 125,000 plus 20,000 more who have retained Syrian nationality living in the Golan. Small numbers of other sects, groups and religions, including those of the Baha'i faith, whose World Centre is based in Haifa, make up the rest.

The position of Israeli Arabs is complex and disconcerting. About 12 per cent regard themselves as Palestinians, albeit with Israeli citizenship. Many have a schizophrenic view of Israel. Some call themselves Palestinian Israelis, some simply Palestinian, while others are equally wedded to Israel. They know that their standard of living and education is higher than elsewhere in the Middle East and that they have the rule of law and greater freedoms than in most Arab states. But they have family members and friends in the West Bank or refugee camps further afield and when their relatives express their anger and frustration it is hard for Israeli Arabs to stay aloof. Adding to their feelings of alienation is a sense that the status of many in Israeli society is that of second-class citizens. Despite this perception, Arab Muslim citizens occupy high office in academia, medicine and the law as well as in the Knesset, and efforts by the government in recent years to encourage and support their development are bearing fruit. But much remains to be done.

Christian Arabs do not quite fit this picture. Their numbers are growing in Israel, perhaps the only country in the Middle East where this is the case, and they are well integrated into Israeli society. A Supreme Court judge, a Minister of Education, 10 per cent of the Judiciary and many of the country's doctors and academics are Christian Arabs, and they are also well placed in the hi-tech industry, the arts and government officialdom.

The future sustainability of the state is dependent on the children now growing up yet there are some potential concerns. Some 50 per cent of children now entering school are from the growing Haredi and Arab populations. Neither of these groups serve in the armed forces and that immediately leads to the conclusion that 50 per cent of school leavers in twelve years' time will not be involved in defending the state. It is not clear whether the government has a plan to deal with this issue or whether it is a serious concern as the growth of both communities continues.

It is in the attitude to the Palestinians where the major distinction between right and left appears and here the population can be roughly divided along 'hawk' and 'dove' lines. Many on the right, especially the orthodox, believe that the whole of the land of Israel, including Judea and Samaria, belongs to the Jews, while the left are more favourably disposed towards a two-state solution in which the West Bank and Gaza are handed over to Palestinian sovereignty. It is a commonplace that any two Jews will have three opinions but an opinion poll in July 2016 revealed a majority in favour of a two-state solution and this was true of both right-wing Jews (51 per cent) and those on the left (74 per cent). The overall majority was 60 per cent with only 8 per cent favouring a one-state solution.[2] Although there was little knowledge or understanding of the Arab peace initiative, a large majority were in favour of a regional settlement involving other Arab states and would support the Prime Minister in embarking on a regional diplomatic effort. However, the public was unsupportive of a return of refugees to Israel.

Those on the left are vehemently opposed to the Netanyahu policies, believing him to be responsible for the failure to make any progress in the negotiations. And the Israeli human rights organisations, of which the best known is B'Tselem, queue up to offer criticism of

Israel's actions in the Palestinian Territories. But despite the fact that there are many nuances in the societal divisions mentioned above, and despite individuals and families voicing their differing views often and loudly, there is a surprising degree of agreement on the idea of two states for two people. But most Israelis see the Middle East as a fragile, threatening environment and seek increased security from their leaders, at least in the short term. There is also an unfortunate perception amongst Israelis that the Palestinians do not want a resolution and as always it is in the detail and implementation where the alligators lie.

Pressures in Palestinian Society

Here there are not the multiple sects, interest groups and religious divisions characteristic of Israeli society. There is a diminishing minority of Christians amongst a predominantly Sunni population that is neither extreme nor fundamentalist, at least in the West Bank. Western dress for women is not uncommon and the wearing of the burqa is unusual in West Bank cities. In a survey of 18–25-year-old Palestinians in the West Bank and Gaza in April 2016, only 48 per cent described themselves as religious, 45 per cent said they were moderately religious while 7 per cent were not religious at all.[3] Less than 2 per cent of Palestinian youth believed that IS represents true Islam and amongst adults, 88 per cent agreed with the youth.[4]

Restriction of movement within a West Bank punctured by settlements and by the large Area C under Israeli military control is a continuing source of frustration that permeates Palestinian society. In his role as Middle East envoy, Tony Blair has done much to improve movement around the West Bank by removing most of the road-blocks and check-points. While there is relatively free movement into Jordan, travel into Israel is dependent on a restrictive permit system. Nevertheless, over 120,000 Palestinians have permits to work in Israel. Palestinians place much of the blame on Israel's 'occupation' but they are also increasingly disillusioned by their own leadership. Their failure to see any movement towards Palestinian statehood or to feel much improvement in their living conditions makes them resentful, leaving fertile soil in which to plant incitement to violence. Official Palestinian media put out a range of vicious anti-Israel and anti-Semitic messages aimed at the young; schools glorify terrorists by being named after them; and the families of Palestinians killed during attacks on Israelis are rewarded thereafter. Yet despite this incitement the survey of young Palestinians referred to earlier revealed that a clear majority would not participate in demonstrations if asked by Fatah or Hamas. Their main concerns were firstly unemployment, then personal freedom and safety and then the costs of education.[5]

The views of the Palestinian public are regularly and reliably monitored by the Palestine Center for Policy and Survey Research and they showed in June 2016 that support for armed attacks on Israelis was declining.[6] Expectations from confrontations were low and diminishing yet a majority believed that an intifada would be more likely than negotiations to achieve national rights.

It is now the case that Abbas's popularity stands at a very low level and two thirds of the population in Gaza and the West Bank want him to resign. Public opinion of Abbas is not improved by the corruption that 80 per cent believe is prevalent in the PLO hierarchy.[7] His failure to hold an election since 2006 has been heavily criticised. And a prominent critic of Palestinian human rights abuses, Bassem Eid, in his publications and media appearances, provides a long list of infringements of basic civil rights.[8] Abbas's appearance in Israel at Shimon Peres's funeral in 2016 won him only more antipathy amongst many Palestinians, especially in Hamas.

In Gaza there is a growing unhappiness with Hamas, but fear of reprisals makes dissent less overt. Here the public sees the battles with Israel as bringing only more death and destruction while it is recognised that materials intended for housing re-construction are being diverted to building tunnels through which to attack Israel. The blockade of Gaza creates disillusion with Hamas and radicalisation against Israel. Palestinians here are caught in a nutcracker, squeezed on one side by Hamas's outright rejection of Israel's existence and on the other by Israel's security needs, played out in its heavy control of their daily lives.

How do these opinions in the public of both sides play out in their governments?

Constraints on the Governments

Israel's government is an extreme version of democracy in which any party that gains 3.5 per cent of the votes at an election is entitled to a seat in the Knesset. Anything more and the number of seats accepted from the party's list is increased in proportion to the number of votes cast. This type of proportional representation has led to a large number of small parties, many standing for single interest groups reflecting the multifarious background of Israeli society. It is inevitable that no party ever gains an outright majority and uneasy coalitions have to be formed. Bargains have to be struck and concessions offered before any potential leader can expect to gain a majority coalition. Room for manoeuvre is extremely constrained.

In 2016 the Knesset of 120 members had no less than ten distinct parties, six of which are on the government side with a total of sixty-seven seats, leaving four in opposition with fifty-three seats. There were seventeen Arab (including three Druze and one Bedouin) members of the Knesset. One of the Arab members has been a Deputy Speaker and while there are twelve Arab members of the Joint Arab List, three, surprisingly, belong to right-wing parties on the government side while two sit on the opposition benches.

Coalitions of this number of parties are always unstable. If, for example, the Jewish Home Party with its eight members, or the religious Shas Party with its seven members, were to switch sides Netanyahu's government would lose its majority and probably fall. Each of them has made demands that Netanyahu has struggled to meet at times. For example the religious parties have ensured that child benefits for their large families are maintained and that their children can avoid national service. Such domestic bargains determine the background with which Netanyahu has to contend and have to be taken into account should he try to negotiate with the Palestinians.

On the Palestinian side Mahmoud Abbas does not have it any easier although he has the capacity to be more autocratic. He has dismissed his ministers, including his Prime Minister, when he disapproves of them. Deeply unpopular, and, according to opinion polls, if there were to be presidential elections his Hamas rival, Ismail Haniyeh, would win, albeit by a small and decreasing margin.[9] The popularity of the parties, in contrast to their leaders, shows Fatah ahead of Hamas in the same polls. Other rivals are snapping at the heels of the ageing Abbas. The most popular and charismatic is Marwan Bargouti, currently serving life sentences in an Israeli jail for his part in the intifada and deaths of Israelis. The ex-Prime Minister Salam Fayyad, who was extremely popular in the West and in Israel for his efforts to try to reduce corruption in government and develop the infrastructure of a future state, is now even more unpopular than Abbas; only 2 per cent of the population would vote for him. Another rival, the charismatic Mohammad Dahlan, is known for his deep antipathy to Hamas, his attempt to clean up corruption and his personal wealth accumulated by uncertain means. He too is unpopular but both he and Fayyad have had plans for negotiation with Israel that may have determined their popularity abroad and some of their unpopularity at home. But anything seems possible in the slow and infrequent transitions of Palestinian leadership. Abbas, for example, became President after Arafat's long reign despite having a popularity rating of less than 5 per cent for much of the time before that.

Abbas meanwhile remains in charge and is able to prevent elections taking place. But he is regarded as too weak to take difficult decisions and at the age of eighty-one in 2016 he may think it best to simply sit it out. The distinct possibility that Hamas might have gained many seats in the municipal elections in late 2016 muddied the water still further until they were postponed indefinitely.

Abbas clearly lacks the leadership qualities of a Sadat or a Hussein. When King Hussein heard about the killing of seven young girls by a Jordanian in the upper Jordan valley, he immediately flew to Bet Shemesh, where they had lived, to kneel before the mothers of the girls. He ensured that his own media recorded the event and broadcast it to his people. And Sadat, even during the 1973 war that he regarded as a precursor of peace, ensured that his military did not gloat at Israeli deaths and that grieving Israeli mothers were shown sympathetically in Egypt. Contrast these leaders' efforts to condition their populations to peace with Abbas's incitement to violence in his population.

CHAPTER 26

External Affairs

THERE CAN BE LITTLE argument that Israel's key relationship is with the United States.

For many years it has relied heavily on the US for security, arms and funds and owes its very existence to that support. The large Jewish community in America has been both influential and financially supportive of Israel, although not always without questioning its policies. The relationship with America is not entirely one-way, however, since the US needs a democratic, pro-Western state in the Middle East to protect its interests there. Despite periods of strong disagreement between their leaders, the links between these allies have remained strong. But the links have been sorely tested during the Obama/Netanyahu era where relations have been seriously challenged and personal relations have reached a serious low. The two clearly have different personalities and approaches to policy and this has caused a damaging rift. Obama's frustration with Netanyahu may have contributed to one of his final acts as President in December 2016 in failing to veto UN Security Council Resolution 2334 that proposed making Israel's settlement policy illegal.

Characteristically cool and unemotional, Obama seems to have allowed anger to creep in to his actions and that is never a rational way to conduct business of such international importance. Senator Lindsay Graham described him as having 'gone from naïve and foolish to flat-out reckless'. He certainly should have recognised that prospects for peace negotiations may now have been set back further. Palestinian victories internationally are hardly likely to encourage them to engage in negotiations with Israel. Why negotiate when the UN can give them what they need? While giving Mahmoud Abbas little reason to negotiate it may also encourage Israel's hard right to resist Palestinian claims. Israel's settlement policy is counterproductive and needs to be resolved, but there is little evidence that the UN Resolution will bring peace any closer.

Despite this setback, American underlying support for Israel and its security continues to be firm. It remains to be seen what President Trump's plans for Israel and the Middle East will entail. His early remarks suggested that he will take a less confrontational approach to Israel, but it is uncertain whether he will have the interest, energy and commitment to press forward on a new peace initiative.

Meanwhile with the fractious Israeli coalition breathing down right-wing Netanyahu's neck and Abbas weak and unable or unwilling to take any risks, the chances of an imminent breakthrough seem remote. However, while making predictions in the Middle East is fraught, even for the next week, a series of movements now occurring across the region may lighten the general sense of depression.

On the one hand Abbas has given up on direct negotiations with Netanyahu. He does not trust him, pointing to the continuing settlement programme, Netanyahu's position on Jerusalem and the right of return of refugees and his failure to freeze settlement building are unacceptable. Abbas failed to respond to President Obama's direct plea for him to re-join the negotiations in 2014 and again, in 2016, refused to yield to pressure from John Kerry to meet with Netanyahu. Martin Indyk, Obama's negotiator, found that Abbas had 'shut down'. Instead he turned to the international community to try to gain approval to declare Palestinian statehood unilaterally. He has had some success in persuading some leaders to support him in the UN Security Council in December 2016 and that has certainly encouraged him. He has now suggested that he no longer feels obliged to be bound by the Oslo Accords, which in any case probably expired sixteen years ago, and is keen to see international pressure being brought to bear on Israel by promoting the boycott movement. In this he has been supported by a group of Palestinian intellectuals frustrated by the lack of progress.[1]

On the other hand Netanyahu has been repeating for some time that he will go anywhere at any time to negotiate with Abbas without any pre-conditions. That is, he will go to negotiation without pre-conditions but that does not mean he will have no conditions for an agreement once at the table. His position is well known and includes recognition by the Palestinians of Israel as a Jewish nation state. His starting positions on refugees, on Jerusalem and on borders are also well rehearsed but it is entirely feasible that this maximalist position, up against the Palestinian maximalist position, can only be the focus for negotiation. That presumably is the whole purpose of negotiation.

While Abbas remains resistant to meeting with Netanyahu, the Israeli Prime Minister can maintain his appearance as the more willing and reasonable partner for peace.

The Middle East

But now the shifting plates in the Arab world around them are offering opportunities to test Abbas's interest in negotiation and Netanyahu's understanding of an acceptable peace. Iranian nuclear ambitions are creating waves across the Middle East and even before the more recent appearance of IS on the scene, the threats posed by Iran to Saudi Arabia and Jordan were soon recognised as the same as those facing Israel. Common security threats have drawn these countries closer to Israel and now there is an obvious thawing of relationships.

The 'cold peace' with Egypt has warmed and the visit in July 2016 of the Egyptian Foreign Minister, Sameh Shoukry, to meet Netanyahu in Jerusalem (not Tel Aviv) is a dramatic demonstration of the change. And the invitation for Netanyahu to Egyptian embassy celebrations in Israel underlined the acceptance of the need for closer working relations. Quite apart from the rattling of nuclear sabres by Iran, both countries face similar threats from the Muslim Brotherhood and its offshoot Hamas as well as a variety of jihadist groups operating in the Sinai desert. Egypt has been working closely with Israel to try to prevent arms smuggling into Gaza, clearing tunnels into Egypt and the Sinai and keeping a very close watch on the Rafah Crossing. Security cooperation in the Sinai is now operating at a high level and is largely effective. And President Sisi is now pressing hard to facilitate a meeting between Abbas and Netanyahu.

Relations between Saudi Arabia and Israel are also changing. Contact has been historically distant and it remains the case that travel for Saudis to Israel is officially banned, as it is for Israelis wishing to visit Saudi Arabia. Israel is still referred to there as the 'occupied territories'. Yet there has been a slowly evolving change in attitudes. The offer, in the 2002 Arab Peace Initiative, of a 'normalisation' of relationships if there was an Israeli–Palestinian agreement came out of the Arab League's leadership under the then Prince, later King, Abdullah of Saudi Arabia. Acceptance that Israel could not be defeated militarily may have played on the minds of the members of the Arab League then. They may also have wanted to gain some credence with President Bush and in any case the offer was carefully worded so that Israel would find little to rush to accept. The Initiative, as I describe later, was reiterated and softened a little in 2007 and was followed, in 2014, by an op-ed article in Israel's *Ha'aretz* by Prince Turki al-Faisal of Saudi Arabia, giving an interesting indicator of the trajectory of travel. The visit to Israel by the former Saudi government advisor Anwar Eshki in July 2016, and the photograph of him shaking hands with Israel's director general of the Ministry of Foreign Affairs, Dore Gold, at an earlier meeting in Washington must clearly have had his government's approval. The Saudi visiting delegation of businessmen and academics who accompanied him, ostensibly to discuss security and the Arab Peace Initiative, was followed by a remarkable bonus for Israel when one member,

Abd al-Mujid al-Hakim, spoke later on BBC Arabic about Israeli society embracing a culture of peace and that the picture portrayed in Arabian society of Israel as a nation seeking death to its enemies was erroneous.

The reduction of America's interest in playing an active role in the Middle East, its deal with Iran and its apparent weakness in its engagement with the Syrian crisis have also focused minds. They have made the Saudis recognise that they can no longer rely on America to help sort out the Israeli–Palestinian conflict. And the new generation of Saudi leaders under King Salman are taking a more pragmatic and less purely religious approach to Israel.

Jordanian rulers have traditionally had more bonds with Israel than those of any other Arab state, despite having a high proportion of Palestinians within their population. Yet Jordan has often been a vocal critic of Israel's policies towards the Palestinians. The Temple Mount has also been the focus of tension. Although the Jordanian King has custodial rights over the Temple Mount the not infrequent clashes there between Israelis and Palestinians threaten peaceful relations with Jordan. However, now, more than ever, Jordan has a need for increased security collaboration with Israel while IS is breathing down its neck in Iraq and threats from Syria continue to loom. Trade and commerce are also increasingly the focus of joint activities. A law allowing investment by foreign countries in Jordan, including by Israel, the 'investment law', was passed in July 2016 and there have been recent agreements on gas and water cooperation. Discussions in Amman between an Israeli delegation and Jordanian ministers, including the Prime Minister, Hani al-Mulki, included a major deal on gas supplies to Jordan. A re-vitalisation of a water-sharing partnership to include the Palestinians is also testament to the bolstering of the relationship. But the strength of popular opinion against deals with Israel and the sensitivity over the Temple Mount will make it difficult for a domestically weak King Abdullah to take more than a supporting role in the Arab Peace Initiative.

There are signs of a Turkish rapprochement too. The *Mavi Marmara* escapade, aimed at breaking the Gaza blockade, marked the low point in Turkey–Israel relations. Not strong before that, President Erdoğan broke off all contacts after it. He remained a vocal critic until the recent tumultuous events in the Middle East changed all attitudes. He became increasingly beleaguered by strained relations with Russia after Turkey shot down a Russian plane straying into its air space, and by the deteriorating situation in Syria. He faces a dilemma there, for the rebel forces and the Kurds are both fighting against the Syrian regime yet Turkey is supporting one but battling against the other. Erdoğan has recognised that he does not need another adversary in an Israel that poses no threat whatsoever to him. Netanyahu's apology for the *Mavi Marmara* incident and the proposed offer of compensation have paved the way for reconciliation. The failed coup in Turkey in August 2016 does not appear to have interfered with its relationship with Israel, fragile though that might be, and the appointment of a new Israeli ambassador to Turkey is a further sign of a thaw.

America's distancing and cooler relations with Russia saw new alliances forming between Turkey and Saudi Arabia, Qatar and the United Arab Emirates, plus Israel. The agreement with Israel for Turkey to help build a desalination plant and electricity generation for Gaza with materials passed through Ashdod was one important outcome of the greater cooperation. New allies are also just visible on the horizon as leaders of the Kurdish opposition and other rebel groups in Syria make positive statements about Israel, and Netanyahu is busily trying to woo a number of African states. The Gulf states are following the Saudi lead and even though Qatari businessmen continue to fund Hamas its government denies involvement.

Of course, not all is sweetness and light between the Arab world and Israel, or even between the states themselves, but there is a sufficient commonality of interest to form a basis for another effort to involve them in trying to resolve the Israeli–Palestinian conflict.

The Arab Peace Initiative

Amongst the flurry of peace initiatives in 2016, the newly re-visited Arab Initiative is the most interesting. The French initiative of early 2017 and the earlier Quartet initiative are high-level schemes proposed from outwith the two protagonists yet neither has fully taken account of the fact that imposed solutions are doomed to failure. Both Israel and the Palestinians have to be directly involved in negotiating a deal that each can find acceptable. And increasingly the more pragmatic Arab states are a vital third party to any agreement.

The initial Arab Peace Initiative of 2002 came at a time when Israel was embroiled in an intifada. Coincidentally the day before it was announced an attack on a hotel in Netanya injured 170 and killed thirty Israelis. Clearly not a time when Israel was ready to accept a peace proposal from Arab countries. This initiative, penned by Prince Abdullah of Saudi Arabia and signed up to by ten of the Arab countries at Beirut, was a complete reversal of the Arab League's three 'Noes' of 1967. Ariel Sharon correctly portrayed it as a 'take it or leave it' proposal that had unacceptable conditions and reiterated Israel's preferred route of bilateral direct negotiations on the basis of Resolutions 242 and 338. It was not absolutely rejected but certainly not accepted.

What was on the table in 2002, and still was in 2016, was normal, peaceful terms with Israel, including full diplomatic relations, on the part of a large number of Arab states in exchange for a return to the pre-1967 borders (including the return of the Golan to Syria), East Jerusalem as the capital of a new and independent Palestinian state and a 'just solution' to the question of Palestinian refugees. Crucially the initiative did not seek 'right of return' of refugees to Israel, at least on the face of it. This did not stop Israeli critics from suggesting that after years of Arab antipathy to Israel they could not trust Arab proposals, that they would soon be overwhelmed by a large influx of returning Palestinians and that their security would be at risk, all in exchange simply for words without guarantees.

The critics may have remembered the words of Manuel Hassassian: 'In the Middle East the language of diplomacy is not supreme. The language of honour, faith, courage and sacrifice outweigh the Western-style art of give and take.'[2] Nevertheless, when the initiative was refreshed in 2007, Ehud Olmert, now Prime Minister, cautiously welcomed it. It is highly likely that if he had remained in office there would have been some further exploration of the opportunities offered. Netanyahu, who followed, was not so willing to pursue it even when, in 2013, the Saudis clarified the initiative further, pointing out that it was not written in tablets of stone but was negotiable and included, for the first time, the concept of 'land swaps' for some settlement blocks.

Then, in a remarkable article in the Israeli newspaper *Ha'aretz* in 2014, Prince Turki al-Faisal, a past Saudi ambassador to the UK and the USA, spoke of his vision for a successful peace initiative. He indicated that the Arab Peace Initiative was 'a template for peace' that was 'not simplistically prescriptive, but could be adjusted'. He went on to describe his vision of a future in which all Arab countries would establish normal relations with Israel in exchange for the conditions set out in the Arab Initiative, to be 'agreed in negotiations'.

> Imagine if I could get on a plane from Riyadh, fly directly to Jerusalem, get on a bus or taxi, go to the Dome of the Rock Mosque or the Al Aqsa Mosque, perform the Friday prayers, and then visit the Western Wall and the Church of the Holy Sepulchre. If the next day, I could visit the tomb of Abraham in Al-Khalil in Hebron, and the tombs of the other prophets … I could go to visit Yad Vashem Holocaust Center and Museum … And what a pleasure it would be to be able to invite … Israelis I would meet to come and visit me in Riyadh, where they can visit my ancestral home … Just imagine too how commerce, medicine, science, art and culture between our two people would develop.[3]

All this was a nightmare for the Palestinians. But al-Faisal clearly saw the advantages of a Middle East that was able to take advantage of the advanced state of Israel's science and technology. Given its leading role in hi-tech, in cyber-security and in medicine and with its array of world-leading scientists and Nobel prize winners it could enrich the wider Middle East and make it a strong trade and innovation block to rival others around the world. A tantalising prospect and what a change from the Arab League 'Noes' of 1967.

Arafat immediately accepted the Arab Peace Initiative in 2002 while Hamas was divided in its response. Some rejected it outright and others were more measured. The Syrian leadership initially objected strongly but signed up to it when it included return of the Golan Heights. Now it is in no position to express a view.

But it is in Netanyahu's and Abbas's attitudes where the issues lie.

CHAPTER 27

Options for Peace

HERE WE MUST EXAMINE the options for a peaceful resolution, leaving aside two unattractive and, to me, unacceptable propositions that are sometimes posited. Firstly, the 'do nothing' idea that, in the belief of some on the right in Israel, the status quo is both sustainable in the long run and desirable. Secondly, the view of Hamas and others that Israel as a Jewish state has no place in the Middle East and should be destroyed. I will not consider these further.

A thorough analysis of all previous peace plans was published in 2004 by Shmuel Bar and his colleagues in the 'Herzliya Papers'.[1] Despite the many variations on the theme, the reasons for failure spelt out in the analysis make sobering reading.

One State, Two States, Federation and Confederation

ONE STATE

Binationalism, or 'one-state-ism', has a long history. Peaceful coexistence between Jew and Arab was certainly in the minds of those in the British Government putting the Balfour Declaration forward and Weizmann and Ben Gurion had briefly toyed with the idea but soon rejected it as unworkable. It repeatedly emerged in the writings of Jewish intellectuals during the 1920s and 1930s. Martin Buber and Judah Magnes, in the 1920s, were sold on the idea of Arab and Jew living in harmony in a unified state. Such a state at that time would have had a minority of Jews, about 160,000 versus 650,000 Arabs, and critics soon pointed out that Jews had had enough of being a minority in countries that were not always favourably disposed towards them. In any case this utopian dream was then shattered by the complete rejection of Jewish immigration by Palestinian Arabs and repeated attacks in which many Jews were killed, underlining their opposition to any suggestion of a shared state.

The idea has re-emerged in recent years when optimistic Western visions based on internationalism, secularism and democracy have been used in arguments in its favour. The historian Tony Judt wrote of the death of the nation state and of Israel's current dysfunctional and 'undemocratic' hegemony. A unified state with equal rights for all was the only answer in his view and, although the Palestinians were not keen on his idea of a secular state, many strongly supported the principle. They and the Israelis could readily see that in a very short time Arab numbers would overwhelm the Jewish population and the Jewish state would no longer exist. Leaving aside the problem of changing birth rates and unreliability of demographic projections, it has been calculated that the current Israeli population of 5.4 million Jews and 1.3 million Arabs would, by 2020, be converted into a country of 15.5 million citizens of whom 8.8 million would be Arabs and 6.4 million Jews. This was hardly likely to appeal to the Jews of Israel, who note the continuing incitement to violence of young children in Palestinian Arab schools. Virginia Tilley, a strong protagonist for a one-state solution, side-steps the issue of Palestinian hatred of the Jews, suggesting that it is after all the Jews' own fault anyway.[2] The examples of Yugoslavia, where ethnic groups were held uneasily together before it descended into a violent split, and South Africa, where the white population is shrinking, do not give much confidence to Israeli Jews. They fear too that the end result will just be another Arab state amongst many.

There are other variations on the single-state solution. Some sort of power-sharing arrangement, joint administration or rule by some external body such as the UN or a great power have been muted. None have found any interest amongst Palestinians or Israelis. Rule by one or the other side, one in the minds of Hamas and the other favoured by ultra-orthodox Jews, is a non-starter as neither side would accept the other's idea of their disappearance from the land.

The most serious ideas about a one-state solution have been advanced by Sari Nusseibeh.[3] As a moral philosopher he wonders if, when Jews and Arabs kill each other for religious values, it is not time to re-evaluate those values. His ideas about a single state involve a distinction between citizenship and nationhood. Why, he suggests, would it not be possible for Palestinians to become citizens of a greater Israel but not have full Israeli nationality? Citizenship would give them all the rights to education, social support, property ownership and employment in Israel but not voting rights, election to government or army service. They would be 'second class citizens' but with sufficient rights to feel as comfortable in Israel as any expat in any country. He thus places human rights higher than religion or nationality. But there are major problems with this idealistic proposal. Israeli suspicion of Palestinian motives and actions would be difficult if not impossible to overcome and there is unlikely to be much appetite amongst Palestinians for anything less than a state of their own. Could it happen at some far distant future? I remain doubtful.

For me, the one-state solution remains a utopian dream, based as it is on the possibility that two peoples, who have spent very many years fighting for irreconcilable differences of opinion, can put those differences aside and live peacefully together. At best, that possibility is remote and in practice stretches credibility too far. It is why the Peel Commission in 1937 and later the UN concluded, albeit reluctantly, that the only workable solution was partition into two states.

TWO STATES

The idea of two states for two people does not have a happy history either. Partition into separate Jewish and Arab states in the Peel Report of 1937 and again in the UN plan of 1947 was only reluctantly accepted by Ben Gurion and Weizmann, who saw it as a further whittling down of the Jewish homeland they thought they had been offered in the Balfour Declaration. But they accepted the idea while the Palestinians and the other Arab states immediately and completely rejected it. They could not abide the thought of a Jewish state in the Middle East and the forced removal of Arabs envisaged in the Peel Report was hardly encouraging. That attitude persists today in Hamas's Charter and in the frequent outpouring of hatred from its leadership. Many Israelis still fear that it is also a deeply felt, if more heavily disguised, opinion of Fatah Palestinians in the West Bank. They remember that it was only in 1988 that Arafat, broken and in exile, began to contemplate the possibility of Israel existing in the Middle East and even then he obfuscated over the details of what that meant. His refusal in 2000 to sign up to the concessions offered by Barak that would have given him a state in the West Bank, including East Jerusalem, led President Clinton to lay the blame for failure of those talks squarely on his shoulders then and later. That was probably a diplomatic error and did nothing to encourage Arafat to consider concessions. But in his speeches in Arabic, Arafat was clear that he regarded any agreement on two states then as being the first phase in the struggle to take over all the land.

Now Israeli suspicions about Abbas's motives are heightened when he refuses to accept that Israel is a Jewish national state. It is hardly surprising then that there is a sense in Israel that the Palestinians are not serious about two states – unless, that is, Israel loses its Jewishness. It is the case, however, that the demand for recognition of Israel's Jewishness has only emerged in the last ten years. It was not an overt part of any negotiations before that, although Dennis Ross has said that it was tacitly understood at Camp David and it is hard to imagine that it has not always been the primary objective of the Zionists. It seems to the Palestinians to be yet another barrier. But their reluctance to accept it suggests to Israelis that their motives are to make Israel another Arab state in the fullness of time. The history of Jews, and

Christians, as minority groups in Arab states across the Middle East is never going to make the prospect appealing to Israelis. Nor does the experience of minority Arab groups at the hands of Sunnis and Shia give them any encouragement. And the unremitting incitement to hatred and violence in official Palestinian media and Palestinian schools convinces many in Israel that there is 'no partner for peace'.

On the other side the Palestinians find little or no encouragement to lower their stance and reach agreement with Israel while they see their potential state being eroded by the pace of settlement building, even though the great majority of building occurs within the boundaries of existing settlements. The concept of occupation does nothing to help Palestinians to move on from their profound antipathy to Israel.

It is the case then that, despite its desirability, neither side has much faith in the prospects for a two-state solution in the near future. The current leadership in Israel and in the PLO are doing little to prepare their people for such a prospect and opinion polls reflect the public's disillusion with what they perceive as the other side's view. Netanyahu is doing nothing to encourage confidence-building measures for the Palestinians while Abbas is not doing anything to curb the messages of hatred of Israelis and Jews in his media.

There are of course men and women of good will on both sides who strongly desire such an outcome. Unfortunately they are currently in a minority, especially on the Palestinian side, where there are few if any of the many movements like Peace Now or the Peres Peace Centre that are characteristically found in Israel.

Into this vacuum a number of alternative scenarios have emerged in an effort to break out of the inertia. A 'step-by-step' approach, in which confidence-building measures by Israel might be followed by movement on some of the dividing issues by the Palestinians, sounds like a rational idea. But it has been tried before, most notably after the Oslo Accords, and it failed miserably. Would it be worth trying again when there is so little confidence of success now?

One avenue that has been largely neglected in Israel is the potential of using the Israeli Arab community as a bridge between Israel and the Palestinians. There are many loyal Arab Israeli citizens who, given the right encouragement and support by the Israeli government, could provide a route to repairing the lack of understanding between these two peoples. However, it is the unfortunate case that such interlocutors might find themselves in danger from their Palestinian counterparts.

Then there is the prospect of a unilateral withdrawal by Israel from the West Bank and the building of a strong separation wall with security installations along the river Jordan. Something along those lines was recently proposed, somewhat surprisingly, by the leader of the Labour Party, Isaac Herzog, picking up the unilateralist ideas of Dan Schueftan in so doing. The experience of unilateral withdrawal from Gaza has, however, not left much appetite in Israel for such a proposition. It would have to include withdrawal from the outlying settlements, containing about 100,000 settlers. Compared with the extensive operation needed to remove 9,000 settlers from Gaza it would be no easy task even if the Israeli public could be convinced. The security issues posed by unilateral withdrawal would be enormous. It would accomplish a two-states position of sorts but only at considerable cost and would leave an unstable and belligerent state on Israel's long border. Even a negotiated withdrawal is unlikely to leave a less belligerent state behind.

FEDERATION OR CONFEDERATION

Ideas about federations, confederations and cantons have been floated from time to time. The most interesting has been the possibility of a confederation of Palestine with Jordan. It has been mooted since the formation of Israel in 1948 and indeed Jordan annexed the West Bank for almost twenty years thereafter. Arafat was not entirely averse to the idea but now the Hashemite King is very unlikely to see a dramatic increase in his Palestinian subjects with any equanimity. Nevertheless it might be attractive to Palestinians; but only after they have achieved independence.

More recently some kind of federation between Israel and the Palestinians of the West Bank and Gaza has been re-visited. Something of the sort had been proposed in 1946, when two cantons of a single state overseen by a British high commissioner were envisaged.

Current ideas about a federation rely heavily on the prospect that Israelis and Palestinians can forget their animosity and work closely together in a peaceful and harmonious dual entity. Each state with its own citizens would have porous borders allowing the free passage of those from one state to live and work in the other in a model not very dissimilar to that proposed by Sari Nusseibeh. There are indeed many examples of Israelis and Palestinians working closely together within Israel, particularly in the medical and scientific fields. Nurses and doctors from Gaza were trained at Hadassah Hospital in Jerusalem before returning home to set up a clinic for children with cystic fibrosis; professors from Hadassah run eye disease clinics at St John's Hospital in East Jerusalem and doctors from St John's train at Hadassah; patients from Gaza and the West Bank flood into Israeli hospitals; the Arava Institute in the Negev runs courses on environmental studies and takes equal numbers of Palestinian and Israeli postgraduate students, who live together on a kibbutz; and many Palestinians work in Israel. But these are all isolated examples and are often frowned upon by the PLO and Hamas, who have to turn a blind eye to allow these examples of collaboration to continue. Witness the case of the Joint Water Committee, set up to coordinate strategy on the water supply to the West Bank, which the PLO has boycotted for some years. The recent arrest by the PLO of four Palestinians who dared to accept an invitation by the Jewish mayor of Efrat to join him during the feast of Tabernacles does not suggest that Abbas has much appetite for conciliation.

The concept of a federation or confederation is based on a Western view of how people of different nations can live and work together and pays little attention to the hatred that seems likely to erupt if the two peoples were to mix freely. Incitement on the one side and fear of terrorism on the other will have to be overcome if there is to be any progress on federation.

Particularly depressing is the failure of both governments to educate their children about the other side. Little wonder that misunderstanding of the other is so prevalent. The recent vote in Britain to remove itself from the EU, largely because of a fear of immigration, suggests that it is not only in the Middle East that mistrust of the 'other' is prevalent.

CHAPTER 28

What Would A Final Status Agreement Look Like?

DESPITE THE GLOOMY PICTURE I have described above I believe that there are signs of what a realistic settlement might look like now and how it might be achieved. I suspect I will be accused of unrealistic optimism in putting such ideas forward but I do so because I cannot believe, as some appear to do, that the status quo is sustainable in the long run. A start has to be made from somewhere.

The constituent parts of an agreement have been clear for some time and look very much like the outline of a number of peace plans as well as the Clinton Parameters of 2000. Both sides had reservations then and it is in the detail and the implementation where problems arose, and in the will to see it achieved.

Near agreement has been reached in past negotiations and presumably could form the basis of new agreements. On borders, the 4 June 1967 'Green Line' was always recognised as being adjustable and acceptable, albeit only reluctantly by the UN now. Debates have focused on what percentage of land in the West Bank should be handed over by Israel. Somewhere between 91 per cent and 97 per cent has been mooted while the idea of land swaps for the large settlement blocks around Jerusalem has not been rejected outright. Arafat argued for 100 per cent of the West Bank and Gaza yet it does not seem beyond the realms of possibility that, depending as it would on modest moves on percentage of land, an agreement could be reached dependent on compromises on both sides.

The nature and extent of security arrangements have been vital for Israel as it contemplates another potentially hostile state on its long border; the more security arrangements, the less Palestinian sovereignty. Although contentious, previous discussions have not fallen on this issue alone. A demilitarised Palestinian state, at least for a number of years, and a defensive system along the river Jordan have been Israel's prerequisites. But the nature of the Jordan defence has ranged from a wide security zone to a mixed Israeli and international monitoring system. Again, somewhere within these possibilities the kernel of an agreement lies. The predominant concern now is not military attack along the river but the smuggling of arms from Iran and its proxies to terrorist groups who would threaten Jordan and the Palestinians as much as Israel.

The two most contentious issues have always been the arrangements for Jerusalem and the right of return of refugees. Netanyahu has stated that Jerusalem will remain the undivided capital of Israel while the Palestinian position is that it belongs in total to the Arabs in general and the Palestinians in particular. Not much room for manoeuvre there. But that has not always been the case, and a number of models of division into East and West, Muslim and Jewish halves, have been presented. Debates about complicated demarcation lines, including horizontal divisions, above and below the Temple Mount, as well as topographic sections, have been endless. And quite apart from what part of the city might belong to which state there is the thorny issue of which party should have sovereignty over the Holy Basin and the Temple Mount, and whether some sort of religious oversight might suffice. An international federation of relevant countries to oversee this focus that is so central to the beliefs of all the major religions has also been in the mix. Every proposal has been found to be unacceptable to one or other party or, more commonly, to both of them.

But the fact that such discussions have taken place at all suggests that somewhere amongst these suggestions lies a compromise that might just be acceptable to both sides when their leaderships climb out of their bunkers.

The pressure for the return of Palestinian refugees has been hyped up by Abbas's talk of the right for every individual and their descendants to reclaim homes in Haifa and Jaffa. Israel's position has been that the refugees, now the children and grandchildren of the original refugees, should be absorbed either into the countries where they currently reside or into the West Bank and Gaza of the putative Palestine. Small numbers could be accommodated in Israel in the case of the elderly or for re-unification of families already in Israel and compensation should be paid for others. Acceptance by the Palestinians of this scenario has proved impossible thus far.

For Israel, a major practical sticking point will be withdrawal from the settlements. Even if the large blocks around Jerusalem remain within Israel there is still the difficulty of what to do with up to 100,000 settlers deep in the West Bank. These are predominantly ideologically driven Israelis, strong in their belief that the West Bank is part of a greater Israel. Numerically a small proportion of the total population, they exert political power beyond their numbers such that even a left-wing government might find it almost impossible to move them. The problem is compounded by the fact that many in the army are from settler communities and it is they who will have to do the removing.

Breaking the Deadlock

If Israel and the Palestinians are ever to break the mould of inertia they have made for themselves they will need international support.

In a wider world distracted by internal tensions caused by stagnant living conditions and inequalities, with rising support for populism and nationalism in the West and the march of authoritarianism in such countries as Turkey, Russia and China, it is little wonder that

Palestinian and Israeli matters have not been at the forefront of interest. Traditionally support has come from the USA but a mixture of the stand-off between Netanyahu and Obama and Abbas's sloth in showing any sign of movement towards negotiation has seen America on the sidelines as Obama has curtailed his interest in intervening in the Middle East. It will be vital for Israel's leaders now to make fresh efforts to capture the interest of President Trump in the peace process. The Palestinians will listen warily to the words of the new President and watch fearfully his actions as it seems likely that he will reduce his predecessor's pressure on Israel.

Although a majority of fruitful Middle East initiatives have started in the region, America's role will remain vitally important and not only in the negotiations themselves. Exerting pressure and inducements to aid negotiations and easing the costs of such difficult examples as compensation for refugees not returning to Israel and for the re-location of Israel's settlers will be critical.

The Egyptian Initiative

President Sisi's offer to host a joint meeting between Abbas and Netanyahu as the beginning of negotiations is an important development. Supported by Saudi Arabia, the Gulf states and Jordan, it has to be taken seriously. If Abbas had been fearful for his life if he was seen to be negotiating with Israel, here is some reassurance that not only are these Arab countries not opposed to him doing so, they are exerting pressure for him to engage. This is an opportunity for him to call Netanyahu's bluff that he really is serious about negotiations 'without pre-conditions' and to take advantage of support from his Arab neighbours.

Some hope lies again in the fact that the Arab Peace Initiative is being re-visited. For Israel, gaining normal and full diplomatic relations with fifty-seven Arab countries would be a seismic change and is a carrot that must be tempting. The Organisation for Islamic

Cooperation includes Iran as member. Although it abstained from the vote, it is remarkable that it did not object. The presumed 'take it or leave it' condition of 2002 has been softened but that has not stopped Netanyahu pouring cold water on the initiative, probably to retain his right-wing support.

The issue has caused a profound split in the Knesset. Some ministers have dismissed it as so much spin but Netanyahu's misgivings are not all entirely invalid. He sees the initiative as a distraction from, rather than a contribution to, the bilateral negotiations that will be necessary. He points out that the suggestion to withdraw to the pre-1967 borders would include handing back the Golan Heights to a dysfunctional Syria. He interprets the 'just solution' to the refugee problem as meaning a return of them all to Israel, choosing to ignore the phrase 'by agreement with the parties' that accompanies this proposal. He has no confidence that the initiative is not an ultimatum, a 'take it or leave it' proposal, despite efforts by the initiators to deny this. He may be correct in putting little trust in the Arab League when he remembers that Olmert's efforts to follow up on a line of communication were ignored by the League after an initial visit by an Egyptian representative. Perhaps too, the failure of the League to be an effective peace mediator between some of its own members was not encouraging. Iraq–Kuwait, Algeria–Morocco and Libya–Sudan are not good examples.

Many on the left in Israel, however, feel that none of these objections, even if partially valid, are sufficient reason to reject the initiative out of hand. It seems to me too that there is sufficient in the Arab League Initiative to warrant further exploration. It is, after all, a dramatic shift from the three 'Noes' of 1967. Former President Bill Clinton found difficulty understanding why Netanyahu ignored the opportunity in 2011. And now it is strongly supported by a series of past and present US Presidents as well as the Quartet.

Israel's mistrust of the Arab League cannot be simply dismissed. There is little said by the League about any confidence-building measures that might be offered to demonstrate its commitment. Why, for instance, has there been no slackening of the bar on Israeli, or even Jewish, visitors to most of those countries and why no offer of the possibility that Israel's commercial airliners could fly over them? The lack of any recognition of the security needs that are so central to Israel's concerns is unhelpful and perhaps the thought of all the Arab states coming together as a negotiating partner of the Palestinians is just too much for Israel to face. Confidence-building measures will be necessary for both sides. Settlement freezes for the Palestinians might oil the wheels and for the Israelis provide some evidence that the words about 'normalisation' with Arab states have some substance.

To my mind the main advantage of this initiative is the support the Arab states may be able to offer to Abbas and the pressure they may be able to exert upon him to resume negotiations.

For Israel, the much more palatable offer by President Sisi to host a meeting between Netanyahu and Abbas is more realistic. However, the stand-off between Saudi Arabia and Egypt in late 2016 underlines the complexity of Middle East relationships. Whatever the cause, Israeli caution about forming a liaison with either is understandable.

So far, towards the end of 2016, Netanyahu has enthusiastically welcomed Sisi's offer while Abbas has remained resistant. Perhaps he is waiting to be convinced that the time is right for meaningful discussions or possibly for some encouraging confidence-building measures from Netanyahu. It would be a not unwelcome and practical sign by a man widely depicted as unyielding. Or perhaps Abbas is just not attracted to the idea of a small isolated Palestinian state standing precariously on its own two feet as the foreign aid that is its current foundation is withdrawn. His success at the UN Security Council in December 2016 will do little to encourage him to negotiate with Netanyahu and attitudes in Israel may well harden. This again is where the support of the UN, the USA and other wealthy nations can make the difference to attitudes.

My belief is that the two-state solution is the only viable option in town, but it is clear that the obstacles in the way are huge and the problems that have to be overcome seem at times to be insuperable for many of the reasons I have outlined. Reliance on the initiatives of others in the region is fraught but each opportunity has to be grasped when it arises. The fact that for the first time since the state of Israel was formed, many Arab states recognise not only its existence but also talk of it as a future partner in a commercially and culturally vibrant Middle East is remarkable.

These are tantalising glimpses of what the future could mean for Israelis and Palestinians. Will it take new leaders with fresh approaches? Probably. Will it take a long time? Certainly. Is the effort and heartache worthwhile? Absolutely.

Britain with the Balfour Declaration recognised the need for a Jewish homeland in Palestine. Now, 100 years later, Israel's Arab neighbours are offering to recognise a similar status for Israel's Jews. A fascinating bookend to this unfinished story.

Notes

INTRODUCTION

1. Hammond 2016; Tilley 2010.
2. Crossman 1947: 8.
3. For example Dershowitz 2004; Glick 2014.
4. For example Morris 1992; Shlaim 2001.
5. For example Pappé 2003; Chomsky and Pappé 2015.
6. Schneer 2010: 279 *et seq.*
7. Cockburn, Patrick 2016.
8. Shikaki, Khalil, personal communication.
9. Eban 1993: 24.
10. Taub, Daniel, personal communication.
11. Rifkind and Picco 2014: xvii *et seq.*
12. Nusseibeh 2009.
13. Nusseibeh 2011.

CHAPTER 1: 1898–1923: TWENTY-FIVE YEARS OF TURMOIL

1. Shavit 2015: 13.
2. Wallach 1996: 77.
3. Doumani 1995: 52 *et seq.*
4. Hourani 1991: 308.
5. Roth 2016.
6. Fromkin 2009.
7. Schneer 2010: 253, 280 *et seq.*
8. Schneer 2010: 49.
9. Doumani 1995: 52 *et seq.*
10. Doumani 1995: 54.
11. Barr 2011: 118.
12. See Sykes–Picot Agreement text, 16 May 1916, available at https://unispal.un.org/DPA/DPR/unispal.nsf/0/232358BACBEB7B55852571100078477C (accessed 30 November 2016).
13. James 2011.
14. Sykes–Picot Agreement text, 16 May 1916.
15. 'Russia and secret treaties: terms published', *Manchester Guardian*, 26 November 1917.
16. 'Russia', *The Times*, 7 April 1881, p. 5.

17. 'Campaign for the return of the Jews to Palestine', *The Times*, 17 August 1840, p. 4.
18. Hodder [1886] 1971, vol. 1, p. 310.
19. Quoted in Stein 1983: 7.
20. Muir 2008.
21. Garfinkle 1991.
22. Weizmann 1949: 31.
23. Beller 1990.
24. Herzl [1896] 1988: 37.
25. Herzl [1896] 1988: 144.
26. Avineri 2013.
27. Dugdale 1936, vol. 1.
28. Adams 2007: 32 *et seq.*
29. Churchill 1942, p. 174–5.
30. Memorandum by Mr Balfour (Paris), 11 August 1919, Documents on British Foreign Policy (DBFP), vol. IV, no. 242, pp. 340–9.
31. Dugdale 1936, vol. 1, p. 433.
32. Dugdale 1936, vol. 1, p. 235.
33. Stein 1961: 502.
34. Beller 1990.

CHAPTER 2: THE BALFOUR DECLARATION

1. Dugdale 1936, vol. 2, p. 221.
2. Dearden 2016.
3. Dockter 2015: 172.
4. Stein 1961: 643.
5. Goodman 1945.
6. Macmillan 2001: 397 *et seq.*
7. Sanders 1984: 640.
8. Macmillan 2001: 397 *et seq.*
9. Wallach 1996: 66.
10. Pedersen 2015.
11. Muslih 1988.
12. Catherwood 2004.
13. *League of Nations Mandate for Palestine (Eretz-Israel). Together with a Note by the Secretary-General Relating to Its Application to the Territory known as Trans-Jordan. Under the Provisions of Article 25*, December 1922, Cmd 1785.

CHAPTER 3: MANY RESOLUTIONS BUT NO RESOLUTION

1. Pedersen 2015: 362.
2. Schechtman 1965.
3. *Palestine Royal Commission: Report*, Cmd 5479, July 1937.
4. Said and Hitchens 1988: 4.
5. *Palestine Partition Commission: Report*, Cmd 5854, October 1938.
6. *Palestine: Statement of Policy*, Cmd 6019, May 1939.
7. Hansard, HC Deb, 23 May 1939, vol. 347, cols 2167 *et seq.*
8. Chomsky and Pappé 2015.
9. Walton 2014: 101 *et seq.*
10. Machiavelli 1961.
11. Crossman 1947: 8.

12. Crossman 1960: 67.
13. *Resolution Adopted on the Report of the Ad Hoc Committee on the Palestinian Question: 181 (II) Future Government of Palestine*, A/RES/181(II), 29 November 1947.
14. United Nations Committee on Palestine 1947: 87.
15. Ross 2015: 6.
16. Weir 2014.

CHAPTER 4: WAR, ARMISTICE BUT FEW INTIMATIONS OF PEACE

1. Rafael 1981: 30.
2. Said Aly *et al.* 2013: 66 *et seq.*

CHAPTER 5: AT THE UNITED NATIONS

1. *Palestine – Progress Report of the United Nations Mediator*, A/RES/194(III), 11 December 1948.
2. Caplan 1993.

CHAPTER 6: MORE WARS AND ABORTIVE PEACE PROPOSALS

1. O'Brien 1986: 391.
2. O'Brien 1986: 398.

CHAPTER 7: THE 1967 WAR

1. For example Hammel 1992; Oren 2003.
2. S/RES/242, 22 November 1967.

Unispal.un.org/DPA/DPR/unispal.

3. 'Security Council Resolution 242 According to Its Drafters', CAMERA, 15 January 2007, www.camera.org/index.asp?x_context=2&x_outlet=118&x_article=1267 (accessed 5 December 2016).
4. Eban, Abba. 1968. The Nine Point Peace Plan – statement to the General Assembly by Foreign Minister Eban – 8th October – 1968. Israel Ministry of Foreign Affairs. Historical Documents, 1947–1974.
5. Ward Barnes, Sir Ernest John. The Intransigent Israel? Letter dated 18 November 1971. Archives of the British Foreign Office (FCO/17 1554).

CHAPTER 8: THE PALESTINIANS

1. Romirowsky and Joffe 2013.
2. Romirowsky and Joffe 2013: 59.
3. Romirowsky and Joffe 2013: 136.
4. *Assistance to Palestine Refugees*, A/RES/393(V), 15 December 1950.
5. Walker and Gowers 2003.
6. Palestinian National Charter (English version), 1–17 July 1968, available at www.iris.org.il/plochart.htm (accessed 5 December 2016).

CHAPTER 9: ANWAR SADAT TAKES OVER IN EGYPT, 1971

1. O'Brien 1986: 512 *et seq.*
2. O'Brien 1986: 512 *et seq.*
3. Avner 2010.
4. Raviv 1998.
5. Rafael, Gideon 1981: 322.
6. Ami Isseroff, 8 October 2009 in www.zionism-israel.com/dic/Agranat_commission.htm

CHAPTER 10: RABIN, BEGIN AND SADAT

1. Avineri 2015.
2. Anwar Sadat, speech to his parliament, 9 November 1977. Reported in Wright 2014: 21.
3. Dayan 1981: 38.
4. Dayan 1981: 46.
5. Peres 1995: 289.
6. Quoted in Gordis 2014.
7. 'Egypt–Israel Relations: Address by Egyptian President Anwar Sadat to the Knesset (November 20, 1977)', Jewish Virtual Library, www.jewishvirtuallibrary.org/jsource/Peace/sadat_speech.html (accessed 6 December 2016).
8. 'Menachem Begin Administration: Speech to Knesset Following Historic Speech by Anwar Sadat (November 20, 1977)', Jewish Virtual Library, www.jewishvirtuallibrary.org/jsource/History/begintoknessetsadat.html (accessed 6 December 2016).

CHAPTER 11: PRESIDENT CARTER AND CAMP DAVID

1. Brookings Middle East Study Group 1975.
2. Wright 2014.
3. 'A Framework for Peace in the Middle East Agreed at Camp David, 17 I.L.M. 1466 (1978)', available at hrlibrary.umn.edu/peace/docs/campdavid.html (accessed 6 December 2016).
4. Wright 2014.

CHAPTER 13: MORE LOST OPPORTUNITIES

1. Peres 1995: 361.
2. Abu Sharif 2009.

CHAPTER 14: TENTATIVE STEPS TOWARDS OSLO

1. Avineri 2015.
2. Beilin 1999.
3. Declaration of Principles on Interim Self-Government Arrangements, 13 September 1993. http://knesset.gov.il/process/docs/oslo_eng.htm
4. Waage 2007.
5. Speech by Yitzhak Rabin at the White House, 13 May 1993.
6. Text available at acpr.org.il/publications/books/44-zero-isr-pal-interim-agreement.pdf (accessed 7 December 2016).
7. Beilin 2004.

CHAPTER 15: HOW EXTREMISTS BEGAN TO WIN THE FUTURE

1. Ephron 2015.
2. Berlin 1997: 40–53.

CHAPTER 16: PEACE WITH JORDAN BUT NOT WITH SYRIA

1. Ross 2004: 168 *et seq.*

CHAPTER 17: MORE FALTERING STEPS TOWARDS PEACE

1. Ross 2004: 269.

CHAPTER 18: THE ROAD TO CAMP DAVID II

1. Ross 2004: 495 *et seq.*
2. Ross 2004: 748.

3. Greenberg 2009: 334.
4. Greenberg 2009: 336.
5. Ross 2004: 801.

CHAPTER 19: ARIEL SHARON ELECTED, 2001

1. Landau 2014: 136.
2. Schueftan 1999.
3. Connolly 2012.

CHAPTER 21: OLMERT TAKES OVER, 2006

1. Winograd Commission Final Report – Council on Foreign Relations. January, 2008. www.cfr.org
2. Swisher 2011.
3. 'Abbas Admits for the First Time That He Turned Down Peace Offer in 2008', *The Tower*, 17 November 2015, www.thetower.org/2580-breaking-abbas-admits-for-the first-time that-he-turned-downpeace-offer-in-2008 (accessed 12 December 2016).

CHAPTER 22: THE SYRIAN TRACK

1. Ross 2004: 587.
2 Hof 2009.
3. Seale 1989.
4. Quoted in Rabinovich 1999: 242.

CHAPTER 23: ABBAS, NETANYAHU, OBAMA AND A ROLLER-COASTER RIDE

1. Ross 2015: 6.
2. Kurtzer and Lasensky 2008.
3. Landler 2016: 204 *et seq.*
4. 'Address by PM Netanyahu at Bar-Ilan University', Israel Ministry of Foreign Affairs, 14 June 2009, http://mfa.gov.il/MFA/PressRoom/2009/Pages/Address_PM_Netanyahu_Bar-Ilan_University_14-Jun-2009.aspx (accessed 13 December 2016).
5. Abu Sway 2002: 84.

CHAPTER 25: PUBLIC PRESSURES AND GOVERNMENT CONSTRAINTS

1. 'Palestinian Public Opinion Poll No. 56', Palestinian Center for Policy and Survey Research, December 2015, http://www.pcpsr.org/en/node/611 (accessed 31 July 2016).
2. Israel Peace Initiative; New Wave Research, July 2016.
3. 'Youth Survey: Political Activism and Awareness', Arab World for Research and Development, 12 April 2016, http://www.awrad.org/page.php?id=Mz5umIerGIa10009275AkYlr2gIHfb (accessed 14 December 2016).
4. Palestine Public Opinion Poll No. 60. Palestinian Center for Policy and Survey Research, 21 June 2016. http//www.pcpsr.org/en/node/658 (accessed 31 July 2016)
5. 'Youth Survey: Political Activism and Awareness', Arab World for Research and Development, 12 April 2016, http://www.awrad.org/page.php?id=Mz5umIerGIa10009275AkYlr2gIHfb (accessed 14 December 2016).
6. Palestinian Public Opinion Poll No. 60.
7. Ibid.
8. See for example Eid 2016.
9. Palestine Public Opinion Poll No. 60.

CHAPTER 26: EXTERNAL AFFAIRS

1. The Prospects for Palestinian Economic Boycott of Israel: Forms and Difficulties. Khalidi Raja. May 2016. Palestinian Center for Policy and Survey Research. pcpcr.org
2. Hassassian 2002: 117.
3. Al-Faisal 2014.

CHAPTER 27: OPTIONS FOR PEACE

1. Bar et al. 2004.
2. Tilley 2010.
3. Nusseibeh 2011.

Bibliography

Abrams, Dennis (2006), *Ehud Olmert* (New York: Chelsea House)

Abrams, Elliott (2013), *Tested by Zion: The Bush Administration and the Israeli–Palestinian Conflict* (New York: Cambridge University Press)

Abu Sharif, Bassam (2009), *Arafat and the Dream of Palestine: An Insider's Account* (New York: Palgrave Macmillan)

Abu Sway, Mustafa (2002), 'Islamic Perspectives on the Oslo Process', in Rothstein, Robert L., Ma'oz, Moshe and Shikaki, Khalil (eds), *The Israeli–Palestinian Peace Process: Oslo and the Lessons of Failure – Perspectives, Predicaments and Prospects* (Brighton: Sussex Academic Press)

Adams, R. J. Q. (2007), *Balfour: The Last Grandee* (London: John Murray)

Avineri, Shlomo (2013), *Herzl: Theodor Herzl and the Foundation of the Jewish State* (London: Weidenfeld and Nicolson)

Avineri, Shlomo (2015), 'Rabin's Strategy: Understanding Security and the Limits of Power', in Johnson, Alan, Greene, Toby and Bell-Cross, Lorin (eds), *The Life and Legacy of Yitzhak Rabin*, Fathom eBook No. 2 (London and Jerusalem: BICOM), pp. 25–8

Avner, Yehuda (2010), *The Prime Ministers: An Intimate Narrative of Israeli Leadership* (New Milton, CT: Toby Press)

Bar, Shmuel, Biger, Gideon, Lotan, Orly and Machtiger, Rachel (2004), *Israeli–Palestinian Peace Plans*, Herzliya Papers, December.

Barak, Ehud (forthcoming), *My Country, My Life: Fighting for Israel, Searching for Peace* (New York: St Martin's Press)

Barr, James (2011), *A Line in the Sand: Britain, France and the Struggle That Shaped the Middle East* (London: Simon and Schuster)

Beilin, Yossi (1999), *Touching Peace: From the Oslo Accord to a Final Agreement* (London: Weidenfeld and Nicolson)

Beilin, Yossi (2004), *The Path to Geneva: The Quest for a Permanent Solution, 1996–2004* (New York: RDV)

Beller, Steven (1990), *Vienna and the Jews, 1867–1938: A Cultural History* (Cambridge: Cambridge University Press)

Berlin, Isaiah (1997), *The Sense of Reality: Studies in Ideas and their History*, ed. Henry Hardy (London: Pimlico)

Black, Ian and Morris, Benny (1992), *Israel's Secret Wars: A History of Israel's Intelligence Services* (New York: Grove)

Brookings Middle East Study Group (1975), *Towards Peace in the Middle East: Report of a Study Group* (Washington, DC: Brookings Institution)

Caplan, Neil (1983), *Futile Diplomacy, Vol. 1: Early Arab–Zionist Negotiation Attempts, 1913–1931* (London: Frank Cass)

Caplan, Neil (1993), *The Lausanne Conference, 1949: A Case Study in Middle East Peacemaking* (Tel Aviv: Tel Aviv University Press)

Catherwood, Christopher (2004), *Winston's Folly: Imperialism and the Creation of Modern Iraq* (London: Constable)

Chomsky, Noam (1999), *The Fateful Triangle: The United States, Israel and the Palestinians*, new ed. (London: Pluto Press)

Chomsky, Noam and Pappé, Ilan (2015), *On Palestine* (London: Penguin)

Churchill, Winston S. (1942) *Great Contemporaries* (London: Macmillan)

Cockburn, Patrick (2016), *The Age of Jihad* (London: Verso)

Connolly, Kevin (2012), 'Charles Tegart and the Forts That Tower over Israel', BBC News, 10 September, http://www.bbc.co.uk/news/magazine-19019949 (accessed 12 December 2016)

Crossman, Richard (1947), *Palestine Mission: A Personal Record* (London: Hamish Hamilton)

Crossman, Richard (1960), *A Nation Reborn: The Israel of Weizmann, Bevin and Ben-Gurion* (London: Hamish Hamilton)

Dayan, Moshe (1981), *Breakthrough: A Personal Account of the Egypt–Israel Peace Negotiations* (New York: Alfred A. Knopf)

Dearden, Lizzie (2016), 'Palestinian President Plans to Sue Britain over 1917 Balfour Declaration and Support for "Israeli Crimes"', *The Independent*, 27 July, http://www.independent.co.uk/news/world/middle-east/palestinian-president-plans-to-sue-britain-over-1917-balfour-declaration-and-support-for-israeli-a7157726.html (accessed 1 December 2016).

Dershowitz, Alan (2004), *The Case for Israel* (Hoboken, NJ: John Wiley)

Dockter, Warren (2015), *Churchill and the Islamic World: Orientalism, Empire and Diplomacy in the Middle East* (London: I. B. Tauris)

Doumani, Beshara (1995), *Rediscovering Palestine: Merchants and Peasants in Jabal Nablus, 1700–1900* (Berkeley: University of California Press)

Dugdale, Blanche (1936), *Arthur James Balfour: First Earl of Balfour*, 2 vols (London: Hutchinson)

Eban, Abba (1993), 'Building Bridges, Not Walls: Israel's Decision to Help the Palestinians to Freedom is Less a Triumph for Idealism than for Realism and Self-Interest', *The Guardian*, 10 September

Eid, Bassem (2016), *Confronting Human Rights Abuses in the Palestinian Authority: An Essential Step for Progress in the Region* (London: Henry Jackson Society)

Ephron, Dan (2015), *Killing a King: The Assassination of Yitzhak Rabin and the Remaking of Israel* (New York: W. W. Norton)

Al-Faisal, Prince Turki (2014), 'Peace Would Be Possible with the Arab Peace Initiative at Its Core', *Ha'aretz*, 7 July, www.haaretz.com/peace/1.599067 (accessed 15 December 2016)

Fromkin, Daniel (2009), *A Peace to End All Peace: The Fall of the Ottoman Empire and the Creation of the Modern Middle East* (New York: Henry Holt)

Garfinkle, Adam M. (1991), 'On the Origin, Meaning, Use and Abuse of a Phrase', *Middle Eastern Studies*, vol. 27, pp. 539–50

Glick, Caroline B. (2014), *The Israeli Solution: A One-State Plan for Peace in the Middle East* (New York: Crown Forum)

Goodman, Paul (ed.) (1945), *Chaim Weizmann: A Tribute on his Seventieth Birthday* (London: Victor Gollancz)

Gordis, Daniel (2014), *Menachem Begin: The Battle for Israel's Soul* (New York: Schocken)

Greenberg, Stanley B. (2009), *Dispatches from the War Room: In the Trenches with Five Extraordinary Leaders* (New York: Thomas Dunne)

Hammel, Eric M. (1993), *Six Days in June: How Israel Won the 1967 Arab–Israeli War* (New York: I)

Hammond, Jeremy R. (2016), 'The No-State Solution to the Israel–Palestine Conflict', *Foreign Policy Journal*, 9 July, http://www.foreign-policyjournal.com/2016/07/09/the-no-state-solution-to-the-israel-palestine-conflict (accessed 30 November 2016)

Hassassian, Manuel (2002), 'Why Did Oslo Fail? Lessons for the Future', in Rothstein, Robert L., Ma'oz, Moshe and Shikaki, Khalil (eds), *The Israeli–Palestinian Peace Process: Oslo and the Lessons of Failure – Perspectives, Predicaments and Prospects* (Brighton: Sussex Academic Press)

Herzl, Theodor ([1946] 1988), *The Jewish State* (New York: Dover)

Hess, Moses ([1918] 2012), *Rome and Jerusalem*, tr. Meyer Waxman (Memphis: General)

Hodder, Edwin ([1886] 1971), *The Life and Work of the Seventh Earl of Shaftesbury*, Vol. 1 (Shannon: Irish University Press)

Hof, Frederic C. (2009), *Mapping Peace between Syria and Israel, Special Report 219* (Washington, DC: United States Institute of Peace)

Hourani, Albert (1991), *A History of the Arab Peoples* (London: Faber and Faber)

Hurwitz, Harry and Medad, Yisrael (eds) (2011), *Peace in the Making: The Menachem Begin–Anwar El-Sadat Personal Correspondence* (Jerusalem: Gefen)

James, Lawrence (2004), 'Sykes, Sir Mark, Sixth Baronet (1879–1919)', *Oxford Dictionary of National Biography* (Oxford: Oxford University Press); online ed., May 2011

Keay, John (2003), *Sowing the Wind: The Mismanagement of the Middle East, 1900–1960* (London: John Murray)

Kurtzer, Daniel C. and Lasensky, Scott B. (2008), *Negotiating Arab–Israeli Peace: American Leadership in the Middle East* (Washington, DC: United States Institute of Peace)

Landau, David (2013), *Arik: The Life of Ariel Sharon* (New York: Alfred A. Knopf)

Landler, Mark (2016), *Alter Egos: Obama's Legacy, Hillary's Promise and the Struggle over American Power* (London: WH Allen)

Machiavelli, Niccolò (1961), *The Prince*, tr. George Bull (Harmondsworth: Penguin)

MacMillan, Margaret (2001), *Peacemakers: The Paris Peace Conference of 1919 and Its Attempt to End War* (London: John Murray)

Montefiore, Simon Sebag (2011), *Jerusalem: The Biography* (London: Weidenfeld and Nicolson)

Morris, Benny (2009), *One State, Two States: Resolving the Israel/Palestine Conflict* (New Haven, CT: Yale University Press)

Muir, Diana (2008), 'A Land without a People for a People without a Land', *Middle Eastern Quarterly*, Spring, pp. 55–62

Muslih, Muhammad Y. (1988), *The Origins of Palestinian Nationalism* (New York: Columbia University Press)

Nusseibeh, Sari (2009), *Once upon a Country: A Palestinian Life*, 2nd ed. (London: Halban)

Nusseibeh, Sari (2011), *What Is a Palestinian State Worth?* (Cambridge, MA: Harvard University Press)

O'Brien, Conor Cruise (1986), *The Siege: The Saga of Israel and Zionism* (New York: Simon and Schuster)

Oren, Michael B. (2003), *Six Days of War: June 1967 and the Making of the Modern Middle East* (New York: Ballantine)

Pappé, Ilan (2003), *A History of Modern Palestine: One Land, Two Peoples* (Cambridge: Cambridge University Press)

Pedersen, Susan (2015), *The Guardians: The League of Nations and the Crisis of Empire* (Oxford: Oxford University Press)

Peres, Shimon (1995), *Battling for Peace: Memoirs* (London: Weidenfeld and Nicolson)

Quandt, William B. (2005), *Peace Process: American Diplomacy and the Arab–Israeli Conflict since 1967*, 3rd ed. (Washington, DC: Brookings Institution Press)

Rabinovich, Itamar (1999), *The Brink of Peace: The Israeli–Syrian Negotiations* (Princeton, NJ: Princeton University Press)

Rabinovich, Itamar (2013), *The Lingering Conflict: Israel, the Arabs and the Middle East, 1948–2012* (Washington, DC: Brookings Institution Press)

Rafael, Gideon (1981), *Destination Peace: Three Decades of Israeli Foreign Policy – A Personal Memoir* (London: Weidenfeld and Nicolson)

Raviv, Moshe (1998), *Israel at Fifty: Five Decades of Struggle for Peace* (London: Weidenfeld and Nicolson)

Reinharz, Jehuda (1985), *Chaim Weizmann: The Making of a Zionist Leader* (Oxford: Oxford University Press)

Rifkind, Gabrielle and Picco, Giandomenico (2014), *The Fog of Peace: The Human Face of Conflict Resolution* (London: I. B. Tauris)

Romirowsky, Asaf and Joffe, Alexander H. (2013), *Religion, Politics, and the Origins of Palestine Refugee Relief* (New York: Palgrave Macmillan)

Ross, Dennis (2004), *The Missing Peace: The Inside Story of the Fight for Middle East Peace* (New York: Farrar, Straus and Giroux)

Ross, Dennis (2015), *Doomed to Succeed: The US–Israel Relationship from Truman to Obama* (New York: Farrar, Straus and Giroux)

Roth, Sheree (2016), 'Were the Arabs Indigenous to Mandatory Palestine?', *Middle East Quarterly*, Fall, www.meforum.org/6275/were-the-arabs-indigenous-to-mandatory-palestine (accessed 30 November 2016)

Rothstein, Robert L., Ma'oz, Moshe and Shikaki, Khalil (eds) (2002), *The Israeli–Palestinian Peace Process: Oslo and the Lessons of Failure – Perspectives, Predicaments and Prospects* (Brighton: Sussex Academic Press)

Said, Edward W. and Hitchens, Christopher (eds) (1988), *Blaming the Victims: Spurious Scholarship and the Palestinian Question* (London: Verso)

Said Aly, Abdel Monem, Feldman, Shai and Shikaki, Khalil (2013), *Arabs and Israelis: Conflict and Peacemaking in the Middle East* (Basingstoke: Palgrave Macmillan)

Sanders, Ronald (1984), *The High Walls of Jerusalem: A History of the Balfour Declaration and the Birth of the British Mandate for Palestine* (New York: Holt, Rinehart and Winston)

Schechtman, Joseph B. (1965), *The Mufti and the Fuehrer: The Rise and Fall of Haj Amin el-Husseini* (New York: Thomas Yoseloff)

Schneer, Jonathan (2010), *The Balfour Declaration: The Origins of the Arab–Israeli Conflict* (London: Bloomsbury)

Schueftan, Dan (1999), *Disengagement: Israel and the Palestinian Entity* (in Hebrew) (Tel Aviv: Zvara Bitar)

Seale, Patrick (1989), *Assad: The Struggle for the Middle East* (Berkeley: University of California Press)

Segev, Tom (2000), *One Palestine Complete: Jews and Arabs under the British Mandate*, tr. Haim Watzman (London: Metropolitan)

Shavit, Ari (2015), *My Promised Land: The Triumph and Tragedy of Israel* (London: Scribe)

Shlaim, Avi (2001), *The Iron Wall: Israel and the Arab World* (London: Penguin)

Shlaim, Avi (2008), *Lion of Jordan: The Life of King Hussein in War and Peace* (London: Penguin)

Siniver, Asaf (2015), *Abba Eban: A Biography* (New York: Overlook Duckworth)

Stein, Leonard (1961), *The Balfour Declaration* (London: Vallentine, Mitchell)

Swisher, Clayton E. (2011), *The Palestine Papers: The End of the Road?* (London: Hesperus Press)

Sykes, Christopher (1973), *Crossroads to Israel, 1917–1948* (Bloomington: Indiana University Press)

Tilley, Virginia (2010), *The One-State Solution; A Breakthrough for Peace in the Israeli–Palestinian Deadlock* (Ann Arbor: University of Michigan Press, 2010)

United Nations Committee on Palestine (1947), *Report to the General Assembly, 31 August 1947* (New York: United Nations)

Waage, Hilde Henriksen (2007), 'Postscript to Oslo: The Mystery of Norway's Missing Files', *Journal of Palestine Studies*, vol. 38, pp. 54–65

Walker, Tony and Gowers, Andrew (2003), *Arafat: The Biography*, rev. ed. (London: Virgin)

Wallach, Janet (1996), *Desert Queen: The Extraordinary Life of Gertrude Bell* (London: Weidenfeld and Nicolson)

Walton, Calder (2014), *Empire of Secrets: British Intelligence, the Cold War and the Twilight of Empire* (New York: Overlook Press)

Weir, Alison (2014), *Against Our Better Judgment: The Hidden History of How the United States Was Used to Create Israel* (San Diego: If Americans Knew)

Weizman, Ezer (1981), *The Battle for Peace* (Toronto: Bantam)

Weizmann, Chaim (1949), *Trial and Error: The Autobiography* (New York: Harper and Brothers)

Wenar, Leif (2016), *Blood Oil: Tyrants, Violence and the Rules that Run the World* (Oxford: Oxford University Press)

Wright, Lawrence (2014), *Thirteen Days in September: Carter, Begin, and Sadat at Camp David* (London: Oneworld)

Index

9/11 attacks 195
'10 Point Plan' (1974) 96
A Defence of Philosophic Doubt 20
Abbas, Mahmood xi, 143, 184
and Arab Peace Initiative 270
becomes president 202
and Benjamin Netanyahu 144, 225–7, 232–3, 248–9, 250,270
and Ehud Olmert 162, 174, 203, 204–8, 209
and Jewish statehood 42
and Palestinian refugees 267
reluctance to negotiate 237, 263, 268
and 'road map' for peace 200
and two-state solution 260, 261
and 'unity government' 229
unpopularity of 208, 227–8, 242, 244–5
Abbasi, Mustafa 44
Abdullah I, King 5, 6, 8, 35, 36, 45, 47, 60, 63, 67, 69, 70–71, 75, 169
Abdullah II, King 142, 199, 232, 251
Abdullah, Prince (of Saudi Arabia) 253
Abraham 176
Abu Alaa 149–50, 205
AFSC (American Friends Service Committee) 92–3
Agha, Hussein 157
Agranat, Simon 103
Ahmadinejad, Mahmoud 223
al-Akki, Sheikh Ismail Abdul 42
Alaa, Abu 205
Alexander II, Tsar 13
Alexander III, Tsar 13
Ali, Abu 184
Aliens Act (1905) 21
aliyah 14
Al-Jazeera 205
Allenby, General 26, 30, 34
Alon, Yigal 59
Amir, Yigal xi, xii, 161, 162
Amnesty International 234
Amritsar massacre 33
Anan, Kofi 183
Anderson, Robert 70
anti-Semitism xiii, 15–17, 21–4, 26, 47, 52, 121, 242
al-Aqsa mosque (Jerusalem) 14, 29, 43, 70, 108, 169
Arab High Committee 66
Arab League xvi, 60, 70, 82–3, 107–8, 120, 121, 143, 253, 255, 269–70
Arab Peace Initiative xvi, 250–51, 253–5, 268–9
'Arab Spring' 11, 121, 223, 229–30, 232
Arab–Israeli War (1948) 58–61, 65, 66
Arab–Israeli War (1967) 77–9, 169–70
Arafat, Yasser 94–6, 169, 265
and 9/11 attacks 195
and Arab Peace Initiative 255
arrest/imprisonment of 95, 107–8
and Ariel Sharon 194–5
and Camp David II Accords 186–8, 191–2
and 'Clinton Parameters' 189–90
death of 202
and Ehud Barak 184–5
and extremist/terrorist violence 113, 159–60, 162–3, 164, 174, 176, 177, 178, 184, 185, 195–6
and Lebanese Wars 125, 126
and Oslo Accords 150, 152, 153–4, 155, 156, 160, 165, 179

Arafat, Yasser *cont.*
and PLO 78, 89, 95–7, 123–4, 125, 135–6, 137, 170
potential conciliation with Israel 137, 147–8, 181
recognition of Israel xvi, 97, 147, 260
reluctance to negotiate 92, 144
and 'road map' for peace 200
and Syrian peace negotiations 215
and UN 'Resolution 181' 62
and Wye River Agreement 178
Arava Institute (Negev) 263
Argov, Shlomo 125, 126
Asquith, Herbert 23
al-Assad, Bashar 142, 203, 216–19, 223, 224, 230
al-Assad, Hafez 97, 107–8, 109, 112, 124–5, 127, 162, 163, 169, 170, 171, 174, 182–3, 212, 213–16
Aswan Dam 71
Attlee, Clement 51–2, 54
Avineri, Shlomo 105
Avner, Yehuda 101

Ba'ath Party 214–15, 216
Baker, James 138, 147
Balfour Declaration (1917) Balfour's motivations 21–2
and British Imperialism 28, 33, 39
drafting of 25–6
high-minded intentions of xii, xiii–xiv, 22, 26
initial reception of 26–8, 38–9, 41–2
and one-state solution 257
and recognition of Israel xviii–xix, 41–2, 271
and San Remo Conference 32–3
validity of xii, xiii
Balfour, Sir Arthur 19–20, 21–2, 26, 32–3, 41
Bar, Shmuel 257
Barak, Aharon 116, 117
Barak, Ehud 128, 174, 179, 181, 182–9, 191–2, 194, 195, 215–16
Bargouti, Marwan 244
Barnes, Sir Ernest John Ward 85
Begin, Menachem 48, 50–51, 57, 82, 88–9, 106, 108–11, 113–15, 116–19, 120–21, 125–7, 151
Beilin, Yossi xi, 149–50, 154, 156, 160, 163, 189, 213
Bell, Gertrude 6
Ben Gurion, David 45–6, 48, 50, 51, 58, 62–3, 70, 72, 86, 157, 163, 257, 260
Berlin, Isaiah 166
Bernadotte, Folke 60
Bevin, Ernest 51–2, 70
bin Sultan, Prince Bandar 187
'Black September' 98, 106–7, 182
Blair, Tony 129, 162, 199, 241
Blood Oil 102
Brandeis, Louis D. 24, 38
British Admiralty Laboratories 19
Brookings Institution report (1975) 112
Brzezinski, Zbigniew 112
Buber, Martin 257–8
Bush, George 129, 147, 162, 222
Bush, George W. 187, 195, 197–8, 199–200, 205, 217, 222, 250

Cairo Conference (1921) 34–6
Cambon, Jules 24, 32
Camp David Accords (1979) 89, 97, 100, 111, 113, 116–21, 151
Camp David II Accords (2000) 186–8, 191–2
Caplan, Neil 67
Carter, Jimmy 108, 110, 111–13, 114–17, 119, 121, 162, 222
Ceauşescu, Nicolae 109
Cecil, Robert (Lord Salisbury) 20
Chamberlain, Austen 11
Chamberlain, Joseph 17, 18
Charles, Prince 162
Chomsky, Noam 49, 58
Christopher, Warren 153, 213, 214, 215, 218
Church of the Holy Sepulchre (Jerusalem) 29, 53, 108
Church of the Nativity (Jerusalem) 53
Churchill, Winston 19, 20, 33, 34, 43, 47
Clemenceau, Georges 12, 30, 31–2
Clinton, Bill 153–5, 162, 171, 175, 176, 177–8, 185–90, 214–16, 223, 260, 269
Clinton, Hillary 227
'Clinton Parameters' 188–90, 199, 207–8, 265
Cockburn, Patrick xiv
Cohen, Geulah 118
Conciliation Commission (UN) 65, 66
confidence-building measures 157, 261, 269–70
Congress of Vienna (1815) 74
Crossman, Richard xii–xiii, 23, 51
Curzon, Lord 12, 31, 32

Dahlan, Mohammad 244
'Damascus Protocol' 7, 9
Damour 123
Daniel Deronda 14
Dayan, Moshe 59, 74, 86, 88, 100, 103, 109, 115–16, 121

de Haas, Jacob 38
Dead Sea Scrolls xviii
Deir ez-Zor nuclear reactor (Syria) 217
Deir Yassin 57
Disengagement: Israel and the Palestinian Entity 194
Disraeli, Benjamin 14
Dome of the Rock (Jerusalem) 29, 171–2, 176
Dreyfus affair 16
Dugdale, Blanche 20, 21–2
Dühring, Eugen 16
Dulles, John Foster 71

Eban, Abba xv, 69–70, 73–4, 82, 83–5, 87
Economic Co-operation Foundation 149
Eden, Anthony 72–3
Eichmann, Adolf 49–50
Eid, Bassem 242
Eisenhower, Dwight D. 72, 75, 222
El Alamein, Battle of (1942) 48
Eliot, George 14
Entebbe xix
Erdoğan, Recep Tayyip 217, 218, 252
Erez Crossing 234
Eshki, Anwar 250
Eshkol, Levi 78, 81–2, 83, 99

FAFO Research Centre 149
al-Faisal, Prince Turki 250, 254–5
Faisal I, King xiv, 5, 6, 8, 9, 27–8, 31–2, 33–4, 35, 36, 42
Faisal–Weizmann Agreement (1919) 27–8, 31
Farouk, King 59, 69
Fatah 95, 113, 201, 221, 228, 244, 260
Fayyad, Salam 208–9, 227, 235, 244
fedayeen 59, 72, 75
federation/confederation proposals 262–4
final status talks/agreement 149, 151, 154, 156–7, 160, 163, 166, 173, 186, 204–8, 209, 265–71
'Framework for the Peace-Making Process between Israel and Its Neighbours' 111, 118
Frankfurter, Felix 27, 38
'freeze' 226–7
'Future of Palestine, The' 25

Gandhi, Mahatma 33
Gaza 60, 66, 92–3, 105, 136, 137, 178, 197, 218, 231, 240, 241, 242–3, 250, 252, 263, 265, 267
  and Hamas 142, 201–2, 203, 208, 228–9, 232–5, 242–3
  and Oslo Accords 147, 149, 151–2, 155–6, 164, 194 violence/attacks in 72, 75, 97, 134–5, 159–60, 233–5 withdrawal of Israeli settlements from 134, 144, 162, 174, 195, 200–201, 262
Gelfman, Gesya 13
Gemayel, Bashir 126
General Assembly (UN) xix, 53–4, 65, 73, 74, 84, 102, 123–4, 227
Geneva Conference (1973) 106
Georges-Picot, François 6, 9, 10–11
Giscard d'Estaing, Valéry 10
Givat Shaul 57
Golan Heights 82, 103, 107, 111, 113, 120, 131, 169, 211, 212–13, 214–19, 255, 269
Gold, Dore 250
Goldstein, Baruch 159
Goldstone Report 233–4
Gorbachov, Mikhail 138
Gore, Al 187
Graham, Lindsay 247
'Grapes of Wrath' 175
'Green Line' border 80, 198, 265
Greenberg, Stanley 187–8
Grey, Sir Edward 25
Gulf War (1991) 138, 195
Gur, Mordechai 108

Ha'aretz 250, 254
Habash, George 95, 98
Hadassah Hospital (Jerusalem) 263
Hadrian, Emperor 33
Haganah 44, 48, 51
Haig, Alexander 124
al-Hakim, Abd al-Mujid 251
Halifax, Lord 48
Hamami, Said 75
Hamas 135–6, 163, 176, 178, 244–5, 252, 255
  attacks by xii, 154, 159, 160, 162, 164, 175, 195, 215, 221
  charter/demands of xiv–xv, 135, 143, 144, 166, 200–201, 225, 259, 260
  and Gaza 142, 201–2, 203, 208, 228–9, 232–5, 242–3
  and Syrian peace negotiations 211, 212, 215, 216, 218
  'unity government' with Palestinian Authority 228–9
Hamdallah, Rami 229
Haniyeh, Ismail 244
Haram al-Sharif (Temple Mount) xvi, 14, 29, 184, 188, 189, 190, 193, 251, 266
Hashomer 45
Hasmonean Tunnel (Jerusalem) 176
Hassan, King 109
Hassassian, Manuel 254
Herzl, Theodor 13, 15–18, 63

'Herzliya Papers' 257
Herzog, Isaac 262
Hess, Moses 14, 16
Hezbollah 127–8, 132, 137, 142–3, 166, 171–2, 175, 176, 183, 185, 203–4, 211, 212, 215, 216, 219, 221
Hirschfeld, Yair 150, 157
Histradut trade union 58
Hitler, Adolf 44, 47
Holocaust 48–9, 50, 51, 52–3, 119, 133, 179, 254
Holtz, Alwin 93
'Holy Basin' 206, 207, 266
Hussein, Grand Sharif xiv, 5, 6–8, 9, 10, 12–13, 27, 31, 42
Hussein, King 78, 83, 98, 107, 109, 131, 132–4, 156, 162, 169–71, 178, 245
Hussein, Saddam 128, 136, 137, 138, 148, 199
Husseini, Faisal 149, 154
al-Husseini, Fauze 75
al-Husseini, Haj Amin 43–4, 47, 48

Ibn Saud 7, 55
Ibrahim Mosque (Hebron) 159
IDF (Israel Defence Force) 46, 95, 121, 127, 196, 233
Immigration Bill (US, 1924) 49
Indyk, Martin 248
Intercontinental Hotel (Amman) 98
'Interim Agreement' (Oslo Accords) 113, 154, 155, 160, 173, 186
International Zionist Congresses 18
intifada 134–5, 136, 190, 193, 194, 195–6, 244, 253
'Irangate' 136–7
Iranian nuclear programme 142, 221, 223, 249–50
Iraq war (2003) 199, 200, 217, 231
Iraqi nuclear programme 128–9
Irgun 36, 48, 49–50, 54, 57, 133
'Irish Free State' 33
IS (Islamic State) xiv, 35, 142, 143, 211, 218, 219, 231–2, 241, 249, 251
Islambouli, Khalid 122
Islamic Jihad 160, 176, 195

Jabotinsky, Ze'ev 50
Jadid, Salah 83
Jarring, Gunnar 83, 84, 86
Jerusalem 28–9, 43, 82, 238–9, 263, 265–7
  and 1948 Arab–Israeli War 60
  and 1967 Arab–Israeli War 78
  and Camp David Accords 184–5, 188–9
  and Egypt–Israel peace proposals 101, 108, 109, 113, 117, 119, 121
  and final status agreement 165, 205, 206, 207, 266
  Israeli claims to xviii, 29, 84, 184–5, 225–6, 248–9
  and Oslo Accords 151, 156, 157
  Palestinian claims to 4, 29, 97, 136, 147, 165, 180, 190, 253
  and Security Fence 196–7
  UN Plans and Resolutions 53–4, 66, 70
  violence in 176–7, 200
  and War of Independence 57
Jerusalem: The Biography 28–9
Jewish Agency 60, 63
Jewish Home Party 243–4
Jewish State, The 15–16, 17–18
'Jewish Problem as a Problem of Race, Morals and Culture, The' 16
Johnson, Lyndon 78, 81, 83
Joint Water Committee 263
Judt, Tony 258

Kach 159
Kadima Party 202, 203, 221
Kahane Chai 159
Kahane, Meir 159
Karameh, Battle of (1968) 95
Karantina 123
Karine A 195
Kemal, Muhammad 115
Kennedy, John F. 75, 222
Kerry, John 237, 248
Kesrawani, Wadia 42
Kfar Etzion massacre 58
Khalidi, Ahmed 157
Khomeini, Ayatollah 120
kibbutz movement 44, 45
King David Hotel (Jerusalem) 50
Kishinev pogrom (1903) 13
Kissinger, Henry 87–8, 99, 100–101, 102, 103, 106, 107, 213
Knesset 108–9, 110, 113, 118–19, 150, 160, 171, 179, 184, 186, 188, 192, 194, 239, 243–4, 269
Kosygin, Alexei 83

Labour Party (Israel) 132, 148, 149–50, 193–4, 202, 262
Labour Party (UK) 50, 51–2
Lausanne Conference 41, 66–7
Lawrence, T. E. ('Lawrence of Arabia') 5–6, 12, 28, 31
League of Nations xiv, 31, 33, 36–9, 41–3, 51, 53, 212

Lebanese Wars 123–8, 132, 203–4
Lehi 49, 54
Lewinsky, Monica 177
Likud Party 118, 131, 132, 134, 160, 186, 188, 190, 193–4, 197, 202
Lincoln, Abraham 141
Livni, Tzipi 202, 205, 221
Lloyd George, David xiv, 12, 19, 20, 22–4, 30, 32
Local Government Board 19
Lueger, Karl 16

MacDonald White Paper (1939) 47–51, 157
MacMahon, Sir Henry 6, 7, 9, 12–13, 27, 31
Madrid conference (1991) 147–8, 213
Magnes, Judah 257–8
al-Majali, Abdulsalam 171
Major, John 162
malaria 34
al-Maliki, Riyad 27
Manchester Guardian 19
maps *xxii–xxiii*
Marks, Simon 19
Mashal, Khalid 178
Mavi Marmara 235, 252
Mein Kampf 47
Meir, Golda 74, 86, 87, 88, 89, 99, 100, 103
Middle East Quartet 199, 205, 269
Mishcon, Lord 133
Missing Peace, The 177
Mitchell, George 194, 227–8
Mohammed 29
Mollet, Guy 73
Montagu, Edwin 23, 24
Montagu, Samuel 23
Montefiore, Sir Moses 14
Montefiore, Simon Sebag 28–9
Morgenthau, Henry 24
Morsi, Mohamed 223, 230, 232
Mossad 178
Moyne, Lord 49–50
Mubarak, Hosni 122, 152, 162, 170, 185, 223, 230
al-Mulki, Hani 251
Munich Olympics (1972) 106–7, 182
Muslim Brotherhood 135, 142, 223–4, 230, 232, 235, 228, 250

Nablus 4, 34, 44, 184, 188
Napoleon 14
Nasser, Jamal Abdal 69–70, 71–3, 74, 75, 77–8, 83, 85–7, 89, 91, 97, 99, 101
Negev desert 53–4, 55, 60, 69, 71, 171, 263
Netanyahu, Benjamin
  and anti-Rabin rally 160
  and Arab Peace Initiative 269
  and Ariel Sharon 197, 200
  and Barack Obama 221, 223, 225, 247, 268
  coalition government of 243–4
  conditions of 225–7
  elected Israeli Prime Minister 164, 175, 215
  fall of 178–80
  and final status agreement 266
  first government of 175–7
  and Golan Heights 213, 219
  and Jewish statehood 42
  and Mahmoud Abbas 225–7, 232–3, 248–9, 250, 270
  and peace negotiations 144, 174, 175–6, 181
  relations with Egypt 249–50
  relations with Turkey 252
  reluctance to negotiate 237, 240, 270
  takes over for second term 209, 221
  and two-state solution 261
  unpopularity of 163
  and Wye River Agreement 177, 178
Neue Freie Presse 16
Nidal, Abu 126
Nine-Point Plan (1968) 83–5
Nixon, Richard 86, 87, 88, 222
Nusseibeh, Sari 259, 263

Obama, Barack 209, 221–5, 226, 227, 247–8, 268
O'Brien, Conor Cruise 73, 74, 100, 101
Odessa pogrom (1905) 13
Olmert, Ehud 162, 174, 194, 202, 203–8, 209, 213, 217–18, 221, 254, 269
one-state solution xx, 240, 257–9
'Operation Cast Lead' 218, 233
'Operation Defensive Shield' 196
'Operation Grapes of Wrath' 128
'Operation Litani' 126
'Operation Musketeer' 72
'Operation Orchard' 217
'Operation Pillar of Defence' 233
'Operation Protective Edge' 231, 233
Organisation for Islamic Cooperation 268–9
Ormsby-Gore, William 31
Osiraq nuclear reactor 128–9
Oslo Accords (1993, 1995) xi–xii, 97, 113, 118, 136, 141, 148–56, 157, 164–5, 166, 172, 173, 175, 179, 181
Ottoman Empire 3–4, 5–8, 26, 35–6

PA (Palestinian Authority) 228–9, 234, 235
Pale of Settlement 13, 19

Palestine National Charter 153, 173, 175–6, 178
Palestinian Centre for Policy and Survey Research xv
Palestinian National Council 95, 135, 154, 175
'Palestine Papers, The' 205
Palestinian refugees 62, 65, 66, 92–4, 126–7, 137, 197, 206, 207–8, 224–5, 226, 253, 267
Palestinian Student League 95
Palmach 48
Palmerston, Lord 15
Pan-Arabism 11, 70, 97
Paris Peace Conference (1919) 10, 28, 30–32
Partition Plan (UN) 42, 45, 46–7, 53–6, 60, 91, 97, 165, 260
Passover xviii
'Peace Now' movement 114, 261
Peel Report (1937) 42, 45–7, 259–60
Peel, Lord 45, 46–7
Peres–Hussein London Agreement (1987) 133
Peres Peace Centre 261
Peres, Shimon xi, 109, 181, 242
  arms deal with France 74
  fails to call election 161–2, 163–4
  and Israeli settlements in Gaza 134
  joins Kadima Party 202
  and Oslo Accords 149–50, 152, 154, 155, 160
  Peres–Hussein London Agreement 133
  steps down from office 175
  and Syrian peace negotiations 214, 215
  and 'unity government' 131–2
Peretz, Amir 204
PFLP (Popular Front for the Liberation of Palestine) 98, 195
Phalangists 126–7
Pinsker, Leo 16
PLO (Palestine Liberation Organization) 85, 132–3, 167, 205, 242
  and 'Black September' 98, 106–7
  Covenant of 96–7, 153
  and Egypt–Israel peace proposals 111, 112–13, 114, 119
  and federation/confederation proposals 263
  formation of 95–6
  and intifada 134–5
  and Lebanese Wars 123–8, 132
  and Netanyahu's conditions 225
  and Oslo Accords 147–8, 149, 150, 152, 153–4
  and Palestinian refugees 94
  recognition of Israel 175–6
  support for Kuwait invasion 136, 137, 138
  and Syrian peace negotiations 212, 215
  and Yasser Arafat 78, 89, 95–7, 123–4, 125, 135–6, 137, 170
Pobedonostsev, Konstantin 13
proportional representation 243
public opinion 237–8, 240–43
Pundak, Ron 150, 157

Al Qaeda xiv, 142, 211, 219, 235
Al-Qibla 27
al-Quwwatli, Shukri 59–60

Rabin, Leah xi, 162
Rabin, Yitzhak
  and 1948 Arab–Israeli War 59
  and 1967 Arab–Israeli War 105
  anti-Rabin rally 160–61
  assassination of xi, xii, 76, 157, 161, 162, 181, 214
  and Egypt–Israel peace proposals 99, 106
  elected Israeli Prime Minister 103, 105
  and extremist violence 159, 160
  and Henry Kissinger 87, 88, 99
  and King Hussein 170–71
  and Oslo Accords 148, 149, 150, 151, 152, 153, 154–5, 156, 160, 165
  resignation of 108
  and Syrian peace negotiations 211, 212, 214
Rafael, Gideon 101, 102
Rafah Crossing 234, 250
Raviv, Moshe 101
Reagan, Ronald 129, 133, 137
'realpolitik' 87
Resolution 181 (UN) 53–6, 60, 62, 68
Resolution 194 (UN) 65–6, 68
Resolution 242 (UN) 79–81, 82–3, 88, 89, 91, 96, 106, 112, 119, 133, 153, 253
Resolution 338 (UN) 106, 253
Resolution 381 (UN) 176
Resolution 393 (UN) 93
Resolution 425 (UN) 114
Resolution 1559 (UN) 217
Resolution 2334 (UN) 198, 247–8
'rights of return' 93, 184
'road map' for peace 198, 199–200
Rød-Larsen, Terje 149
Rogers Plan (1969) 88, 99, 100, 101
Rogers, William 87, 88, 99, 100, 101
Rome and Jerusalem 14
Roosevelt, Franklin D. 55
Ross, Dennis 171, 177, 187, 215, 216, 260
Rothschild, Lord xiii, 25
Russian Revolution (1917) 12, 26

Sabra camp massacre 123, 126–7, 134, 193
Sachar, Harry 19
Sadat, Anwar
assassination of 75, 92, 121–2, 125
becomes Egyptian President 99
and Camp David Accords 51, 111, 116–17, 121, 151
and Egypt–Israel peace proposals 106, 107, 108–10, 111, 113, 114, 115, 119, 120, 212, 245
peace proposals 99–100, 101, 170
recognition of Israel 91
and Yom Kippur War 100–101, 102
Said, Edward 46
Salisbury, Lord (Robert Cecil) 20
Salman, King 251
Samuel, Herbert 19, 25, 43
San Remo Conference (1920) 32–4, 37
Sartawi, Issam 75
Schueftan, Dan 194, 262
Scott, C. P. 19
Seal, Patrick 218
Security Council (UN) 54–5, 62, 63, 73, 78–9, 84, 103, 129, 227, 248, 270
Security Fence 196–8
Shaftesbury, Lord 14–15
Shah of Iran 75, 109, 114, 120
Shalit, Corporal Gilad 203, 233
Shamir, Yitzhak 131–3, 136, 147–8, 170, 213–14, 237
Sharif, Bassam Abu 135, 176
Sharon, Ariel 189, 190
and Arab Peace Initiative 253
death of 202
and Egypt–Israel peace proposals 114, 117–18
elected Israeli Prime Minister 193–4
and intifada 194, 195–6
Israeli withdrawal from Gaza 134, 144, 162, 174, 195, 200–201, 202, 233
and Kadima Party 202, 203
and Lebanese Wars 126, 127
and 'road map' for peace 199–200
and Security Fence 197
Sharon, Omri 195
Shas Party 243–4
Shatila camp massacre 123, 126–7, 134, 193
Shia Muslims ix, 11–12, 35, 127, 132, 231, 261
Shikaki, Khalil xv
Shoukry, Sameh 249
Shultz, George 133, 136
Sieff, Israel 19
Siege, The 101
el-Sisi, Abdel Fattah 121, 144, 224, 230, 232, 235, 250, 268, 270
Al Solh, Riad Bey 71
Sokolow, Nahum 24
Spanish Inquisition 29
Special Fact Finding Commission 194
SS *Exodus* 52, 70
SS *Struma* 49
Stalin, Joseph 62, 63
Stanley, Venetia 23
'step-by-step' approach 107, 184, 227–8, 261–2
Stern Gang 133
Straits of Tiran 72, 74, 75, 77, 81, 118
Suez Canal 5, 6, 11, 52, 71–4, 86–7, 100, 118
Sunni Muslims ix, 4, 11–12, 35, 89, 208, 231, 239, 241, 261
Sykes, Sir Mark 6, 9–10, 22
Sykes–Picot Agreement (1916) xiv, 8–13, 22, 26, 30
Syrian peace negotiations 211–19
Szold, Henrietta 15

al-Tal, Wasfi 98
Talleyrand, Charles Maurice de 74
Tancred 14
Taub, Daniel xvii
Tegart, Colonel Charles 196
'Tegart's Wall' 196
Temple Mount (Haram al-Sharif) xvi, 14, 29, 184, 188, 189, 190, 193, 251, 266
Tenet, George 195
'three noes' xvi, 82–3, 253, 255, 269
Times 14, 27
Touching Peace 150
Treaty of Lausanne (1949) 41
Trotsky, Leon 26
Truman, Harry S. 51, 52, 55, 62, 222
Trump, Donald 88, 122, 248, 268
B'Tselem 240–41
Tuhami, Hassan 109
Twain, Mark 34
'two frameworks' proposal 115–16, 117
two-state solution xv, xx, xxii, 91, 97, 142, 145, 160, 206, 225–6, 240, 259–62, 270–71

'Uganda' scheme 18, 22
Ugglas, Margaretha af 157
UN (United Nations)
and 1948 Arab–Israeli War 58–9
and 1967 Arab–Israeli War 77, 78
and Abba Eban 73–4
Conciliation Commission 65, 66
General Assembly xix, 53–4, 65, 73, 74, 84, 102, 123–4, 227
and Palestinian refugees 93–4
Partition Plan 42, 53–6, 60, 91, 97, 165, 260

UN (United Nations) *cont.*
recognition of Israel xiv, xviii–xix, 38, 41, 54–5, 62
recognition of Jordan 36
recognition of Palestinian state 227
Resolutions of *see* Resolutions
Security Council 54–5, 62, 63, 73, 78–9, 84, 103, 129, 227, 248, 270
UNESCO (United Nations Educational, Scientific and Cultural Organization) 234
United States Institute of Peace 218, 222
'unity governments' 132, 228–9
UNRWA (United Relief and Works Agency for Palestine) 93–4
UNSCOP (UN Special Committee on Palestine) 53–4

Vance, Cyrus 115

Waage, Hilde 153
waqf land 228
War of Independence (1948) 57–8
Washington Declaration, The (1994) 171–2
al-Wazir, Khalil 95
Weir, Alison 55
Weizman, Ezer 114, 116
Weizmann, Chaim 18–19, 36
and Arthur Balfour 19–20, 21
and David Ben Gurion 45–6
and David Lloyd George 22, 23–4
and Faisal Hussein xiv, 9, 27–8, 31
lobbying and diplomacy of 38, 42, 51, 62–3
and one-state solution 257
and Partition proposals 45, 54, 55, 259–60
and Zionism 13, 15, 26, 165
Wenar, Leif 102
West Bank 131, 134, 135–6, 137–8,163, 164, 165, 195, 206, 223, 232, 239–40, 241, 242, 263, 265, 267
and Camp David Accords 111, 113, 117–18, 119
Israeli claims to xv, 36, 67, 70, 78–9, 105, 141, 214
and Jordan 67, 81, 82, 170
and Oslo Accords 147–8, 151, 152, 155–6
Palestinian statehood claims 60, 170–71, 176, 179, 189, 260
proposed Israeli withdrawals from 109, 117, 162, 174, 184, 194, 200–202, 262
violence in 97, 196–7
Wilhelm, Kaiser 18
Wilson, Woodrow 24, 28, 30
Wingate, Major Orde 44
Wise, Rabbi Stephen 38
Wolf, Lucien 23
Woodhead Committee 47
'world opinion' xix
Wright, Lawrence 118
Wye River Agreement (1998) 173, 177–8

Yad Vashem Holocaust Center 108, 254
Yadin, Yigael 59
Yassin, Sheikh Ahmed 135, 178
Yom Kippur War (1973) 86, 100–101, 102–3, 106, 193
Young Turks 8

al-Za'im, Husni 69
Zionism, birth of 13–15